End

These stories are raw and deeply vulnerable, not for the faint of heart. But then, neither is faithfully following God in a broken and beautiful world. Grab a box of tissues and let these tender stories usher you into the holy presence of a loving and pain-carrying God. No matter where you come from, where you live, and what you have walked through, you are not alone.

—Rachel Pieh Jones, author of *Pillars* and *Stronger than Death*

How do we cling to hope when our faith is tested, at times severely? When circumstances seem beyond what we can bear? When we wonder if it's worth the cost? In this collection of sacred stories from our sisters serving around the globe, you'll smile, tear up, and words will resonate as you read of unexpected sacrifices, scars that heal slowly, and those secret struggles we rarely voice. But more than that, you'll see how God intentionally and faithfully pursues each one and reveals Himself, giving strength, renewed hope and intimacy to thirsty, weary souls. A timely read for all of us 'for such a time as this'.

—Suzy Grumelot, co-author of *Sacred Siblings: Valuing One Another for the Great Commission*

Yet We Still Hope invites us into the lives of women who unveil their stories of hope-filled courage. When threatened with fear, anger, or guilt, they found hope, forgiveness, and peace. For any woman in cross-cultural ministry who feels alone in their struggles, these accounts of God's grace will stir their souls to remember truth. With our eyes fixed on Jesus, though despair seems inevitable, he overcomes it with hope.

—Sue Eenigenburg, author, speaker and global worker

If you have ever known the loneliness, grief, joy, and excitement that comes with a life abroad, this book will surely comfort you while also tingling your senses with vivid memories. The words on these pages offer hope, affirmation, and healing to the wanderer's soul...you will find a whole host of best friends you've never met as you escape into a shared experience with these brave, curious, and faithful women.

—Lauren Pinkston, Ph.D.,
Executive Director of Kindred Exchange

As I read through these stories of women serving cross-culturally from various places around the world, three words came to mind: honesty, openness, and transparency. Women serving cross-culturally today face multiple challenges that can test one's faith and dependence on the Lord. I was overwhelmed by the spiritual courage and strength demonstrated in each story. If you are serving or have served in a cross-cultural setting, this book is for you. You will be encouraged deeply through each account of God's abiding presence amid real-life experiences.

—Perry Bradford, Executive Director of Barnabas International

In these pages you will encounter the boldness, brokenness, and beauty of a throng of women who are living heroes of faith. We are thirsty for hope that springs from the depths and not superficialities; herein you'll find stories and perspectives forged in the fires of suffering, honest questions without easy answers, and the rich fare of truly inspiring faith. I believe every woman with a heart for cross-cultural work will have their faith galvanized through this book. Whether to nourish your own soul or encourage a friend's, I wholeheartedly recommend tuning in to the powerful chorus of these women's genuine journeys with Jesus. I know I will be gifting a great many copies to all those I hope to see echo the refrain, "Yet We Still Hope."

—**Brian Gibson, Executive Director of TRAIN International**

Since the day Velvet Ashes began, the heart of this community has been to provide a place for our authentic stories. When we offered a space for women to be raw and real in their journey to follow God onto foreign soil, the connections and comments started firing across the globe. A life-giving community was born. Almost a decade later, it's a true joy to see this collection of stories bound as a testament that will sit on shelves and in hearts for years to come. In these pages you will see reality, the soaring mountain tops, the deep valleys, and the long plateaus that one traverses on a journey such as this. Through it all you will see our common Hero. As you read these stories, you will be drawn to the One who bids us, "Come and follow." You will see his tender care, his indwelling strength, and his transforming power. May this book help you "root and ground yourself in his love... that you may know the love of Christ that surpasses knowledge. And may you be filled to all the fullness of God."

—**Danielle Wheeler,**
Founder of Velvet Ashes and Director of Spiritual Development

Yet We Still
hope

Stories of Courage from Women Serving Around the World

Edited by
Denise Beck and Sarah Hilkemann

VELVET ASHES
PUBLISHING

To all the women whose stories are impacting the world that we will never read about in the pages of a book.

Table of Contents

Foreword

Most of the women who contributed to this book will not be famous. You will not read their names in a history of Christian missions book or watch a movie of their lives on the big screen. However, they represent a new generation of the countless unnamed women who for centuries have been counting the cost, taking up their crosses, and following the Lord Jesus to the ends of the earth. Today, the ends of the earth do not seem quite as far away as they once did, but the unique influence that living cross-culturally has on one's faith remains. The vignettes that the contributors of this book have written about their lives reflect that influence. Whether you are a woman, like them, who is living cross-culturally, or you pray for and support those who do, within this book's pages you will find hope and courage to face what is in front of you today.

Missionary autobiographies played a formative role in my own journey of faith. As a teen, I began devouring historical missionaries' stories, drawn in first by the lure of adventure in their tales. As I read, though, the authors inadvertently became mentors in the faith. While there certainly were stories of miraculous and awe-inspiring "God moments," much of their writing was filled with the mundane, hardship, sickness, longing, devastation, loss, waiting, and suffering. Through their raw writing, I began to realize that the real adventure did not lie in distant, exotic lands, but in the moment-by-moment trust in God wherever one might be in the world. I credit those historical missionaries with nurturing my faith at a critical time. So too, the contributors of this compilation offer stories that "go there." The brokenness of life is very evident throughout their writing and not all the stories have happy endings...yet. But as they courageously share their hard stories of the stresses of cross-cultural life, illness, betrayal, rape, and death, they still extend hope to their readers.

As a young adult, I lived and served cross-culturally. Now my years of serving overseas are starting to fade distantly in the rearview mirror of my life but reading the stories of the women in this volume brought me right back to that time and to many of the truths that I learned while living in a remote region of Kenya. Although the circumstances are different, the tender voice of God is still the same. Through the pages of this book, you will hear it comforting, lifting, challenging when necessary, and giving courage.

For the past decade or so, I have been immersed in the world of mission scholarship. I have had the privilege of learning from the best in the field of intercultural studies, read many histories and theologies of mission, and made some of my own contributions. Such work is fueled by those who serve cross-culturally and share their stories. Therefore, it was a privilege to be invited to become a board member of Velvet Ashes and then to hear and learn from the women in this book who are the front-line workers. Historically, the vast majority of missionary women will never write or read a formal theology of mission, but through the pages of this book, through the stories that the authors tell, you will read their theology. They worked it out as they were serving and again as they were writing and rewriting their stories. It is a theology of risk, suffering, disappointment, and hope. It is a theology born out of being on mission with God.

—*Laura Chevalier Beer, PhD*

September 2022

A Word from the Editors

I remember walking with her in the bush of S. Sudan. The stories she told about the life she had lived there were so courageous that I was nearly speechless as we navigated the bends in the land forgotten by the rest of the world. As a mom of four, my dreams of what the Lord could do were very much mixed with fear of the unknown. The unknown of this wild place and of the strength I wasn't sure I had for the job ahead. As we stepped in pace with each other into the parched riverbed before us I remember telling her, "Someday I will be reading the story of your life and I'll remember this moment with you right now".

Little did I know that a few years later I would be sitting in the Executive Director seat for an organization that stewards and gathers stories in all formats from courageous women in every bend in the path and forgotten place in the world. Little did I know that at that moment there were others living courageous stories that I would have the honor of adding to the pages you hold in your hands right now.

Serving with the Velvet Ashes team from this seat has been the privilege of my life. What started in S. Sudan and Uganda changed my husband and me forever. And from that changed place we now navigate serving cross-cultural workers from the Midwest while our four TCKs amaze us with the brilliant adults they are becoming.

I pray that wherever you find yourself these stories change you. I pray they fill you up and give you courage as you walk the bends in your land, forgotten or not.

—*Denise Beck, Executive Director of Velvet Ashes*

I grew up reading the stories of Elisabeth Elliot, Gladys Aylward and so many other brave men and women who followed God across borders and into new cultures. These stories inspired me to say, "Here I am, Lord" and then pack all of my life into two suitcases and step off a plane to breathe in the humid air of Cambodia.

Stories are powerful. They challenge and inspire us, move us to laughter or tears. We pause and ponder and look at our own lives with a fresh perspective. Story drew me into the Velvet Ashes community in those hard and beautiful days living in Cambodia, bringing encouragement and the reminder that I wasn't alone in all that I was experiencing.

The stories in this book, the words these women have bravely shared, are precious treasures to me. Now on staff with Velvet Ashes after my years overseas, I couldn't be more grateful for the opportunity to be part of this project and get this book into your hands. May you see God's faithfulness, feel the power of his hope and hold fast to courage as you follow him.

—*Sarah Hilkemann, Velvet Ashes Program Director*

Introduction

7 days. That's how long it takes for the earliest symptoms of malaria to develop.

7 days. That's how long we had been in Africa when my 6-year-old spiked a 105° F temperature and the fear I had hoped to have more time preparing for became a reality.

30 minutes. That's how long it took for her to show up, load us in her truck, and get us to the clinic. To me, malaria was a nightmare that ended in me burying a child. To her it was a minor inconvenience (most of the time), and fear didn't even register on day one of a diagnosis. Just sitting shoulder to shoulder with her and seeing her calm, hearing her calm, I felt my courage grow. I felt hope ignite. What began as a competition between my heart and stomach as they battled for exit from my body in response to fear, ended in a puzzle piece being snapped together in the picture of what life in rural sub-saharan Africa would look like. Literally within hours of his first dose of malaria meds his fever left and never came back. I survived one of the big fears I had about my new life. She showed me how.

A puzzle is actually a good analogy. We have one nearing completion on my thick, wooden coffee table right now. The arms that sprawl around the unfit pieces are always reaching for the lid of the box. The place that shows them what they are striving for.

The place that makes sense of the mess in front of them and inspires them to keep going one piece at a time.

The women that go before us in many ways are the lid of the box. Maybe it was the complete picture that you had heard about at Vacation Bible School or as bedtime stories that motivated you to want to live your life in this way.

Maybe it was the complete picture that you studied in college that caused you to dream of this adventure with the Lord.

Maybe it was and is the complete picture of the women who have gone before you that remind you why you are where you are, even when you are so in the middle of your picture you can't tell what it looks like anymore.

Either way, because Elisabeth Elliot allowed the people that killed her husband to love on her child—I am braver.

Because Dr. Helen Roseveare did not get angry at the Lord when she was beaten and raped but instead looked at her life and body as His to use to reach the lost at all costs—I am challenged.

And because Dorothy Carey's picture taught me to value mental health, I am better equipped than others have had the chance to be.

Each of us has a story that offers courage to someone. Maybe our pictures aren't ones we want to hang up for the world to see, but here, in the right hands, women have had the courage to share them, and they are seen as beautiful.

At Velvet Ashes our unusual name is a constant reminder that we exist to help women thrive in the most unlikely places. Like the

Velvet Ash tree, with the right care, we can weather the extremes in climate and culture. And our shared experiences give us the courage and the hope to do just that.

What we have worked to do in this book is get a few more puzzle box lids into your hands. The famous stories may have inspired you to go. But these are the stories that may inspire you to stay. These are the pictures that may help you with the decisions you are making or will be making. Not every story has a happy ending. But every story is from a woman who understands the joys and challenges of living a cross-cultural life for the sake of the lost. Every picture is personal and is being held up for you so that from their picture, you can look at the pieces you are trying to make sense of and say, "I think I can see it now."

And maybe like me and my hero in her truck, you will feel the shoulders of other women who have gone before you pressed against yours. I pray that their courage will wash over you and you will realize that although there may still be fear, Yet We Still Hope.

—*Denise Beck, Velvet Ashes Executive Director*

Up the Mountain
with Isaac

Part One

>>>>>

Up the Mountain with Isaac

"So Abraham called that place The Lord Will Provide.
And to this day it is said, "On the mountain of the
Lord it will be provided."
—*Genesis 22:14 NIV*

We begin counting the cost before our feet land on foreign soil. We say yes to God's call but that means a brave no to living near family and operating in our heart language. We sell our possessions, decide what absolutely must fit into two suitcases per person, and take one last glance back at precious loved ones as we walk through airport security.

The surrender doesn't stop there, though. If only it did!

Abraham waited patiently for the fulfillment of the Lord's promises to him in his son Isaac. And then came the call to sacrifice his only son to this same God. His heart must have ached with confusion, yet he opened his hands in surrender with faithful steps of obedience up the mountain.

We follow in Abraham's footsteps, but instead of firewood and the knife, we carry our dreams of marriage and babies, our expectations for what overseas work looks like. We open hands that hold the safety of our children, our agendas, even our very lives, in surrender to the One who provides in the moments of joy and sorrow, doubt and disappointment.

Elisabeth Elliot is an example of a woman who walked this daring surrender path ahead of us throughout her entire life. Before she was the wife of Jim Elliot, the mother of Valerie, the missionary partner of Rachel Saint, Elisabeth said yes to Bible translation work among the Colorado people in the jungles of Ecuador in 1952. She laid her relationships, work and life on the altar of sacrifice. Knowing she loved Jim but putting their relationship on hold, she endured bugs, heat, isolation, mud, and tedious translation work.

After the death of a dear local friend and later in that year when her language informant died, she wondered if God was the one who had failed her. Did she hear right? Did she somehow get this calling wrong? We've been there too, when the pain rushes in and hope feels buried like a seed deep in the soil.

It's one thing when we get to see the miracles, the beautiful end result of all our patience, waiting, suffering. We can look back and say, "It was all worth it." But that's not how surrender works usually. Like Abraham, Elisabeth Elliot, and so many others, we know it's that daily, moment-by-moment trudge up the mountain through loneliness and loss.

And so we keep climbing.

May these precious stories of surrender encourage your heart in each moment as you hold fast to Jehovah Jireh, the God who provides.

—*Sarah Hilkemann, Velvet Ashes Program Director*

Chapter 1

SUFFICIENT GRACE

My grace is sufficient for you,
for my power is made perfect in weakness.
—2 Corinthians 12:9 ESV

That familiar feeling overwhelmed me. *How am I going to do this?*

We were headed back to the field after an intense home assignment. This season was spent in countless hours helping my daughter who has cerebral palsy access health care and services in the U.S. Gracie was finally settled into a lovely routine with a good situation at school and specialists who were helping me fine-tune her health. As a wheelchair-pushing mama, I was thoroughly enjoying conveniences like ramps, elevators, electricity, and clean tap water.

Our treasured daughter is now seventeen years old and fully dependent on me for her health, hygiene, mobility, nutrition, hydration, and medications. She represents more than a full-time job with no holidays, no lazy sleeping-in mornings, and no guaranteed nights of sleep. Meanwhile, I have five other children, and I am committed to supporting my husband, our local church, and community, while I also serve as a medical doctor in a limited capacity. The full-time task of taking care of Gracie in the U.S. seemed that much harder in our host country with so many more barriers.

We were on this foreign missions journey before we adopted Gracie. I went to medical school to become a missionary doctor overseas, but it turns out that God had even greater plans for that training. It's a running joke that I went to medical school in order to be Gracie's mom. A month after we adopted Gracie from West Africa, it became clear that the extent of her disabilities was far greater than we had been informed. Since we were starting the field scouting process, we focused on looking for places with proximity to the health care that would be needed, and, one by one, God closed each of those doors.

Shortly after one of those trips, feeling completely at peace with not joining the field we had just visited, Gracie underwent a life-changing surgery for her epilepsy. Her epilepsy stabilized, and God opened the door to move to Uganda.

Throughout the journey of preparing for moving to a foreign missions field with a daughter with special needs, I searched far and wide to network with and learn from seasoned missionary special needs families. During that time of preparation, we never met another family in overseas ministry whose child had even a hint of special needs. Undaunted, we packed up Gracie's equipment, stockpiled her medications, and made the move with our three little children to a country the kids and I had never seen.

I tackled setting up a house in a new country, learning language and culture, one-on-one homeschooling and providing therapies for seven-year-old Gracie, along with her very precocious three-year-old sister. Meanwhile, our cheerful one-year-old boy thrived in the red dirt underfoot. Anxiety threatened to overwhelm me, and the tasks and challenges were exhausting. How did local moms fetch water with a child who couldn't walk? I could barely manage, and we had so many luxuries, such as running water (usually) in the house. How do I keep a belly-crawler clean and parasite free? I had no one to ask for advice because local children with disabilities were hidden, and other missionary families didn't have children with significant special needs.

A few months later, I was pregnant, and we were adopting a traumatized five-year-old when our directors abruptly left the rookies in charge of the ministries. I knew I needed help. We were stretched thin. But where would I find someone who would be comfortable helping with Gracie? Whom could I ever trust to care for my very vulnerable daughter?

A friend who had become quite dear to me during our first year on the field approached me one day. "We're leaving the country, and we're looking for someone to hire our very trustworthy nanny. Would you be open to meeting her?" Monica came to our house, graciously sat with us, and spent time getting to know Gracie. She asked for time to pray about taking this unique caretaking job. A short time later, God brought our Auntie Monica into our lives. She became Gracie's best friend and most loving auntie. I trained her to bathe, change, feed, and teach Gracie. She delighted in Gracie's growth and cried with her pain. She named her daughter after her and made sure her children all spent time with our Gracie.

Five years later, we were finally going on our first furlough, and Monica was now passionate about God's great purpose and beauty in disabilities. She wanted to pursue full-time community based ministry to families impacted by disabilities. We released her with great enthusiasm, knowing that Monica's impact on her own community was going to be ten-fold our potential impact as foreigners.

Coming back from that furlough to a new community, I was pregnant again and sick. Gracie had major orthopedic surgery during that furlough and was in pain much of the time. I didn't know how I would possibly manage with Gracie who was now so much bigger and had to be positioned just right to avoid pain. Our new teammates hired a lady they knew to be reliable, but Gertrude had never cared for "one such as this."

The first month was rough, and Gertrude wasn't sure that this caregiving work was for her. By month two, Gertrude would hear nothing of leaving her Gracie girl. I trained her to provide all aspects of Gracie's care in case I was ever not available to be there. Gertrude rose to the occasion and loved the challenge and the joy of being close to our very spunky nonverbal daughter. During our next furlough, Gertrude started working at the local disabilities ministry full-time and subsequently went to school to be more qualified for the work, leaving us without a one-on-one for Gracie again. But Gertrude has joined the growing community of Ugandans who are passionate about God's love and design through disability and suffering..

Time after time, God has been faithful. Time after time, God has provided help for me in Gracie's care. Time after time, God has not only provided for us but also has transformed lives with far reaching ripple effects through this nonverbal treasure in a jar of clay. "But we have this treasure in jars of clay, to show that the surpassing power belongs to God and not to us" (2 Corinthians 4:7, ESV).

Gracie has thrived on the field. She has not been a passive recipient of services as she would likely be in the U.S.. She has been an active member of our local community. She is the loudest "singer" in church, and the dancing gets a little more lively when Gracie starts jumping out of her wheelchair. Church members cleared the bush around the church shelter so that her wheelchair could approach without getting snagged on all the tree roots.

With her vibrant personality, neighborhood children have learned not to fear approaching someone who looks and acts differently. Shy giggles erupt when Gracie plays a silly game with a reticent five-year old. Myths and misconceptions about disabilities have been shattered when people have come into our life to help me with Gracie.

Life with disabilities is hard. I can't just jump on a motorcycle taxi with her or even take her into the local market. Gracie struggles to sleep at night, and many dark nights find me curled up with her under her mosquito net willing her battery powered fan to keep cooling her off. Trips to the city always involve counting her medications and networking with pharmacies to restock her medications months in advance. Her specialists have helped me switch her to medications more common to Uganda. International flights are feats of Herculean strength and endurance matched with unmeasurable acts of kindness and mercy.

We thought we were going to Uganda to serve the local church by training pastors and participating in mercy ministries. We never imagined the huge impact of living as a real family in the community. We are needy, flawed, and pouring it all out for the least of these. We need help from our neighbors, and we are not self-sufficient.

Life with Gracie has helped to transform our understanding of what missions truly is: living life as if before the face of God (coram Deo), hand in hand with our community, pointing together to Christ and not to ourselves or our program.

We are once again packing for Uganda and that fear is creeping in. How will I become fluent in this new language, homeschool the kids, and give Gracie what she needs? How will I meet all the expectations that I feel so acutely? Where will I find Gracie's next caregiver? It always seems impossible and yet...

> *"My grace is sufficient for you, for my power is made perfect in weakness." Therefore I will boast all the more gladly of my weaknesses, so that the power of Christ may rest upon me. For the sake of Christ, then, I am content with weaknesses, insults, hardships, persecutions, and calamities. For when I am weak, then I am strong (2 Corinthians 12:9-10, ESV).*
>
> —*Abigail Rattin*

Chapter 2

RE-FORMING HOPE

Life is not supposed to turn out like this! I'd gone overseas with high hopes, called by God to Asia to share His Good News with people who'd never heard before. Sure, I had read lots of biographies since I was a kid, and I knew there would be challenges, but I didn't know it would be like this!

I was in a teaching job in a university that I really loved, but very few of my students or friends were interested in hearing the Gospel or even discussing spiritual things. Instead, I had my students ask me questions like, "Why do the foreigners keep telling us about Jesus? Why don't they respect our culture? Don't the foreigners know it's against the law to come onto our campus and try to make us believe in Jesus?"

The work seemed so impossible. And somehow the expectations on us always seemed to be growing. Before I went overseas, people encouraged me to share my faith. Then leaders in our campus group said really our goal is to make disciples. When I went to seminary, the focus was on church planting. In the early years of being overseas, we started hearing about church planting movements and the ten (or fill in some number) steps toward working with God in making that happen. Later, leaders started talking about the DNA for cross-cultural work being in these new churches from the beginning. We wanted to see multiplying movements of churches reaching out cross-culturally and planting more cross-culturally-minded churches! And, honestly, that is a beautiful vision of what the global church can be. But I was sinking under the expectations!

In those early years when my students were asking all those challenging questions about why foreigners were trying to share with them, my closest friend, Yvonne, had made huge steps of faith toward God. One night we were sitting together with her husband's friend. As this guy shared about all the problems his family was going through, Yvonne told him, "You all need to believe in God. There is a Creator God who loves you." I was so excited to hear her sharing her faith with someone else!

But later, Yvonne turned away from God. She told me, "I wanted to believe. I tried to believe. But I couldn't believe. The stories in the Bible seem like children's fables to me."

When I got together with other foreigners living in that city, they asked me, "Why doesn't your friend believe in Jesus yet?" Over and over people asked me this, and I simply answered, "I don't know." But I felt so ashamed.

My hopes for my students, my hopes for Yvonne, and, if I'm being honest, my hopes for being considered by others to be a good cross-cultural worker were crushed.

I was also crushed in my personal life. I was single when I left for Asia, but I assumed that God would provide a husband for me at some point. I'm not sure why I assumed this considering all those biographies that I'd read didn't usually turn out that way! But for years people had quoted, "God gives us the desires of our hearts!" He especially gives us the desires of our hearts when we desire Him and follow Him to the other side of the world, right? Among all the foreigners working in the whole region, I found the single female to single male ratio to be about 40:1. I'm not exaggerating! Also, there were no local single men my age who were followers of Jesus.

A few years after arriving in Asia, God put a single guy with similar values and a similar ministry focus in my small group with our Sunday fellowship. We got along well. We spent a lot of time hanging out together with a young couple with kids. I had several different ladies who knew us both come up and ask me, "Hey, what's going on with you two? It's obvious he likes you." It wasn't just in my head. I had high hopes. But, in the end, he wasn't interested in me.

It felt like in every area of life, I was crushed. I was bitterly disappointed. I wondered, *Really? Really, God? This is how life turns out? This is what working overseas looks like? Your Gospel is so great, but the people don't want it. And why, God, did you set me up for heartbreak?*

Up the Mountain with Isaac

Out of all the small groups in all the places in Asia, that guy ended up in mine?

In my disappointment—even disappointment with God, no, especially my disappointment with God—He was gracious to me. God brought me to a deep examination of my motives for being overseas and to repentance for my sin. I repented for the pride of wanting people to love Jesus so that I would look good. It was like God pressed a reset button in my heart so that the work here is truly about Jesus—His beauty, His love, His grace to set people free. Jesus deserves our worship and the worship of the local people here. And the local people have the right and the need to hear about the love of Jesus. That's my motive. That's my joy and ambition. And when I start to get off track, I try to be quick to repent and turn away from those sinful, prideful, arrogant motives.

God also wooed me again.

The following summer after my broken heart, I had the opportunity to travel to Vietnam for a teachers' conference, and I tacked on a few weeks of vacation to the end of my trip. None of my friends could travel with me, so I was on my own in that exotic and fascinating country. I was processing many vivid sights and strange smells. With no one there to talk to, I found myself praying often, just experiencing these new things with Jesus. I'd look up at the mass of crazy power lines, and think, *Wow, Jesus! It really does look like power line spaghetti!* I'd taste the pho and say, "Oh, Jesus, I can't believe the people here eat hot noodle soup when it's over

40°C (104°F). I think I'm going to sweat to death!" I came to think of these weeks experiencing all these new things as "traveling with Jesus." It wasn't "journeying with Jesus." It did not feel like a spiritual, metaphysical "journey." It felt like a road trip with Jesus! It was so precious to have that time with Him, with so few other voices or conversations, just the two of us experiencing life together.

After a few weeks of "traveling with Jesus," I decided to join a tour group going to the Mekong Delta. I got on the big tour bus and sat with my earbuds in, listening to music. At the next hotel, we picked up another group of passengers. The bus was filling up, so a man sat down in the empty seat next to me. We silently rode for a while to the stop where we had lunch. When we got out and sat at various tables, the same tall, dark, and handsome guy came and sat down next to me. He wasn't with the other people like I originally thought he was. Like me, he was traveling on his own. So, we started to chat. I found out that he was a piano teacher at a conservatory in Spain. I asked him, "What's your name?" He answered, "Jesús." I had to turn my face away because I started laughing to myself, *I'm still traveling with Jesus, only this time he's a handsome Spaniard!* God has an incredible sense of humor. The whole trip I kept laughing about how I was "traveling with Jesus."

During those weeks, I also thought about how to have hope again even in the midst of my deep disappointments. I studied in the Bible about hope and learned that *hope* doesn't just mean "wish," like in English. It means a "confident expectation." I listened to a series of Tim Keller sermons on Habakkuk about not understanding what God is doing but still trusting Him. I was encouraged to believe that God is still working out His good purposes—His Kingdom come—in this world, even when we can't see this happening. I was encouraged to persevere in hope because of God's character.

During that season of crushing disappointment, God showed His kindness to me in forgiving me and resetting my motives in ministry. Out of deep discouragement, God deepened my trust that He is good, as is His Gospel of grace. He also wooed my bruised heart after unrequited love. In my season of deep pain in realizing I would probably never be married or have kids of my own, I was, after all, quickly approaching that age, God graciously poured out His love to me again in such sweet ways. God's love reformed hope in my heart.

A few years later, after I had moved to a different city, I ran into a foreign lady who was also friends with Yvonne. She excitedly asked me, "You know Yvonne got baptized, right?"

—Anonymous

Chapter 3

LOOKING FOR THE LIGHT

God is our refuge and strength,
a very present help in trouble.
Therefore we will not fear though the earth gives way,
though the mountains be moved into the heart of the
sea, though its waters roar and foam,
though the mountains tremble at its swelling.
—Psalm 46:1-3, ESV

The penetrating rays of last sunlight streamed through the airport windows, straight into my broken heart. I put my phone down, sank to the floor, beyond awareness of the flow of people around me, internally crying, O God, O God, O God. How long I knelt there, I am unsure, only as long as the light hit my wet face. When the sun finally sunk below the horizon, I stood, dusted myself off, grabbed my backpack, and boarded my first flight.

Up the Mountain with Isaac

Comfort us, O God, in these hard
and early hours of loss.
Be to us a strength and light,
for we are shocked, numbed.[1]

Thirty-hour travel days, alone, after a massive family tragedy—we are not made for this—I was not made for this. I squeezed past two large men to my window seat and turned to keep my face to myself. No, I did not want to talk; I did not want to be seen. It would be a long time before I could be hugged, be with someone, be with anyone who knew me and knew what loss had hit me.

God, I am so alone. In the middle of all of this, I am so alone. These desperate cries flooded my ears, the weeping of my heart, the shroud of my grief. I rested my head against the window, keeping my eyes on the last lights of the runway, shallow breaths coming, the familiar nausea and anxiety hitting along with the intense grief and shock. I needed light, O God, any light, to pierce this vast darkness overcoming me.

Be nearer, O Christ,
Than I have ever known.
Be near to me, be near to those
Who also share this grief.[2]

My mind went to the memories, of course. When had I last seen him? I could hear his voice, the way he said, "Aunt Bethany," the turn of his nose, and the piercing blue of his eyes. My eleven-year-old nephew, my brother's son, my children's cousin, my flesh and blood. No, no, no. This cannot be; this cannot be true. These were the random tragedies that happened to others, not to our family. Why did it have to be him? This cannot be real; this cannot be part of the story—it is all so wrong, so random, so cruel.

> *My thoughts are torn and tossed. They make little*
> *sense... how can I or anyone make sense of this? Make*
> *peace with this? Have words for this?*[3]

My body lurched back into my seat as the plane took flight. I closed my eyes; the music in my earbuds drowning out the announcements, the chatter, the plane sounds, the screaming in my head. *Deep breaths, you are not truly alone.*

I pulled my woolen poncho tighter around my shoulders, shivering not from cold but from aching. My heart ached for my husband and children already—how would they process this without me? My heart ached for my brother and sister-in-law and niece—what does life look like without him? And then my heart ached because I did not want to do this, because this was not to be part of the story, because life overseas away from loved ones is hard enough in stable times, and I could not imagine how to do this life when my heart could not be whole on one continent.

"In the day of trouble," the psalmist laments, "I seek the Lord; in the night my hand is stretched out without wearying; my soul refuses to be comforted. When I remember God, I moan; when I meditate, my spirit faints" (Psalm 77:2-3, ESV). Praying feels more like moaning in times like this: thinking incoherent thoughts, mumbling for strength, begging for peace that cannot flood my soul. What is courage in the midst of great tragedy? When the next breath is labored, the next step a mountain of its own, the next day inconceivable? Perhaps courage is in the muttering, in the moaning, in looking up in times of deepest need. Courage manifests in the expanding of the lungs for necessary air, in the movement of muscles for forward motion, in the opening of our eyes to the sun rising on another day. Courage, at times, is simply surviving.

My brother and I paddled silently through the shallow channel that had been my nephew's favorite fishing spot. *How can I leave this place?* I silently asked God. My return trip was scheduled for the next day, but my soul was restless, burdened by the needs of my family here and my family there. *How do we continue to live and work there when there's so much hurting here? I can't leave them!* I silently screamed at God, resentful of my complicated life, for the work which took us so far from family. *What about me? How am I supposed to live my life after this?*

It wasn't only about my hurting family; it was about my own hurting heart as well. I knew the demands of my life in southern Africa. I could not imagine jumping back into all of the responsibilities and ministries when even just another breath, another step, felt like such work.

I cannot yet know what it will mean to live daily with the wounds of this loss. I cannot yet know what to do

or where to go. Only do not let me go through this
alone, O God.[4]

There was a bitter wind blowing, my fingers numb on my paddle, but the sun was shining brightly. Every day since the airport, I found myself looking for the light, wherever I could find it. I lingered in it, basked in it, warmed myself, asked God to let it flood my soul, over and over again. *Behold, I am making all things new... yes, He will wipe away every tear from their eyes, and death shall be no more, neither shall there be mourning, nor crying, nor pain anymore.* Oh, how we longed for that—*why does this seem so far off, Lord?* And what about the rest of this life in the meantime, when there's so much pain and brokenness and darkness?

> *"The people who walked in darkness have seen a great*
> *light,"* the prophet wrote, *"those who dwelt in a land of*
> *deep darkness, on them has light shone"* (Isaiah 9:2,
> *ESV).*

I inhaled deeply, closed my eyes, and turned my face toward the sun. Grief is lonely and will be especially lonely on that side of the Atlantic, far from my family. I knew this; I dreaded this. Yet graciously God reminded my fractured heart that I am not alone, not ever.

The Light of the World incarnated to walk with us, in the most physical sense, body and spirit. His feet took labored steps on this dirt; His lungs labored for breath in this very air. He knew the pain of a loved one dying, and He wept bitterly. Deep anger welled up within Him at the brokenness of this earth. He knew depths of brokenness beyond our human experience and in the bravest act of history carried Himself to His own death to show us that He would indeed conquer it, for all time.

> *Hold me now, O Christ—I am undone—*
> *and I have nowhere I might run but to You.*
> *If Your Spirit is not present, or your promises not true,*
> *there is nothing we can do but crumble in despair and*
> *disbelief,*
> *defeated by this enemy—death.[5]*

God, in His abundant mercy, Calvin says, is "dispelling the darkness of death, and restoring to the people of God the light of life." This is what it means to grieve in hope, I realized. Yes, there is so much pain, so much grief and gratefully, in Christ, so much hope. Without Christ, "there is no life-giving light in the world, but everything is covered by the appalling darkness of death."[6]

I trust You, the tiniest whisper my soul had ever made to God, but there it was. Oh, all that I needed to entrust to Him—it felt like my whole world. It was my whole world. He would carry them—my brother and his family, my parents, the many others who loved and grieved my nephew. He would carry us—my husband and children—so far from the loss, the grief. And He would carry me—my broken, conflicted heart, my darkened path, my loneliness. There is nothing about this journey that would be easy, but I would not be alone.

I sit on the wooden bench on my back patio, back in Africa, back with my husband and children, back to my life and home. I pull the woolen poncho around my shoulders again, against the winter chill, and warm my hands with my mug of steaming coffee. I am waiting for the light again, in these predawn minutes. The vast sky streaks with shades of orange and pink and purple, as if laying the royal carpet for the coming of the light.

I take a deep breath, the clean air cleansing my lungs, and I pause to think on how my nephew's lungs are now enabling breaths in another body, sustaining another life. Gratitude floods my soul. Such grace, in the midst of so much sorrow. Such light, in the midst of deep darkness. This is life, I am alive, and the sun is rising.

> *Through the heartfelt mercies of our God,*
> *God's Sunrise will break in upon us,*
> *Shining on those in the darkness,*
> *those sitting in the shadow of death,*
> *Then showing us the way, one foot at a time,*
> *down the path of peace.*
> *Luke 1:78-79 MSG*

—*Beth Barthelemy*

Chapter 4

THAT YOUR FAITH MAY NOT FAIL

I sat across the table from the young Thai doctor, a can of Coke at my elbow. I never drink Coke. Beside me, my friend's reassuring presence was a bulwark against my slowly rising tide of dread. More experienced in these situations, she had handed me the Coke when we sat down, saying, "You might need the sugar and caffeine." Beginning to feel alarmed, but not yet aware this conversation would divide my life into "Before" and "After," I listened uneasily as the doctor began to explain what was wrong with my daughter.

She lay sleeping in the bed behind us, her tummy full of the watermelon she'd begged for, which my sweet friend had miraculously found in the hospital food court, even though it was out of season. My little girl's tummy was also, apparently, full of cancer. That's why it was so distended, why her tiny face was pasty white, why she was too weak to walk very far and wanted to ride in her stroller everywhere, even though she was almost three and a half.

Cancer.

My mind slid past the word, unable to find purchase. A word full of darkness and death. No one I knew had gone through chemotherapy, but I had heard the horrible stories. I felt like Alice falling down the rabbit hole.

"It's very curable," the doctor was saying, reassuringly. "The kind of leukemia she has has a very high success rate. She will be cancer-free; don't worry; don't worry." He smiled his cheery Thai smile. I was a block of ice. Numb. Uncomprehending. I longed for my husband who had stayed behind in Central Asia with our two boys while I flew to Thailand with Grace for what we thought would be a straightforward set of tests. He was on speakerphone in the middle of the table, listening, helpless. I could feel him through the phone line, wrestling incredulously to understand.

My friend pushed ahead, asking all the questions. I sat there reeling. I took an automatic sip of Coke, tasted sugary sourness in my mouth. "Excuse me," I blurted, feeling the tears rise, not wanting to wake Grace.

I slipped into the bathroom and collapsed onto the toilet lid, holding up my heavy head with trembling hands. All my life, I'd been waiting for the other shoe to drop. A pain-free childhood and young adulthood coupled with a careful reading of Scripture and biographies meant I was acutely aware every human experiences excruciating pain at some point in their life. I had dreaded mine with every fiber of my being. I'd prayed for years that when the crisis came, God would make me ready, that I wouldn't disappoint

Him by losing my faith, that somehow He would make me able to bear it.

Now the tunnel mouth yawned blackly in front of me. *Cancer.*

In that bleak moment, words emerged in my mind: *Shall I receive good from the hand of the Lord, and not evil?*

Job, I thought dully. It was Job who said, "Shall we receive good from God, and shall we not receive evil?" (Job 2:10, ESV) My body began to shiver. *No. No.* I pushed both hands out in front of me, holding it all at bay. *Jesus, I know You allow both good and evil. But... how can I receive this? Really, Lord?*

That night by her hospital bed, I felt like Abraham, being asked to lay my child on the altar. My heart could not lift her up high enough to place her small body on the cold stones. The whole thing was too heavy. I wrestled for hours. *Why our family? Why our smallest, most vulnerable person? Why now? We've given our lives to serve you overseas, God; You would really bring this into our story? I thought Your plans for us were good.* Even as my heart quietly whispered more of Job's words, *When he has tried me, I will come out as gold* (Job 23:10, ESV), my mind and body writhed against the suffocating, terrifying dark.

We slept forty-six nights in the hospital in Bangkok, pumping Grace's tiny body full of targeted drugs until every speck of leukemia and lymphoma had disappeared. The tumors in her organs melted away, the percentage of mutant blood cells steadily reduced, while the medicines shredded her mouth and digestive system and she sunk deeper and deeper into a listless stupor of narcotic-dulled pain. We were buoyed up by incredible "aunties" and "uncles" who dropped their own lives to be by our side—looking after our boys, taking turns staying with Grace, bringing food, helping us talk with doctors, researching, doing whatever needed doing. We were children again, helpless, desperate, trusting God to bring what we needed, to do whatever it took to heal her.

At the end of six weeks, exhausted and relieved, we flew back to New Zealand with a living—smiling!—cancer-free toddler, who at just 12.5 kilograms (25 pounds), looked like a concentration camp survivor. All that year we plodded through the rigorous program designed to ensure the poisonous cells would never return.

In November, with Grace out of danger and the boys in school, a semblance of normalcy began to return. But we had been "on" mentally, emotionally, and physically since February, and fatigue was taking hold. I slid into a fog. I felt disassociated from my own body, like I was watching myself from a distance, which frightened me.

God felt impossibly far away. (Or maybe I was so numb I couldn't feel anything.) He was a stranger; I felt I needed to get to know Him all over again from the beginning, which, coupled with my new doubts about His goodness and wisdom, plunged me into depression.

I began seeking help for the various physical needs I had and for my spiritual needs as well.

Up the Mountain with Isaac

I let myself grieve. This was not the life crisis I had imagined—one of my parents dying early, my own body getting sick—this was so unbelievable, such a low blow. How could God do this to our sweet little girl? I started to feel some of the anger I'd pushed down, the shock, the incredulity, the outrage. My mind knew God was still good, I just couldn't believe He would allow this kind of thing to happen to a child—*my* child. I was also disturbed and guilty about my total lack of awareness of childhood cancer up to this point. Every week we entered a ward full of kids with a whole spectrum of diagnoses, many with worse projected outcomes than Grace's. In the world of cancer, we actually had it... good. I felt sick to my stomach. *How could I not have known? God, did You know about all this?*

My local friends from our little village back in Central Asia texted regularly to find out how Grace was doing. I was plagued by new thoughts: *How many kids in our village will go through these same horrors, but in a poorly equipped, archaic medical system with minimal resources to ease the journey, and a depressingly lower survival rate? How many more would survive if they could get to where we are?*

Just before Christmas, a friend invited me to go on a silent retreat with a local college group. I boarded the bus with a bunch of strangers, weirdly comforted by not having to talk to anyone, though I was known for being outgoing and extroverted. Despite my lethargy, I felt a faint stirring of hope as we approached the forested mountains where we would stay for two nights.

It rained, and I went for long walks, relishing cool air, wet leaves brushing my face, mist droplets in my hair. There was no pressure to talk. I journaled a little, but mostly I walked, ate, slept, thought, tried to pray, walked again. I crouched for long, slow minutes, drinking in the tiny ferns along the path, absorbing their vivid green. I wandered around the base of an enormous tree, head tipped back, worshiping, my heart sinking ravenously into roots and earth, reaching upward in the solid immensity of the trunk.

It felt like coming up for air.

That weekend I tramped through the fresh, wet green, feeling my insides slowly expanding. Toward the end of the second afternoon, I curled up in my bunk to nap but found myself wide awake, unable to sleep, journal, or even move. I just lay there, completely still, allowing a rare sense of safety to well up all around me. No needs to meet, everyone safe at home, no one to hear or see. I was completely alone with God.

A sob welled up from my gut and tore free. Great wrenching heaves, my soul turning inside out. Stomach convulsing, lungs burning, mouth stretched in a silent scream, groping blindly down through the maelstrom until I found what I was screaming:

What would I have done if you had let her die?

How would I have LIVED?

I was sobbing, inconsolable. Choking the words out. *Would I still believe in You? Would I still love You? What You let happen was horrible enough. But You could have taken her. Then what?*

Kids... die. I'm finally absorbing this, and it's wrecking me. Parents lose their children—the heart of their heart—every day.

Then what? What do they do? How do they keep going? How do they live all those years, all those awful, empty days, one by one, between the death of their child and their own death?

When I tried to lay Grace on the altar in that hospital room, I was giving her up to God, entrusting her to the Great Physician. It nearly broke me. But this was harder. Now I was grappling with the writhing reality of this broken planet, the destructiveness of sin, the fact that God does not always step in and intervene. *He saved my little girl but allows other children to perish.* I was facing the incontrovertible fact of God's utter sovereignty over all things, including the things I love the most and take for granted He will protect. I had known there are no guarantees of safety. Now my heart tried to swallow the bitter implications.

Cocooned, exhausted, I lay limp on the floor of the utmost bottom of myself. Everything became extremely still. I heard my heart beat.

Then came that same quiet voice, gently: "I let My own Son die."

A slow, seeping realization of the grief of God. A oneness. A familiarity. A promise of presence. An actual presence. "Would I not be with you?" A peace I had never known stole over me. My tired heart stirred, faintly.

"Lord..." Hesitant. Testing the words in my mouth. "...to whom else... would I go? To whom else would I go? You—You have the words of eternal life."

That I could say those words, and mean them, was God's

answer to years of fear my faith would fail at the crucial moment. I was flooded with weak relief. I had faced the abyss. He had not let my faith fail.

> "I have prayed for you," Jesus said to Peter, "that your faith may not fail. And when you have turned, strengthen your brothers" (Luke 22:32, ESV).

> When you pass through the waters, I will be with you; and when you pass through the rivers, they will not sweep over you. When you walk through the fire, you will not be burned; the flames will not set you ablaze. For I am the Lord your God, the Holy One of Israel, your Savior. (Isaiah 43:2-3, NIV)

Epilogue:

Two years later Grace had finished chemo and was still in remission, her immunity counts back up to normal. We resumed our life and ministry in Central Asia with a newfound awareness of the fragility of all things, and God's unbreakable faithfulness.

Nearly three more years after that day, I'm typing this in the heat of a Central Asian high summer, flowers and veggies growing outside, my husband working in his orchard, the kids swimming in the irrigation canal.

We've shared Grace's story many times, testifying to God's goodness and faithfulness. On the other side of that terrifying word—cancer—is a whole world of people I can now hold inside my heart. Even now, I'm aware we might not be finished. Every blood test finds me holding my breath; each normal result brings a fresh sigh of relief in my bones.

God is good. All the time.

All the time.

—*Carolyn Broughton*

Chapter 5

COUNTING THE COST

How did I end up here again? I did everything in my power to prevent this from happening. I had learned lessons along the way and made adjustments accordingly. I knew what I needed to thrive on the field; I had learned so much. And yet, I have ended up here again, feeling empty and lost.

My story is one of trauma and difficulty, but also of God's great faithfulness and of small miracles along the way. I wanted to be a missionary for as long as I can remember. I come from a country in Scandinavia, but as a child I played with children on the street in Bangladesh when our family lived there for a time. I saw real poverty. I knew there was no other path for me; I needed to live a life in service to people. Everything I did as a teenager and young adult was deliberate. I had a plan; I was going out on the field as soon as I possibly could. I made my decisions based on this plan, including the decision to go to England to study, which is where I met my future husband. One thing led to the other; God led me through it all. It was so exciting.

In 2007 my husband and I moved to a country in the Middle East. I was so excited to start language studies and to connect with people. It did not turn out how I had expected. That dream I had had since I was a child turned out to be filled with struggles. All the training in the world could not have prepared me for the culture shock or for the difficult journey through language learning. My love for the people kept me going, but I struggled to like the culture. The limitation that comes with being a woman in that part of the world was hard for this Scandinavian to bear.

As if this wasn't enough, we also had two children within our first three years there. When our second child came along, I really started to struggle. By this time we had moved five times, including moving to another city. I had moved with morning sickness, during pregnancy, with one baby, with two babies. I was exhausted. The months went by as if I was in a fog. I started to have panic attacks. Not knowing what they were, I started to fear that something was wrong with me. I had dreams about demons during this time, attacking the baby or lashing out at us.

When our son was about four months old, he started to sleep poorly. He would sleep for only half an hour at a time. When he woke up, he would be inconsolable. Soon I started to expect him to wake up. I would lie awake and just wait for him to cry. There were many nights when I had to get up to take care of two kids still in diapers and didn't sleep at all. Weeks turned into months, and it started to take its toll. My body started to react. Tiredness, stomach issues, body pain, they were all reactions to stress. I started to once again fear that something was wrong with me. I constantly felt nervous and fearful. At night the fear would get so strong that I wasn't able to rest. I was convinced something was going to happen to our family; I just knew it. At the same time I refused to give up. If God had called us, we were going to just hold on and fight.

In August of that year we went on furlough. Our son was by that time not gaining weight. He also wasn't eating well. I knew something wasn't right, but I convinced myself it was allergies or something really simple. Two weeks before we were due to go back to the field, he got a fever. Little did we know that a simple trip to the doctor that afternoon would change our lives forever.

On the morning of October 1, 2010, we were waiting in a hospital room expecting to be told that our son had a simple infection and that we could go home. At the same time this nagging feeling and dark thought had entered my mind. The doctor had tried to conceal it the night before, but with my nursing background I knew. High white blood cells and low hemoglobin could only mean one thing. It all started to make sense. Yet I just couldn't believe it. It just couldn't be true. When waiting turned into hours and the doctors didn't show up, we started to suspect that something was going on. Finally, as a whole team of doctors entered the room, we were told. Our nine-month-old son had leukemia.

Up the Mountain with Isaac

During the whirlwind of activities, examinations, and decisions in the following weeks, we walked around in a fog. Not sure what to think or do. The reality started to sink in. Not only would we spend two years going through a difficult cancer treatment with our son, we also could not return to the field. Looking back, God sent small gifts showing us He cared throughout that time. The taxi driver that drove us to a different hospital was a believer and wouldn't let us pay him. Nurses and doctors at the new hospital were members of my church and came to us to pray and encourage us.

My husband, who is American, was given a residential visa right away because of our circumstances. It might seem like small things, but they were actually true miracles. I still remember phone calls from dear friends from this time that kept me going for a few more days. Sometimes I lived hour by hour, but these phone calls and messages kept me going.

Dealing with this diagnosis was hard enough. We also had the added complication of not having lived in my home country together and not being able to return to the field. We were grieving two things at once. Both things were hard to deal with and get through.

During the first months of the treatment, as the chemo started to break down our sweet son's little body, we entered a darkness that broke us down completely. We felt abandoned by God. We just didn't feel that He was there. Everything had fallen apart. We could not understand why He would call us to something and then not let us continue in it. It seemed so cruel. I could not see a meaningful future. We struggled to find meaning in our new jobs and situation. The dream I had since childhood was taken away from me. At the same time, our son was really struggling, and we were dealing with anxiety and fear daily, or actually, hourly. I planned his funeral. For me this was a way of dealing with what was going on; I felt that it would be easier to bear if I had prepared for it. I am not sure it helped.

Afterwards, when things had calmed down a bit, I asked God for an explanation. I wanted to know why in the most difficult time of our lives He hadn't been there. God showed me a picture of the hospital room. I was standing over my son's bed, praying. I felt abandoned and didn't think God was there. A little further away, over by the window, I saw Jesus. He was crying. This is the only explanation He gave me. Jesus was there. I just didn't feel it or know it at the time. But He was there, and He cried with us.

As the years went by, we continued to struggle with our lives in my home country. We just didn't feel the passion that we felt for our work on the field. Slowly our son's health improved, and we also had a third child. Life went on. I struggled with panic anxiety for a long time and also with depression. The relentless physical fatigue after something like this is overwhelming. I still struggle with it.

In August 2017 our son was given the all clear. Against all odds, in September that same year we went back to the field. It was a miracle. A dream come true that we had never expected.

Up the Mountain with Isaac

There is a lot to be said about missionaries. Resilience, strength, fearlessness. But there is another side to it. There is stubbornness and a tendency to be blinded by our calling or by our tasks. I am so thankful that I was able to come back. God has done so many things that we never would have expected. It has been so exciting. At the same time it has come at a great personal cost. The thing is that the fatigue that I mentioned is very real. I struggle with it every day. It is like a fatigue of the soul. It is so heavy. I still struggle a lot with panic anxiety and feelings of hopelessness and sadness. I also very easily get overwhelmed and stressed.

After another four years on the field I can only say this: I am not who I used to be, for better and for worse. I have learned so much more about God's faithfulness, and I am so much more resilient as a result of what I have gone through. I am not someone who gives up easily, but I also need to realize that I have my limits. The constant cultural difficulties, work challenges, kids struggling with school and social life, kids who are sick and need care that they can't get, it just wears you down. Add that to the fatigue and struggles that come with having had a severely sick child, and sometimes I wonder how I am able to do what I do. I know that God cares for us wherever we are and whatever we do. He does not love us more because we are on the field.

God brought us back in His timing. He made what seemed impossible, possible. I am so thankful. Whatever happens in the future, I know that there is a time for everything and that God is in control. Whatever you are going through, there is a future. It may not look the way you had expected, but God has great plans for it. Whether you make the decision to stay on the field or go back to it or if you decide that the best thing for your family right now is to leave, these decisions are difficult, but God honors them all. Whatever you decide, this is not the end. It might be the start of a really exciting new chapter.

—*Elisabeth*

Chapter 6

NOT THE END OF THE STORY

Perhaps they call it your "period" for a reason. Period. Full stop. It's so final, so cruel. Hope dashed anew as you learn it didn't happen this month either. You wonder if it's worth continuing to hope. The pain is so great it overwhelms you. You cry out to the Giver, Creator of Life, and wonder why He doesn't change it all with the snap of His mighty fingers. You wonder if you should dare ask for *anything* when He already gave you *everything*—His only Son. Yet doesn't He tell you to ask? Jesus told the parable of the widow before the judge, relentless for justice (Luke 18:1-8). He tells of the friend knocking at the door persisting he needs bread at an ungodly hour (Luke 11:5-10). His Word says that you have not because you ask not (James 4:2).

My husband and I moved to West Asia in our mid-twenties, with two years of marriage under our belts. We decided to spend a year adjusting to life overseas before trying to have kids. The first month that we tried but didn't get pregnant, I was a little disappointed, a little relieved. By the third or fourth month, I began wondering if something was wrong. During a brief, yet tearful consultation, a doctor at a women's conference reassured me that it was too early to worry and that I should give it a year.

That first year of trying to conceive passed quickly. I had plenty of things to keep me distracted. All the hard work we had put into language and culture learning was finally paying off, and exciting things were happening. Our friendships with locals were beginning to go beyond the surface level. I had a new mentor. My husband and I traveled often to different parts of the region for conferences.

After a year of trying to conceive, my husband and I were both tested. The doctors couldn't find anything wrong. I began to question whether we should pursue a medical solution or continue to pray and wait on God. Perhaps it just wasn't God's timing yet, and I needed to be patient. Would seeking medical help show a lack of faith? Would it be taking matters into our own hands? Would it be good stewardship of the support we had raised?

Around this time, I was encouraged by a wise, respected leader to "pour out my heart before God" like Hannah and to be open with God about my feelings. I hadn't always been completely honest with myself, God, or those around me during previous trials in my life. I had tried hard to keep it all together around friends and even before God. But now, for the first time in my life, I was going to make a conscious effort to lay it all out before God: the good, the bad and the ugly.

Up the Mountain with Isaac

My quiet times became less traditional as one year turned into multiple years. Some evenings after my period came (again), the physical pain of cramps coupled with the pain of despair left me curled up on my bed barely able to utter a word before God. Other times I turned to worship. With the help of the Holy Spirit, I willed myself to get off the bed and dance to a worship song. Music became key to unlocking the deep, hidden emotions I might otherwise have had trouble uncovering. Sometimes I paired Scripture with a simple melody and offered up the song to God—not a grand song to be sung in churches worldwide but one that would stay in that intimate moment with my loving Father. Through this trial, I was learning to keep the line of communication with God open and to hear His still, small voice during my daily life.

One moment with God is still so vivid. I was reading a Christian book while enjoying a ferry boat ride as part of my commute home. The author described the process by which a pearl is formed. It starts when an irritant like a grain of sand enters the oyster. "[The oyster] secretes a substance that produces a soft, smooth coating around the grain of sand—a substance called pearl.... Eventually, that which vexed and pained the oyster is the very thing which produces something of great value and beauty."[7] Instantly I knew God was speaking hope into my years-long struggle with infertility. In addition to deeper intimacy with God, I felt that something else precious would come forth from this incredible difficulty. God planted a seed of hope that He would give us a child. In the days and weeks ahead, the word for *pearl* in the local language kept popping up all over the place. Never before and never again have I been inundated with such a powerful reminder from God.

Besides being open with God, I tried to be transparent with others. When people asked if we wanted kids (and believe me in that culture, this question comes up a lot!), I was honest and said that we did. Being open wasn't always easy. There were some well-meaning people that said thoughtless, hurtful things. There were times when it was very tempting to isolate myself. However, transparency also made it possible for people to speak into my life and to share the burden with me. Eventually hundreds of people on our newsletter list from all over the world were praying for us to be able to have a baby. Several shared that they had a strong sense that God was going to give us children. Though I did not take their words as a guarantee, they gave me more seeds of hope.

After nearly four years of infertility, God ordained a new friendship to encourage me. Rachel (not her real name) had just had her second child. Miraculously after five years of secondary infertility, several failed intrauterine inseminations (IUIs), and miscarriages, she had conceived naturally. Rachel's frank yet compassionate demeanor and her experience with spiritual directors made her uniquely gifted to walk alongside me. She encouraged me to scour the Scriptures for examples where God opened the womb and for the promises that God gave to barren women. She then had me talk to God about His promises in those

Up the Mountain with Isaac

Scriptures as I asked Him to grant me the desire of my heart. At one particularly low point, Rachel recommended I sit quietly before God and ask Him what He would say to me. Tears flowed as I prayerfully penned His response of deep love and approval over me.

Hearing about Rachel's experience with fertility treatments also helped us feel more certain of our own convictions about the place of medical intervention. Right around the five-year mark, after a few unsuccessful rounds of taking pills to help boost my fertility, my husband and I decided that we would try IUI. Thankfully, this procedure is much less expensive in West Asia than back home.

Several aspects of the process were unpleasant to say the least: the exams, the shots I had to administer to myself daily, and the medicine-induced hormonal mood swings. Rachel encouraged me to invite a few close friends and family to pray with us through each step of the process. This turned out to be a lifeline on days when I felt that I didn't have the strength or words to pray. Their prayers carried me through the disappointment of the first month's canceled IUI and the second month's failed IUI. They were also some of the first to hear the news I had only dreamed of sharing for five and a half years.

My hands were clammy as I ascended the stairs to the lab on the second floor of the local clinic, where I had taken a blood pregnancy test earlier that day. I anxiously jammed my thumb into the edge of the envelope that contained the results and peeked in at the numbers on the page. I collapsed into a chair, amazed at the number that peered back at me. Quickly I snapped a picture of the report and texted it to my doctor. She soon confirmed. I was pregnant. Period. Full stop. The wait was over!

I'll never forget one night, a few days after we brought our daughter home from the hospital when the reality finally sank in. I was overtaken by emotion—the sweetest devotion and the deepest relief. I cradled my brown-eyed girl and pulled her close in a tight embrace as I wept openly. Tears of joy and groans of gratitude flowed from my innermost being, from my very soul. After all those years of waiting, praying, and persisting in faith, I finally held in my arms that precious pearl.

But my journey didn't stop there. During all those years of sharing openly with others, I had heard many accounts of those who had become Fertile Myrtle after having trouble conceiving their first child. I had heard this story so many times that I assumed it would be the case for us too. By the time our daughter was two, however, we realized that we were once again failing to conceive month after month. I had always wanted to have two children, and I now saw my little girl in need of a permanent companion in our transitory lifestyle. God knew the desire of my heart was not to just have one child but two.

You would think the second time around in the same trial would be easier. And in some ways, I guess it was. I could not deny that God had heard every prayer and saved every tear. He had covered me with grace and filled me with peace before, and I knew

Up the Mountain with Isaac

He would now. I also had a toolbox filled with hard-earned lessons. But for some reason, it also seemed to bring me right back to the deepest point of despair I had felt the first time. The sense of loss and grief. The desperation. It was going to be a daily battle to lay down my will and surrender to God's.

We went straight back to the same group of friends for prayer, and this time we didn't wait to seek out medical help, beginning monthly IUIs again right away. After several whirlwind months of shots, exams, and procedures, we found ourselves at our seventh failed IUI attempt. The doctor said that statistically there was no reason to continue with the same approach. We had already decided not to pursue more invasive treatment, so that was it. We were done. This time the prayers and procedures had not produced the desired result.

After years of praying and listening, my husband and I had both felt in our hearts that God would give us more than one child. But where did that leave us now? It was incredibly tempting to turn bitter and cold toward God. I decided the healthiest thing for me to do was to move on. I had spent most of our married life consumed by infertility, and my heart couldn't afford any more disappointment. It was time to give up the dream of having a second child. My heart teetered on the fence between surrender to God and stubborn reliance on my own strength.

To our surprise and delight, in the month immediately following that final failed IUI attempt, I became pregnant *naturally* for the first time in our twelve years of marriage! Now, at night we have a new family tradition. All four members of our family pile onto a bed. Our two girls snuggle together, and my husband and I form bookends around them. We sing a worship song together and say a bedtime prayer. In those moments I am awestruck by what God has done. I am certain that only God could write this story. And I know He will write yours too. Sometimes a period isn't the end of the story.

—Esther Seifert

Chapter 7

SAFETY IN MY STRONG TOWER

"Today is January 17, 2000," I wrote in my weekly letter to my parents. "There is a demonstration in the governor's field this morning. They are protesting recent reports of Christians killing Muslims in other parts of the country. We have been told to stay at home, but we are not alarmed." We were accustomed to hearing news of this kind of "tit-for-tat" unrest. While on paper Indonesia allows freedom for five religions, in practice the majority wins. And rumors alone could incite crowds to anger and retaliation.

I turned from my writing as my husband arrived with visitors from our company. As I heard their report, my nonchalance faded. On their drive from the airport, they had seen a church on fire less than a mile away, as well as smoke rising above other parts of the city. The demonstration had become destructive. I felt the first seeds of alarm forming.

Throughout the day, the violence escalated to include homes and businesses of Christians. While we didn't know it then, this was not a haphazard mob, but rather about twenty thousand clearly organized demonstrators given specific targets throughout the city, and later, the whole island of Lombok.

At noon, our local coworker called in a panic. A Muslim friend had warned her, "After they burn the churches, they will find all the Christians and chase you out. Flee while you can." Taking this threat seriously, she left the island in the first wave of eventually thousands who evacuated.

We weren't sure what to do, so we prayed and conferred with teammates and local friends by phone. All afternoon we discussed options and grew more anxious with each report of violence. We finally decided to leave our home following supper and seek safety in the tourist district.

Grabbing bags, I quickly packed clothing, school books, and a few toys that had just arrived from Maw Maw that very day. Then because of the uncertainty of the situation, I filled a separate bag with precious photo albums, important papers, credit cards, passports, and my address book. We also grabbed the money that we had taken out of the bank in preparation for the Y2K scare. God, who "knows what you need before you ask him" (Matthew 6:8, NIV), knew banks would be closed that day.

Fifteen minutes after deciding to leave, we were on the road. During the thirty-minute ride to the hotel, my son asked to sing. I lifted my voice, reminding myself of the truth we had sung in worship the day before: "The name of the Lord is a strong tower; the righteous run to it and are safe" (Proverbs 18:10, NKJV). We arrived at our destination ahead of the riotous mob that crowded the same road later that evening. My Strong Tower was indeed reliable.

The next day a steady queue of helicopters airlifted tourists, expatriates, and locals to the safety of a neighboring island while I watched with rising panic. When our team met to assess our situation, I began to cry. I wept for the loss of my physical home, my belongings, my settled routine, the beautiful island, and the peaceful life my children enjoyed. As far as I knew, it was all going up in smoke.

I wanted to abandon it all, to just get on a plane and fly to the States. As I wept, I sensed the Lord speaking to me: "Release everything—your home, life, ministry, and the island you have come to know and love. Holding tightly to these things will not provide safety."

Perspective came, and I surrendered. And with surrender came peace. My security was in the name of the Lord. In Him I found strength for the next challenge.

"Wake up! Gather your belongings and meet in the hotel lobby!" Banging on the door aroused us from the beds we had settled into minutes earlier. Frantically we followed orders and joined our teammates and other guests to await our fate. There we received the news we had feared—the mob that had burned churches and ransacked houses for the last two days was headed up the road toward our hotel.

An hour later word came that police had stopped them just three miles away. Although momentarily safe, the hotel manager realized he could not keep us protected. He decided to immediately evacuate all guests and shuttle us up the coast and off the island.

"Women and children first," the manager called out when the first vans arrived.

Amused by the *Titanic* reference, but too nervous for melodrama, my two sons and I complied, stuffing ourselves into a large van with all the other women and children. My husband joined the men in several smaller vans, and the convoy headed out for the ten-minute ride.

As the old diesel engine of our overloaded van grunted up the first hill, the smaller, faster vans quickly flew by. Thirty minutes later, after praying the vehicle over each hill, I knew the driver was lost. When the men realized the women and children were no longer first (!), they sent out a search vehicle. We eventually joined the men—in last place—but in time to catch the boat.

The scene was surreal—escaping violence and destruction on a beautiful, starry night. Enjoying an "adventure" with friends while fleeing the anger of enemies. The large capacity jet-boat arrived around 1:30 A.M. and transported five hundred people to the safety and comfort of another hotel bed five hours later. It then headed back to Lombok, completing three trips that day, and evacuating around twelve hundred in total.

Up the Mountain with Isaac

I still didn't know when or if we'd ever return to Lombok or in what condition we'd find our home and car. As it turned out, at the time we were settling into our interim lodgings, a crowd came up our street and inquired about us. Our local helpers, who were guarding the house, told them truthfully that the home was owned by Hindus and so the crowd left it alone.

God used our loyal helpers to defend our home and our belongings. However, other families in our neighborhood were not so fortunate. All totaled, fourteen churches were destroyed, and at least two hundred homes and businesses were burned or ransacked throughout the city during four days of rioting (though the exact figures vary by report).

While looting and vandalism continued on Lombok, we set up a temporary home in a hotel suite, and I tried to maintain some routine for our family. My husband and our teammates focused on finding our local Christian friends and coworkers. Once they were located, we purchased tickets so they could evacuate and provided food, clothing, and shelter for as many as we could.

We also debriefed each one. I listened in horror to their stories of escape, hiding out in forests and rice paddies, sheltered in police barracks, listening to gun shots, and eating ramen noodles three times a day. Many lost their homes or at least all their belongings—burned by angry crowds of Muslims, shouting, "Kill the Christians!"—but not one lost their life.

While I waited for the outcome of this senseless destruction, I poured out my thoughts in my journal and wrote updates to family and prayer warriors who were lifting our needs before the Father. As I went to the Lord, God's Word flooded comfort and promises into my anxious soul: "In quietness and trust is your strength" (Isaiah 30:15, NIV). "You will keep in perfect peace all who trust in you" (Isaiah 26:3, NLT). "Those who trust in the Lord find new strength" (Isaiah 40:31, NLT). These promises from my Strong Tower gave me courage to live in limbo, to explain hard things to my children, and to help those who had suffered far worse than I had.

Three weeks after we evacuated, we returned to our home. In retrospect, we believe this was an attempt to incite an on-going battle between Christians and Muslims. Fortunately, no Christians retaliated, and Lombok began to rebuild.

Coming home from the airport, everything looked pretty normal, even quieter. But we saw destroyed buildings and gutted homes with their insides all black. I was especially devastated to see churches burned, as well as the homes of our dear friends.

I still did not feel safe at night. Rumors flew of continued unrest and potential robberies. There was still a slight chance that the president would not be able to control his military and the country would go to war. We needed great wisdom to know when we should leave again, if at all. I packed a few bags for emergency getaway just in case.

We saw mixed reactions in the folks around us. The most callous seemed to think the riot and destruction was no big deal or that it was the fault of the believers themselves. Others seemed remorseful, but not really embarrassed or repentant. But there were a few who felt genuine concern for their Christian friends.

During those fearful days, I was buoyed up by Jesus' reminder to His twelve apostles that there are risks involved in my calling:

> "*I am sending you out like sheep among wolves. Therefore be as shrewd as snakes and as innocent as doves. Be on your guard.... Do not worry about what to say or how to say it.... Do not be afraid of those who kill the body but cannot kill the soul*" (Matthew 10:16-17, 19, 28, NIV).

I had seen what this meant first hand. The task of sharing about God's Kingdom was tough, frightening, and certainly not safe. Even though my status as an expat might provide some safety, I needed to be ready to face the risks of serving God nonetheless.

On my desk I found my abandoned letter to my parents from the day the riots broke out. I continued from where I had left off:

"We picked up our mail today. There were two letters from you, Mom. One had this footnote: 'I see you in the arms of Jesus Christ.' Do you remember writing that? Well, it was a very special message meant for today. We are in His arms here and that is a very safe place. Please pray for peace and contentment to live in the midst of unrest and uncertainty."

When the next rumor came, I ran to my Strong Tower who had proven to be my place of safety. He emboldened my weak heart. I reminded myself, "Surely the righteous will never be shaken.... They will have no fear of bad news; their hearts are steadfast, trusting in the Lord" (Psalm 112:6-7, NIV).

God answered my mother's prayer. With a steadfast heart, I kept going.

—*Eva Burkholder*

Chapter 8

CORAZON

"Known but to God" is written on select crosses in Manila's World War II American Cemetery. While most crosses in the American Cemetery bear names, the unidentified soldiers have their remains marked by that simple phrase. As I sat among the crosses, I grieved for a child I wanted to hold, but could not. I cried for a child that I desperately wanted to know, but could not. Still, I clung to the fact that my daughter was known by God.

In overseas work we prepare for and anticipate culture shock, frequent transitions, different communication styles, and language learning. Moving cross-culturally is not for the faint of heart. Hudson Taylor, famed missionary to China, once said, "Attempt great things for God; expect great things from God." I was ready to see the hand of God move. I, however, did not prepare myself for failure, unanswered prayer, and the deep loneliness that would follow.

We named her Corazon, which means "heart" in Tagalog. "Corrie" was much prayed for and loved. When I boarded a plane from the Philippines to Malaysia to attend a weeklong international teaching conference in March 2017, I was only filled with excitement. Here was Corrie's first plane ride, the first of many as a TCK. This was Corrie's first trip to another country, another first of many! As I looked in wonder at the sea anemones in the harbor of Kota Kinabalu and listened to world-class speakers, like most expectant mothers, I wondered, *What kind of person will you become?*

Cramping. Spikes of pain. Blood. This was my first pregnancy, and I was unsure about the specifics. Was this level of cramping normal? I hugged my belly and pleaded that God would keep my baby safe. My husband, Dennis, and I had known that starting a family could be challenging because I have Polycystic Ovarian Syndrome (PCOS). Yet a year and a half into our marriage we were overjoyed to find ourselves pregnant. God had answered our prayers.

While I basked in the excitement of the conference, my symptoms continued. With little sleep, I got dressed for another day at the conference. I attended the morning sessions, but the pain was unrelenting, and I was bleeding heavily. I excused myself from lunch with coworkers and took a Grab taxi back to the hotel. There I googled "Hospitals near me" and sent a message to a coworker, "I'm pregnant, and I think I'm having a miscarriage. Can you come with me to the hospital?"

Up the Mountain with Isaac

Being checked into a hospital is not easy in any context, but it is especially unnerving outside of your home country. The Philippines had been home for almost four years, and I had my medical go-to's for the dentist, eye doctor, and a gynecologist. However, I was outside my "second home" of the Philippines. I was in Malaysia. I fumbled over the paperwork asking for my address, medical identification number, and other personal information. The nurses and doctors spoke to me in Malay and switched to English when I explained that I was an American. Instead of a hospital gown, I was given a fabric tube—a sarong—that I held in my hands, unsure of how to put it on until a nurse helped me. *This is fascinating*, I thought, enjoying the cultural learning, while my own trauma was unfolding.

I waited until after the doctors had examined me and confirmed that I was in the process of miscarriage to call my husband. I knew it would be a roaming phone call, but I was desperate to hear his voice.

"Dennis, we lost the baby," I sobbed. "How can I come to Malaysia with a baby and then leave here without one?"

The two days that followed were agonizing. I stayed in the hotel to rest, listened to *Hamilton's* "It's Quiet Uptown," and wrote letters to Corrie in my journal. When I flew home to Manila and Dennis met me outside our home, he held me tightly in his arms—sharing the grief we had both faced apart.

My heart and body held onto the trauma of the miscarriage. My doctors did not recommend a D&C, and so I bled for forty days. Then, for over a year, my period did not return. At all. We pursued medical treatment for my PCOS in the Philippines with doctor after doctor. They had no answers for our infertility, and with each new doctor, we became increasingly discouraged. I was developing a hatred and fear of hospitals.

A doctor's visit in Manila may take between three to five hours depending on factors like the traffic, waiting room times, and availability of hospital technicians. I yearned for the efficiency of North American healthcare, where, by and large, if an 11:30 A.M. appointment was scheduled, I would be seen close to 11:30 A.M.

Our family in the United States and Canada even asked us to consider returning for medical treatment, which was very tempting. But our hearts were rooted in the Philippines, and to think of leaving, even if for a valid reason like my health, was painful to consider. What did trust in God look like for this decision? Do we return to North America for medical aid and trust God for the care of the ministries we were involved in? Do we stay in the Philippines and trust God for my health? Dennis and I entered a time of dedicated prayer. We did not tell anyone about the possibility of leaving the Philippines, we desired a clear answer from God—untainted by our loving community and the pull of ministry. After a few months, we both received confirmations from God: We would stay.

Manila, like many mega-cities, is a symphony of the senses: people on motorbikes, bright advertisements, the call of street vendors selling snacks, and never-ending movement. In my grief,

Up the Mountain with Isaac

I yearned for quiet and nature, like the American Cemetery in Manila. Its green lawns and orderly white crosses reminded me of the Arlington Cemetery outside of Washington, D.C., another city I have called home.

We chose to remember and celebrate Corazon's life at the American Cemetery. At an unknown soldier's cross, we placed a pink rabbit and flowers. Just like the American soldier never returned home to his family, Corrie would never return home to us. We can go to her, but she could not come to us.

Outwardly, I continued ministry in the Philippines, pouring myself into my role of teaching children. Inwardly, I was folding into myself. I was a mother, unable to mother my own child in heaven. Was I only ever meant to love other people's children? I felt fragile and forgotten by God. I was angry at God. How could He grant numerous children to those who could care less, when I desperately wanted a child? I would love and care for one with my life, and yet I couldn't bear one. Each new baby announcement on social media pierced my heart. Trust in God was reaching an all-time low. Reading Scripture was tedious, and my prayer life was scant. Anxiety and depression were ever-present companions. I believed the lie: I wasn't feeling broken; I was broken.

Christian community, however, was my saving grace. My ladies' Bible study and our field team met each week. Best friends, though an ocean apart, were only a text message away. They were all safe havens. With them I did not need to put on a brave face, I could bare my soul, and I could be loved and accepted in my brokenness. I started meeting regularly with a local psychiatrist who prescribed medication for my anxiety and depression. The medicine was a buoy, a lifeline, keeping me afloat in the processing and healing. My therapist challenged me to lean into my complex emotions and anger towards God through lament in Scripture.

God used the people in my life to be a tangible expression of His care and love. While enfolded in loving and intentional community, my soul began to trust God again. It did not happen at once. I had days of doubts and moments of rage. However, I started to see that God's promises did not waver even if my faith wavered. I learned that God's love is unfailing, even if my love is conditional.

Have you had to trust God in the dark? In Isaiah 30:20-21, it says: "And though the Lord give you the bread of adversity and the water of affliction, yet your Teacher will not hide himself anymore, but your eyes shall see your Teacher. And your ears shall hear a word behind you, saying, 'This is the way, walk in it,' when you turn to the right or when you turn to the left" (ESV). We made the difficult, but obedient, decision to trust God, believing that we would see God, that He would guide us.

Trust is costly. What does trust look like? Trust is putting a pink rabbit and flowers on the tombstone of our grief, knowing that one day we will hold Corazon in our arms.

—*Evangeline Chow*

Chapter 9

STILL WAITING

Two positive lines on the fifty-cent cassette pregnancy test caused me to plan the rest of my life in a matter of minutes. Those two lines instantly had the full eyelashes of their father, our blue eyes, and the blonde hair of our childhoods. Our children would have friends from around the world, speak several languages, and need a little help sorting out who they were in this big world. It was a big task with which we felt entrusted.

We were planning to move to a remote area in a few months, and I instantly pushed those dates back in favor of traveling back to my passport country to give birth. We had worked tirelessly to learn the national language and pass our exams. After being away from our passport country, we would get to be by our family and friends for the birth. In a matter of a few minutes, I joyously rearranged my whole life to make room for this new life.

At a remote village resort for our annual conference, the bleeding started. I clung to the future that we had dreamt for our family, but the blood smeared its ugly, red stains across each dream and drew me into the nightmare of miscarriage.

The hotel room was full of white sheets, and the cleanliness of the white-tiled bathroom floor seemed to mock how dirty and ashamed I felt that my body had failed me. I did not want housekeeping to know my shame, but I could not hide the betrayal of my body.

Without cell reception, I could not call any of my friends who had walked the journey of miscarriage before. In desperation, I shared with our coworkers. I needed to find someone who could tell me that this would be okay—no one had walked this road. I felt alone.

Each morning and evening we gathered for sessions of worship and times of prayer, but I could not stand, and I could not sing. The physical pain was immense, but the spiritual pain, sense of betrayal, and loss that I felt were increasingly stronger. What was supposed to be a week of refreshment turned into a dreadful nightmare that I couldn't leave.

One of the things that I did not realize about miscarriage is that it is a process. The physical process of losing a baby can take weeks, and life goes on while death is sinking in its claws. As the conference week drew to an end, I felt like I was finally set free from the mountaintop prison cell that was housing my nightmare. I thought I could somehow escape and return to a different reality. Yet, as we drove away, I felt like I was leaving a piece of myself forever.

Up the Mountain with Isaac

When we finally returned to our apartment, I wanted to crawl up in bed and stay there for days. I felt shattered. I did not think I would walk back through those doors without holding my child.

On the advice of a medical colleague, I arranged to go to the hospital for an exam.

With a heart wrapped in shock and pain in my abdomen, I drove my scooter to the newer hospital in town. I was grossly unprepared. I naively anticipated an experience similar to my passport country. Duped by the new facade and decent English that everyone spoke inside, the culture shock hit me like a punch to my already sore abdomen.

There was a unit on medical terminology in our language program, and I had been to the clinic for immunizations, but I had never been to the hospital. I took another expat friend who had recently made a trip to this hospital. She knew where everything was and could pick up medicine or pay the cashier for me between appointments and departments. In Nepal, one does not go to the hospital alone.

Entering the hospital, we made an appointment at the front desk and then navigated our way to the maternity ward. Like a pair of mockingbirds constantly chirping from a wire, the women's department was full of swollen bellies and anticipation. I did not belong, and I felt as though my flat stomach and tear swollen eyes proclaimed my emptiness as we sat in the waiting room.

My name was called, and I walked alone into a tiny room that looked like it was built around the doctor's massive, wooden desk. I felt small and unimportant. The doctor sat behind her fortress as I undressed in front of her and the nurse. Like a piece of forgotten furniture, the examination table was crouched in the back corner. The table was made for someone under five feet, and I let my feet dangle off the edge. The doctor poked and prodded at me as tears leaked from the corners of my eye.

She asked how long it had been since the bleeding started and when my last cycle began. The whole event felt like just another medical procedure rather than the loss of life, loss of a future, and so many dreams.

My blood type is rare, especially in Nepal. When the doctor asked me about it, I felt shamed for my answer—like I had done something terrible by having blood. I hung my head to hide my grief and shame, wanting to run from her office, wanting to run away.

I wondered how this experience would have been different in my passport country. I blamed the jumble of emotions on the foreign environment that I found myself in rather than on the waves of trauma and grief I was drowning in. I concluded that doctors in Nepal do not care about their patients, lack any bedside manner, and show up just for the status and paycheck. The enemy tried to make me think that this would all be different if I could go back—if I could just be home.

The doctor wanted to check for any remaining tissue that could result in an infection. We walked to the ultrasound department where I filled up on fluids for the imaging. The broom closet that was converted into a two-bed ultrasound room was divided by a paper-thin curtain. My feet hung off the edge again as the cold gel allowed the wand to glide across my flat abdomen.

Seeing those images on the screen made me feel like a hollow, decaying tree that had no life left in it. Part of me was relieved that this nightmare of a hospital visit was going to end, and part of me felt like I was watching the last straggling vapors of a hoped-for-miracle blow away in a burst of wind.

The day wasn't over, and we had to stay a little longer. My blood type meant that I needed an immunization. We sat in the pharmacy for over an hour as the staff tried to locate an immunization that few women in Nepal need. I wanted the day to be over, and I was beginning to worry that we would have to repeat the day tomorrow.

The immunization was finally located, and I carefully checked the expiration date—something I had learned to do when picking up anything from the pharmacy. We quickly rushed back to the maternity ward. The lights were dim, the waiting room was empty, and I was overcome with frustration with the day.

Suddenly, a nurse popped out from behind the nurse's station. She beckoned me back, "I stayed so that I could give you your immunization. I could have left an hour ago." For the first time in that dark, foreign hospital, I felt cared for that day. This woman owed me nothing—she could have left and had me return the next day. She showed me love and kindness when I was engulfed with the emotions that the day and the week had brought. Like the rays of light that push forth from a dark stormy sky, the Lord used her kindness to soften my heart and the judgments I had made about the entire medical system in Nepal and the individuals at the hospital that day.

In the following months, I wrestled with the Lord. I did not know why He would give us a child and allow her to be with Him already in such a short period. We asked "Why?" more times than I can count.

Over the years, I have walked this path of healing and grieving. I have talked with friends in my passport country who have also suffered from miscarriages. I realized that my passport culture does not have a developed or appropriate grief response to baby and infant loss either. The lie that I would have somehow known how to process or grieve if I had been somewhere else was untrue. Grief is like a fog that hangs heavy and low, obscuring clarity and causing confusion.

We asked "Why?" when I did not conceive again. I watched as children were born to my friends during my daughter's birth month while my belly was still flat, and my longings surged. I waited still as those same friends went on to have other children, and I let my hope wane.

We moved to a more remote location of the country and began working with a smaller, isolated mountain people group. Plugging into a new community meant that I was met with questions every day: "How long have you been married?.... Oh, almost seven years?... Where are your children?" These questions were meant to be welcoming and enforce the social norm, but they fell on my ears as a condemnation of my shame, my dead daughter, and my worthlessness as a wife and woman. We were not having kids, and I had to tell people I didn't know why.

Degrading jokes would follow: I could be taken off my husband's hands, or my husband could take a second wife. These comments made in jest held elements of socially accepted solutions to our problem—that society automatically decided was me.

The doubt and questions crept in once more. If I were back in my passport country, I would have access to better medical care. We could run tests, get advice, and figure out what was wrong with us. Rather than trusting in Him, I schemed and plotted. I wondered if the commitment we had made to these remote mountain people was worth trusting Him with all my longings and desires.

Staying through the difficulties is hard. Our first term was nearly four years, and at each anniversary of my daughter's passing, due date anniversary, or friend's pregnancy announcement I wondered at how things could be different if we were somewhere else. However, things could just as easily not be different. We could have "unexplained infertility," and I would still feel stuck.

Choosing to stay in Nepal during this difficult journey of miscarriage and infertility has caused us to dive deeper into friendships with local friends and dependence on Him. I could easily rely on medicine or science, but as the months pass, I must rely on prayer. I must rely on God to meet me in my longings and to weep with me. As we stay through the difficult seasons, we solidify this new and foreign place as home. We have learned that He will meet us in this place and that He is faithful.

Initially, as I talked and bargained with the Lord, I felt a sense of injustice. I believed the lie that He owed me something for this arduous life that we had chosen to live in obedience. Life was rugged and harsh enough, water was unreliable, and no other foreigners lived anywhere nearby. Why was He adding these extra difficulties and withholding the blessing of children in our lives?

I had reasoned that for God to be glorified in this situation, I needed to fall pregnant. It was then that I could tell of the miracles and work that He had done. Like Mary and Martha who ran to Jesus and pleaded with Him to come and display His power by healing their brother Lazarus right away, I argued with God about how His glory would be displayed in my life. I had a narrow and pitiful definition of glory that was couched in my own desires and longing.

This story feels like it is full of trauma and fear, but I am learning to embrace the ways in which He is sculpting courage and perseverance through this long season.

Up the Mountain with Isaac

He is still working to write His story of glory. He is teaching me to trust Him with my longings, desires, and frustrations. After years, I am learning to acknowledge that I don't know how His glory will come to full realization in the story of my family. I do know that I've seen glimpses of it, and He has allowed me to see His glory in new ways. I'm still waiting for it to unfold in its fullness.

—*Gwen Elm*

Chapter 10

MOTHERHOOD AND MISSIONS

Before leaving for the field, we all have our vision of what ministry will look like once we get there. We excitedly share this vision with friends, churches, and supporters. We get our team on board and are ready to get to work. We hear the statistics that many have to change their plans once they get to their host country, but that will not be us, we say. This is what we are called to do. It is what we have been preparing to do. What happens when the vision does not match reality though?

Ever since I was old enough, I have worked with kids. As a pre-teen I helped in the nursery. When I turned sixteen, I got a job working at the church daycare. God called me to missions at seventeen, and I knew I would be working with kids. I got my bachelor's degree in Family and Child Development knowing this was the plan.

My first term in Botswana I volunteered at a preschool training national preschool teachers. We moved halfway through the term, and I volunteered at an orphanage preschool. There I was able to teach, train, and work on curriculum development. I loved the work, but the kids' needs were greater than I was prepared to help. When I got sick and we had to end our first term to get medical treatment, I knew I needed more training.

Between sickness, debt, and both my husband and I getting graduate degrees, it took five years for us to get back to Botswana. We were foster parents during this time, and we adopted our son. Fostering and later adopting taught me more about trauma and children than any of my classes. It seemed God was continuing to prepare us to work with children with trauma and disabilities. That was our vision for our second term.

During our second term it was no longer just my husband and me. We were parents now. We worked with our organization on how this term would be different as parents. We thought we were prepared, but things did not go according to our plan. We did start working with a new church that was focused on children. It seemed a good fit. We were living out our vision. Then COVID-19 hit and other circumstances we were not prepared to have happen. Our son no longer felt safe or accepted at that church. The vision was shattered.

I wrestled with God for a long time. How could He bring us here for this to happen? Wasn't this what He had been training me for all my life? Surely, He just wanted us to push forward and find a way to continue the vision and meet our son's needs. There had to be a way to do both. That was not what God was calling me to do. I knew it, and I fought it. He called me to stop and focus on my son. Mothering was what my ministry needed to be.

Walking away from helping ninety kids to take care of just one seemed wrong. In my pride I thought, *God, are You really going to waste my education, experience, and talents to just stay at home? I have a graduate degree. I have decades of experience working with children. I have studied countless hours learning how to help children with trauma and disabilities.* All of my accolades came rushing out. I, I, I and me, me, me. Oh how I am ashamed to admit the depths of my pride in my plea to the God of the universe. I stomped my feet in defiance. I tried finding a way that I could convince Him that He was wrong. This could not be the plan. No, I did not leave my home, family, and friends to stay within our gate just being a mother. No way could I be hearing correctly.

My protest lasted a few months and wounded my family plus our ministry. The screaming match was no longer just with God, but I lashed out at my husband and son. We were spiraling fast and about to fully burn out. Thankfully in God's mercy, He called me to repentance. He showed me the darkness of my heart during this battle. He revealed sin and areas that needed repair. I was finally ready to repent and surrender.

Shakily, I reached out to dear friends, our organization, and the ladies in my Velvet Ashes Connection Group. I shared that God had told me to step back and focus on taking care of my son. I expected backlash and doubt. I was met with such kindness and acceptance—absolutely you should do what God is telling you to do. Our organization reminded me that I am called to obedience, no more and no less. God confirmed through so many people that this was what He wanted of me.

So motherhood became my mission. That means most days I don't leave our property. Some days the only adult I encounter is my husband. Other days I get to talk with neighbors, mostly through our gate, or talk to my son's teacher that comes twice a week. Not the grand stuff you write in newsletters and are excited to share back home. In the dark corners of my mind, I even question if I really am a missionary anymore. My husband talks with nationals each day and is getting ready to teach at the new seminary. He's the real missionary. I am just a mom, and it doesn't even feel like that because I don't even hold that title in my son's eyes.

I am just a Jen.

I start to doubt. Then my son starts asking about Jesus. As I have focused more on him and worked on connection, my son has been more open to the Gospel. He's asked what Jesus looked like and drew a picture of Jesus holding his dad's hand. He's asked why Jesus let there be evil and why can't there be two heavens instead of one heaven and one hell. He's hearing the message again after being closed off for a season.

It's not just him.

A neighbor told us he's learned about faithfulness through watching our family. Another neighbor said she was able to share about God's love and how He meets us in our weakness to her niece whose son has the same disability as our son. God can use even our simple, mundane lives.

I am learning from this area of surrender too. After a bad day, I weakly implore, "Are you sure, God?" My heart is reminded of the parable in Luke 15. He leaves the ninety-nine for the one. God's deep love for my son says, "Leave the crowd and focus on the one I have entrusted to you." He is my mission and that is enough.

—*Jennifer Ball*

Chapter 11

IRISH COURAGE

Screaming into the phone, eleven-year-old me informed my father that he had to pick me up. "I'm not spending the night at my best friend's house!" I had been staying there every other weekend since second grade, but all of a sudden, I was afraid of accidents, death, illness, and couldn't be without my parents. For five years I struggled with homesickness until one night, in grade eleven, I laid in bed and prayed, "God, I don't want to be afraid anymore. I put my fear in You!"

Weeks after praying those words, I headed off to a youth conference for five days and never looked back. That was the beginning of my independence and freedom. In 1996, I moved to another country for Bible college and met wonderful friends from East Africa (where a heartbeat for Uganda began). Then I moved over to the Netherlands to serve as a nanny for a year and learn about my ancestral heritage. Of course, I couldn't stop there, so I moved to the Philippines, where I tutored missionary children for three years. I experienced times of house arrest there when the Abu Sayyaf (a Jihadist militant rebel terrorism and pirate group) came into town for supplies. Yes, I was probably naive, but I was at peace.

People would tell me that I had an abundance of courage. Flying and traveling to almost twenty-five different countries alone was a grand adventure. Living single on the foreign mission field opened many doors for me to get into homes or places where the married families couldn't go. Trying any new foods that locals placed in front of me was a privilege—including flying ants, balut, grasshoppers, blood sausage, desert camel yogurt, and so much more. It took sixteen years before the Lord opened doors for me to move to Uganda, but I had finally reached the Africa that I had loved for so long.

Serving under a mission agency in Uganda, I delighted in sharing God's Word or touring wherever I could. If that meant driving through districts of cattle raiding, gun-shooting Karamojong herders, I went. Camping next to warthogs and hippo—why not!? Speaking to ten thousand youth at an outdoor conference and sharing that I was a forty-year-old virgin—sure, yes please! I even stayed on the field and prayed that truth would set me free when false accusations were piled against me. I wasn't going to leave the mission field until God wanted me to go, not mankind.

But in 2017, everything changed. Early in the year I started feeling weak and tired. Doctors in Kampala couldn't find anything wrong, so I headed to Kenya for five weeks to rest and stay with my college roommate. I came back to Uganda not feeling much better, but my spirit was renewed. When my parents called for my birthday, they said, "Hey, do you want to meet us in Ireland for an eight-day vacation?" Yes, I thought, that is just what I need. I hadn't seen my family for two years.

I traveled to Kampala and had one final medical exam before I left the country. Everything was coming back normal. During the flight from Entebbe to Dubai, I experienced a horrible cramp in my right calf. I tried stretching it out during the layover, but it remained tight. I slept more on the flight to Dublin and landed with great expectation at seeing my parents. As I weaved through immigration, my small purse seemed to get heavier and heavier. When I talked to the customs officer, I felt like I was getting winded, and the air was harder to breathe. As I looked at the luggage carousel, I feared I wouldn't even be able to lift my big travel pack off of the conveyor belt. I was going to black out. But my parents were waiting just on the other side of the arrival doors! I could do it. I grabbed a luggage cart and leaned on it until my bag came around the belt again. I dragged it onto the cart and pushed my way into my parents' arms.

Immediately they knew something was wrong. Airport security made their way over, and soon I was connected to oxygen and sticky heart tags were all over my chest. An ambulance escorted all of us to the nearest hospital. Doctors placed me in quarantine because when you fly in from Africa with unknown illnesses, people fear the worst—Ebola, malaria, sleeping sickness, typhoid, you name it.

After a few X-rays, two massive blood clots were found in my lungs. These pulmonary embolisms were stressing my heart, and I was in an extremely dangerous medical state. After ten hours of being in my own quarantined ER room, I was transferred to the oxygen ward, and when I was rolled to my bed, in the middle of five other women, I thought for sure I had come to die. Machines whirred. Chests gurgled. Older ladies were battling lung cancer after a lifetime of chain smoking. I couldn't do anything but sleep. If a wire fell off my chest, nurses came running. This Irish hospital only allowed visitors for one or two hours in the evening, so my parents struggled to be tourists without me. The following day I was told that I would have to wait four to six weeks before I was allowed to fly again. The blood clots had to be completely out of my system before I could even think of getting on a plane. It didn't make sense. I had flown so often, and this was no way to spend an eight-day vacation. And yet, the Lord gave me peace. He knew my needs and my condition.

On the third day, an older couple stopped by to see me. They had received word from our mission headquarters that I was in the hospital, and within twenty minutes of meeting, they had offered to host me once I was discharged from the hospital. I had a place to stay for the six weeks of recovery! The little, old ladies in my room couldn't believe that I had readily accepted to stay with complete strangers. But I was excited. The husband was an Irish

Up the Mountain with Isaac

Baptist pastor, married to a Canadian woman, and they were a year younger than my parents. I believed it to be a divine appointment. I love the family of God.

I left the hospital after five days, and for a few weeks I rested, joined church activities, toured a little, and looked forward to going back to Uganda. After a month I returned to the hospital for a follow-up appointment, and there they told me that the pulmonary embolisms were completely gone, but they had noticed a large dermoid cyst growing on my left ovary. They had spotted it when I went for a CT scan the day I was discharged, but had no way of contacting me. I had not left a forwarding address.

All of a sudden, another trauma. I now had an aggressively growing dermoid cyst, the size of a football. It was vital that I have it removed before returning to Uganda. The doctors figured that the dermoid was probably squishing the veins to my legs, and that's what had caused the blood clots in the first place. I was not allowed to have surgery for at least three months because of the embolisms, but if the dermoid exploded, I was also in danger. Lord, help me. All I wanted to do was go home to Mom and Dad's.

Graciously, insurance flew me back to Canada, since we knew it was now going to be a long journey. I crashed at Mom and Dad's house. Thinking the worst was behind me, I settled in to wait for a surgery date. But my legs were getting more and more painful. And for the first time in my life, I started experiencing anxiety. Long days home alone. Every leg cramp reminded me of the plane ride to Dubai, and I constantly thought I was going to experience another pulmonary embolism.

I had left the mission field so quickly and completely unexpectedly, that some things fell apart and other ministries were put on hold. My heart ached for community. In Uganda, you are never alone. I had to keep the faith that the Lord knew all things. Jesus was my constant comfort when I feared my body so much.

The eight day vacation had turned into an eight month leave of absence. My body was recovering nicely, albeit slowly, but my stress levels had been increasing. My family doctor finally recommended that I return to Uganda because it would be better for my mental health to once again be in my own apartment, surrounded by friends and neighbors I loved, and have a purpose. It was the scariest flight of my life. To go all the way to Africa—alone. But I wasn't about to give up the calling God had placed on me: That I was to go and make disciples in Uganda.

A month after I settled back home, the Lord sent a young couple from Canada to stay with me for two months. The Lord knew I needed companionship more than ever. They played games and cooked with me, jumped into ministry alongside me, and prayed over me.

The following spring, my best friend in Uganda proposed to me, and I was blown away, for many reasons. One—someone would love me and be with me. Two—he understood my stress and anxiety. It has now been four years since that life-changing trip to Ireland. I've been married for almost two years, and even though there are days when I still feel courageous, there are also times when I am still scared. I'm not afraid to meet new people or try new things. I'm not afraid to drive through Kampala traffic or move to another tribe and start over (which I did last year). But there are times when the anxiety comes back. What if I have another pulmonary embolism? Or a heart attack (it runs in the family)!?

> Be still, and know that I am God. I will be exalted among the nations, I will be exalted in the earth! (Psalm 46:10, ESV)

I'm beyond thankful for a husband who sees when I begin scratching my neck, a sign that I'm feeling anxious. Sometimes he notices even before I do, and he finds an activity for me to get involved in. Or he cuddles beside me as I cry on the bed, "If I don't wake up in the morning, just know that I love you!" And I am eternally grateful that the Lord continues to see and know my weaknesses. He is always there when I call out to Him, and He watches over me in miraculous ways. I shall continue on. I will not be overcome by fear. The Lord knows the plans He has for me, and so I will live, one day at a time, doing my best to answer His call. Until His Kingdom comes.

—*Karen M. Lubbers Odel*

Chapter 12

UNUSUAL GIFTS

Shaving her armpits and legs, my mind wanders to what might have been had my daughter been born with all her chromosomes intact. At eighteen her bedroom might have music coming from a set of Bluetooth speakers as she fills out college applications. There might be photos of friends framed on her shelf and white lights dangling from her ceiling. Instead, her room is filled with stuffed animals, building blocks, and anything Toy Story. This summer she might have been biking with her sister or hitting up the local night market with her brother. Her fingers might have been tapping away as she texted back and forth with a friend while sipping a passion fruit red tea.

Instead, my eighteen-year-old daughter listens to a kid's radio program while building with Duplo blocks or splashes around in the pool meant for a toddler. Most likely I would be worrying about boys, treasuring every single minute knowing that she will be going away in a year, or worrying about what university she would choose. All normal things that parents of teenagers worry about. Instead, I worry that she might get into the kitchen and choke on a homemade cookie or that I did not get the car door locked and she might open it while the car is moving. But what plagues me the most is what she will do after graduation. As I rinse off the razor, I know for sure she would be taking her own shower and shaving her own legs. But she is missing part of her fifth chromosome. And it affects everything. It has since the day she almost died.

My biggest fear at the age of 28 and six months pregnant with my second child was having a child with special needs. My daughter was not diagnosed until she was ten months old, so I had many months where I believed all was normal and fine. I believed this fear to be silly and unmerited. Then one early morning I woke to a baby with a high fever and rasping for breath. This was the beginning of those forgotten fears becoming a reality.

We braced ourselves at the first hospital when the doctor confirmed that she had pneumonia and needed to be hospitalized immediately, but they did not have any oxygen tanks available. We called another hospital to hear a similar conclusion: oxygen tanks, but no pediatric care. We lived in a city in Taiwan that was fairly modern. My mind yelled, *What in the world?* The third hospital had oxygen tanks, so we traveled an hour through town in a taxi to find relief for our seven-month-old daughter. This hospital was small. We were told that they did not have a private room or medical equipment to measure her vital signs, but they had an oxygen tank:

a tall tank with green paint peeling off with a hose and face mask attached. The tank was located near an empty bed in a room with six other children of various ages all coughing. At that moment I honestly didn't care. We had oxygen and medicine. But, twenty-four hours later we were medevaced to a different hospital in a different city. Thankfully, my husband's mind works better than mine in critical moments. At the new hospital she had a private room and all the beeping machines needed to check her vital signs, especially her oxygen levels.

It was here that questions were asked about previous health concerns. She had been hospitalized a few months earlier for a lung infection. With the doctor's strong suggestion, I took her to the U.S. for further testing. Those next two months were a time of waiting as she saw more doctors and specialists and had all kinds of tests run to see what was going on. Those two months fed into the fear that was growing inside my gut. When the doctor told me her diagnosis, the fear that I had earlier believed was "silly and unmerited" became my reality: Matthea was going to be mentally and physically handicapped; she was going to be one of those kids with special needs.

Matthea means "Gift of God." She was given that name before her diagnosis, before we knew anything about Cri-du-Chat Syndrome. Gifts of God are easy to call a blessing when the gift is financial, an unexpected friendship, healing from illness, or children who have no diagnosis. But what about the child diagnosed with a rare chromosomal deletion who you are told by the specialist will probably never walk, never talk, and mentally only be around the age of two when she becomes an adult? Honestly, I felt like her name was a slap in the face. Her diagnosis also revealed that she no longer could eat by mouth. She aspirated, which means her food went into her lungs instead of her stomach. So a super thin NG-tube came out of her nose like a long worm attached with white medical tape to the left side of her smooth cheek in hopes that she could not pull it out.

She did. Multiple times.

I learned to hold her head still while poking that long tube back through her nose down to her stomach. I never wanted to be a nurse, but here I was doing things I thought only a qualified nurse should do. She would now only be allowed to have liquid diets pushed through this tube. This beauty-look only lasted a few weeks because she had surgery to insert a Mic-Key gastrostomy feeding tube. This tube was attached above and a little to the left of her belly button. She now looked like she had two belly buttons, but no one could tell as her clothes covered it.

She was given a machine that would pump the liquid food into her stomach from an IV bag that hung from either her stroller or a metal pole by her highchair. Baby spoons and sippy cups were put away, and then eventually thrown away as it became clear this was our new normal. And as this new normal became routine, I found that the meaning of her name, *gift of God*, became my lifeline, anchoring me to the Rock of my salvation.

God was in this. None of this was a surprise to Him. He did not abandon us. During those unsettling months He provided what was needed and answered most of our questions. Including the question, "What do we do now?" After discussing with her therapists and surgeons about our options, it was decided that we could return to our host country. So packed with extra feeding tubes, all the cans of liquid food she would need on the flights along with the machine, we boarded the plane and flew back.

We were able to stay in that location another two years, but then due to the need for speech therapy we moved to Taipei. God was part of that decision and made it clear that this was the place for our family. Since that diagnosis seventeen years ago, Matthea has surprised us with what she can do. She was able to have the feeding tube removed at the age of seven. She loves fried rice and dumplings. Though her balance is not the greatest, she walks and even runs. Mentally, she is probably around the age of four on a really good day. I have been a mother to a child with special needs for eighteen years now. My fear did become my reality, but God has given me the grace, the peace, and the strength to do it thus far.

She has two more years of high school left, and my one big worry these days is what she will do after graduation. I have anxieties about that. I have concerns. *Will she be at home with us? Will we need to move again? Will our time on the field be over? Where would we go? What would we do?* My heart rate increases, and I just want to take a nap to escape it all. I have noticed in the last year the frequency and the intensity of these questions revving up. Those days are heavy and honestly suffocating. I feel almost paralyzed. I also feel like the pandemic has just sprinkled a heavy layer of fear over everything.

In the past when I have battled anxiety of the unknowns, I have been able to put in some praise music or read the Psalms to change my perspective. But this past year has been different. I do think the pandemic has been part of it, but most of it is that there are so many unknowns in our life and the biggest unknown is coming quicker than I would like. I have started to take walks in the morning without music or a podcast playing. Just me. The path. And God. It is time out of the house where the demands of "Mom" can be overwhelming. It is quiet. It is peaceful. It is a gift.

—*MaDonna Maurer*

Chapter 13

THE LAND OF THE LIVING

Sometimes you feel like you're at the bottom of a deep pit with no way to get out. I imagine God hovering over the pit in a helicopter ready to throw down a rope ladder the moment I cry for help. Reassuring words come back to me through memory channels, such as, "For you have delivered my soul from death, my eyes from tears, my feet from stumbling; I will walk before the Lord in the land of the living" (Psalm 116:8-9, ESV).

I know that looking up, I will clasp the strong arm of my Father in heaven who reaches down to save me. I was in the pit once again. The story of how I got out is like following the breadcrumb trail back to the heart of God. Follow it with me.

Several years ago, I came to the field with my dear husband, Jake. We had married later in life and were riding the wave of adventure. Before coming to the field, we would see each other after a normal eight-hour workday with a kiss and dinner on the table. Now that we were full time global workers, we fell off our proverbial surfboard and plunged awkwardly into language school and a strange foreign culture with determination. Our love for each other and the Holy Spirit kept us from drowning. It was extremely different in every way than our former life, including the fact that we spent twenty-four/seven with each other. That also took some getting used to as we were being stretched in many directions. We felt that our relationship was a gift of grace from the start, and even more so when it was tested on foreign soil.

After two years we finally made it out of formal language study and were living in the city to which we felt called. Then came our first home assignment, and we headed back for a short four months with a sense of accomplishment. I remember getting off the plane, jet lagged, and going straight from the airport into the Sunday morning service of our sending church. I guess we thought we were invincible. Initially, a whirlwind of activity had us meeting with friends and supporters almost nonstop. We crammed a lot into that first month.

The second month included a road trip to upstate New York to visit family, and toward the end of that week, while on the road in Pennsylvania, Jake complained of pain in his leg. It grew worse until he was admitted to the hospital with sepsis from cellulitis in his leg.

From that point on, things were a blur. During his short hospital stay, there was only one day that he didn't continually grow worse. On that day, I celebrated with a piece of lemon meringue pie with friends from my organization who had flown in to be with us. I felt helpless as Jake was fighting for his life, and after one week, he lost the fight and died of a rare autoimmune disease that we didn't even know he had.

My world had shattered. My life was so entwined with Jake's that I couldn't imagine a future without him. I didn't want to write an obituary, I didn't want to face our supporters, but the embrace of the Body of Christ surrounding me is what kept me upright. I had friends who walked with me through grief counseling and offered their companionship until I was ready to focus on the future. During this time I clung to words from a popular song that reminded me God's ways are perfect. This struck a loud chord in my heart.

I'm usually quite pragmatic but for my own mental and emotional health, I took the time I needed to collect my thoughts rather than rush into the next thing. I remembered an important lesson from my first year on the field. That lesson was to never doubt the goodness of God. I clung to that like a lifesaver in a hurricane. When you doubt, you start to sink.

In the following months, I had to learn my husband's role and all the things he handled so effortlessly before, which was a gigantic learning curve for me. Think of the feeling in the pit of your stomach when you crest the top of the first giant swoop of a roller coaster. This is how I felt. I realized during my grief journey that I needed to do things the way I understood how to do them. They wouldn't be as perfect as Jake's flawless administration, but they would be tools that I would use to cope with life and business from then on.

Ten months after Jake passed away, I came back to the field as a widow. God had called me as well as my husband and hadn't changed His mind about reaching the unreached people groups on our island in Southeast Asia. Returning to the field was not only an act of obedience, but it was also the next chapter in a continuous love story. The story did not end with the death of my dear husband, my protector and provider, because my Heavenly Father has become those things to me and more. His love is beyond compare.

It's now been nearly five years since Jake went home to be with Jesus. Even though I'm responsible for myself, I am not alone. God is never away, sleeping, or uncaring. He IS a good, good Father and He's MY Father and He's YOUR Father. Give yourself time to adjust and grace to relax and just enjoy sitting on your Father's lap. It's easier to hear what He says when you're not running down the path ahead of Him. He says, "I am good (Psalm 119:68); I am enough (2 Corinthians 12:9); I am on time (2 Peter 3:8-9); I've got this (Jeremiah 29:11-12)." The land of the living is not our destination; it is our present reality.

—*Maggie V.*

Chapter 14

IN EVERY CRASHING WAVE

I always thought I'd become a mom one day. We were going on an adventure, moving to a new country, and learning a new language and culture. We were leaving behind the U.S. Southern culture of having babies early and leaving behind my Los Angeles friends who had plans and careers first. We were breaking the mold of what we should be doing and moving to our new home. There would be time to do the mom thing, and kids would be part of the journey. They would be missionaries too, and they would join us on this adventure. But God didn't use my blueprints, my plan for our life. Somewhere in my head I thought, *I agreed to the adventure; He will follow the plan.*

In a new culture, the first question asked is "Why are you here?" In Romania, the second question that follows is often about family. "Do you have kids?"

"Oh, not yet." "Nope." "It's all in God's timing."

Memorize and repeat. I admire the ties and commitment to

family here in Romania and how they take care of each other. Yet, it can easily feel like you're not a family until you have children. "Oh, you're married. How many kids do you have?"

"None, yet." "Yet," I add hopefully.

But month after month, every time we travel to a new village or city, the same question and answer is on repeat. I have found after a few years of marriage, they ask this question no matter the country we live in or visit. I repeat, "No, not yet." again. It's another month of grief and despair.

Other missionaries would comment how great it was that we could solely focus on language learning and our ministry instead of having to feel split in our time. What they didn't know was that I felt split already. Fracturing in my identity, in my spirit, and in my understanding of God as a good Father. They didn't know the pain I held. And I wasn't willing to share with others yet, especially not knowing if they knew how to hold it with me.

In infertility, you begin to live life two weeks at a time. Get ready for ovulation, drink water, take vitamins, exercise but not too much, and stay positive. Try again to make sex with your husband not about the making of a baby and don't let the pressure into the bedroom. But somehow it always finds its way in. Then there is the two-week wait. What is this pain, this feeling? Is this nausea from bad food, my period, or a baby? Is God still good when another month passes us by again? Is God still good when years pass us by as we wait for a baby?

I felt like a failure. My body felt like a failure. My value as a woman and wife felt under attack. My identity as a missionary felt fake. Because surely a missionary didn't have the kind of conversations I had been having with God. I wanted to spend time with friends, but I was worried they would be the next ones to share their good news, "We're going to have a baby!"

I didn't know how to talk about this with people in English, let alone in another language. This pain had no language but anger, despair, grief, and depression. I was not sure how to understand God providing and intervening in every aspect of life, except infertility. I watched Him raise thousands of dollars to keep us on the field and in ministry. I found it hard to accept His sacrifice for me as enough. I circled inward in my pain.

My husband was at a loss as to how to help me. He prayed and tried to understand. We often felt the pain of infertility at different times and had different triggers. We had to learn how to communicate those feelings with one another and how to adjust our social commitments to support each other when we needed to place boundaries.

Family would ask questions like, "Would it be easier if you came back to America?" Or make comments like, "I hope I live long enough to see my great-grandbabies."

I finally tried to share with friends here and asked for help to find a doctor. The doctor ran all the tests. "Okay, everything is normal; it all looks great. Maybe just try not to stress?" she said. "Try not to stress!" I repeated. "I live in a foreign country with a foreign language, and you want me not to stress." Then there are the cultural beliefs people liked to share, "Don't sit on the cold concrete, you will freeze your ovaries." I thought to myself, *That's stupid! Also, I wonder if I did freeze them?* Then a doctor told me I was lying on my back too much and that lying on my stomach would help. *Oh Lord, where have You brought me!*

The doctor said the next test we should do was an HSG test to see if my fallopian tubes were open and clear. When we told our families, they pointed out how many people they have heard get pregnant after this test. No pressure. We invited a friend along because high stress situations didn't make my new language brain work well. I called to set up the appointment and found out that I couldn't do it in the newer, private hospital because they didn't own this machine. I had to go to the public hospital with the reputation that makes the "just don't stress" advice laugh in my face.

On the day of the test, we met our friend at the hospital. The doctor doing the test was different from my usual one. He invited me into a room, and my husband and friend waited in the hall. He told me to get undressed on the bottom half and climb on the table. He then proceeded to ask me where I was from and why I was living here. While I got undressed, he injected the dye and prepped to take the X-rays, and I tried to explain why, in my broken, can't-find-the-right-word language because I was stressed, I was living in Romania. He heard "U.S." and immediately decided to talk to me about politics. I cried silently as he went on and on, trying to breathe as I looked up and stared at the peeling paint on the ceiling. He came to my side to tell me it was done and I could get dressed when he noticed a single tear that had rolled down my face hanging from my ear. "What's this?" he asked. "Oh a tear!" he exclaimed with surprise. I tried to say I was fine, and he began to talk about things he knew about America again.

Once back in the hall, my usual doctor walked by and saw us. She looked at the X-rays and said everything looked good, again, but casually mentioned that IVF may be the next step for us. We got outside, and I broke down and bawled my eyes out in my husband's arms, in front of my friend. She later commented on how she appreciated my honesty and openness of my fears and emotions, to the point of crying in front of her. I guess sometimes ministry just looks like sitting in the mess of it all with others (do not read "everyone"). But it didn't feel like that at the time.

I continued to question how to keep going with ministry and not let my anger with God seep in. How could I share about God's goodness when I didn't feel it? Often it has felt like a clash of emotions between joy in ministry or joy for others and sadness for us. Once we put on a workshop to talk about God and our work. That morning my period showed up, and I prayed to God I would feel well enough to get through the morning. While setting up the space, two of our team members arrived visibly pregnant and excited to share the good news with everyone. I unsuccessfully held back tears to congratulate them and quickly found something else to do on the other side of the room.

Up the Mountain with Isaac

I once heard infertility explained like rain. It's always raining, but some days it is just a light drizzle and others it is a massive downpour. But it is invisible to everyone except you and God. Thankfully, we were able to see a counselor while stateside and continued that relationship via Skype. After being unsure about how much to share with family, friends, and our mission organization, we finally had a safe space. A safe space to share about the pain, to discuss the wrong interpretations of God we had believed, and to begin to reconstruct a correct view of God.

We went to Croatia with friends on vacation one year. Some of them talked about how they were nervous because they were not great at swimming. We talked about how we grew up swimming, and we were excited to be at the beach again, finally. But once we arrived on an island in the middle of the Adriatic Sea and began to swim, I began to panic. The water was too deep. The unknowns were too great. And what I had known was not supporting me enough to keep me afloat. To my friends' surprise, I borrowed a floaty. The same happened with my faith. I didn't know I had been believing promises never promised or that I had certain ideas about God until the water was too deep and the pain of infertility was too great. The faith I had was failing me. I needed to borrow a floaty while I deconstructed and reconstructed my understanding of God. The Psalms became a floaty, as I could only cry out to God and hope He would cling to me harder than I was pushing away, because, again, another month passed.

I have never seen a positive pregnancy test. I can't count how many I have taken. I look at the ovulation tests with hope and wonder what it will be like to see two lines on a pregnancy test one day. Six years and counting, with an entirely new relationship with God, all while being sent to share with others about who He is, and still no baby.

I have learned to never speak Christian clichés over people. I have learned that I need to expand my view of God. He is a loving Father. He sacrificed for me to know Him more and for eternity. We do live in a broken world where there can be healing, but it is not promised to me. He is sovereign over all and still sits right beside me and comforts me in every single crest of hope and trough of despair. I have learned no matter the location or culture, God is still in control, and moving to a new place or back to an old one will not change the outcome. I have learned that we are living in the war already won and the battle still being fought. I have learned that I put too much of my identity in other things and that identity work is always long and hard. I have learned that if I do not remind myself of these things daily, then that monthly reminder of failure will (and still does) suck me back under waves at times. While I wait, God is still good.

—Michelle

Chapter 15

EYES TO SEE THE BLESSING

On the twenty-minute drive to our friends' home, I tried to smile and not let my face betray to our youngest son the dread that was coursing through my heart. We had done this once before, and yet here we were *again* making our way to a house—not a hospital—where we would have him undergo a small "surgery" that I would be terrified to undergo myself. The voice of reason that told me this was necessary was waging a battle with my mother heart, and hot tears threatened to spill from my eyes and onto his head at any moment. The giant motocross helmet that we had purchased for him before the move stood out sorely in this country where laws only required adults to wear them, a symbol of the ridiculous situation we were in.

Less than a year before, our family had made the move to our new home in Southeast Asia. We had boarded the plane with our two, four, and six-year-old children in tow, ready for adventure and confident that we had heard God's call to go. Looking back, that confidence was a necessary gift and a balance to the naivety we had carried with us in our suitcases. In all the planning and dreaming, preparing, and praying that had gone into our decision to come to this place, we had somehow forgotten to factor in the potential cost to our children.

Now, as motorbikes passed on either side, a sick feeling of panic was rising in my throat. Noah laughed as we drove, not understanding what was about to unfold. Somehow this made my own fears multiply. His right eye, pink and nearly swollen shut, distorted his little face. What had begun months before as a minor irritation around his left eye had developed into a stye. Typically, a stye would be considered a common ailment, easily treatable and quick to clear up. However, Noah's eye infection just would not seem to improve no matter what we did.

Medical care in our host country was lacking at this time, which compounded our feelings of helplessness as parents. It was a constant temptation to think that if only we were "at home," we could take him to his pediatrician, and all would be well. Yet, here we were nine thousand miles from his pediatrician, wrestling with the guilt that came from feeling as if Noah was having to pay the price for our decision to be here. Was it worth it? Were we forcing our son to suffer for something he had never asked to take part of in the first place? And, in addition to these feelings came another conflicting type of guilt: *Did we think we were better than all the other parents in this country whose children faced the same issue? Did our child deserve more than their children just because we were used to a higher standard of care and had more money to pay for it?*

I often clung to words that a former missionary had shared with me before we left for the field. When I had voiced my concerns about taking our young children overseas, she had told me that God does not call parents and disregard their children. When He calls parents, He calls their children. Not only that, He loves them and wants their best even more than we do as their parents. Did I really believe that? *Did I really trust that God could see my baby in the middle of this crowded city street, on his way to undergo what felt to me like torture?*

Despite the challenges of obtaining quality medical care, God's grace towards us during this time was evident. An eye surgeon from Korea, along with his family, attended our tiny international church community. They had moved to our host country to minister under the auspices of his vocation. While his days were filled with serving nationals, he made himself available to serve our family as well. So, when Noah got his first eye infection, our friend monitored it over several weeks before finally having to lance his lower eyelid to treat it. Though this was difficult to watch as a parent, it did not compare to the anguish of what we were about to have to watch Noah endure.

When his left eye recovered from the infection and subsequent procedure, we were thankful and hoped the minor medical ordeal was over. Little did we know that it was only a precursor to what would become a more significant infection in his other eye. As time passed, it appeared as if the infection had not healed, but had simply transferred to the other eye with a vengeance. It soon became clear that it was not going to heal on its own.

A well-meaning friend also serving in our new city offered suggestions as to the cause of Noah's troubles. While I did not allow these speculations to hold much weight, they did leave me further confused and guiltily questioning if we had somehow placed Noah in the enemy's crosshairs. *Had allowing him to be near our dog (which happened to have been given to us as a gift) put him at risk? Was it the local preschool we had enrolled him in where he was surrounded by altars and teachers who might have "spoken something over him"?*

Whatever the cause, Noah's eye could not be left untouched any longer. We had read and inquired enough to know that if we were in our home country, a child Noah's age would be placed under sedation in a sterile environment for the procedure. Yet that was not an option because it would be too risky for him to be placed under anesthesia in a local hospital.

Pulling up to our friend's house, we ambled off the motorbike. Noah ran over to the swing on the sidewalk, not knowing this surgery would be more invasive than last time. My stomach knotted, and I prayed silently, a plea wracked with fear, desperate for God to somehow let this be okay. *Who brings their child on a motorbike to have eye surgery at someone's house?*

Our friend welcomed us in. His wife, sensing my struggle, hugged me. I wondered if she thought this was as unorthodox as I did. *Surely her husband had never performed surgery in their house in*

Korea. They ushered us into a bedroom where a coffee table had been placed at the end of a bed. *A coffee table. What were we doing to our child?*

By this time, Noah's carefree laughter had turned to apprehension. The adults in the room were too serious, and he could sense it in our hushed whispers. It was time, and delaying was not going to make it any easier. We lifted Noah onto the coffee table, and he began trying to wiggle himself free. As he realized we were going to hold him down, fear kicked in, and he started to cry. There was nothing to do but hold him and speak in comforting tones, hoping he would somehow be calmed.

Our friend took a syringe and proceeded to inject anesthetic medicine in multiple places around Noah's eye. Next, he placed a clamp on his lower eyelid and turned it inside out. It was beyond painful to watch as our son stared up at us, wide-eyed with fear, looking as if we had betrayed him. Over and over in my mind, I frantically repeated my question. *What are we doing to our child? What are we doing to our child?*

Our friend had to ask his teenager to come and help hold Noah down, another proof of the insanity of the situation. His wife placed her arm around my shoulder and prayed softly as he took a scalpel and lanced Noah's eyelid. I turned away, unable to watch. I just wanted it to be over, and it was not happening quickly enough. Noah cried and kicked. I cried and prayed, and my earlier questions turned into emphatic statements. *We are never doing this again. We are never doing this again.*

I could not bear to look as I held Noah down with my head turned. Finally, my husband said it was finished. There had been a lot of infection, but it had been removed. Noah, relieved to be free, laid in my arms as I kissed his head and whispered how brave he had been. It was such a strange event with too many emotions seeking the spotlight. We were grateful that our friend was available and willing to help Noah. At the same time, the afternoon had been traumatic.

When we left, I took Noah home in a taxi. Holding him in the backseat, I sang over him. *The Lord comes with healing in His wings. The Lord comes with healing in His wings.* It was as much a song of wanting to believe as it was actual belief. I was a mother, but I could identify with the begging father's words to Jesus when he said, "I believe; help my unbelief!" (Mark 9:24, ESV)

In the coming weeks, we prayed and hoped. Noah's eyes did heal completely, but the coffee table eye surgery ended up being minor in comparison to the other issues he soon faced. Months later, almost overnight, Noah stopped speaking. He developed a stutter that caused his face to distort with the effort of producing even one syllable. We have a video where he tried *thirty-eight times* to pronounce the first syllable in the word *elephant*. This resulted in using our savings to fly to a nearby country to visit a developmental clinic. From there, he was referred to a specialty hospital where he had an MRI of his brain to rule out a brain injury. He was then diagnosed with a stuttering disorder. We were told that it was an eight on a scale of one to ten and that it would likely be lifelong.

So much had happened in our little boy's life since moving to our host country. As I reflect back on this time now, ten years later, I see a young mother who loved God, loved her child, and was trying to flesh out what obedience looked like in the midst of a hundred doubts and questions. Miraculously, our little boy regained his speech within a year. That, too, brought questions about the power of prayer. *Had I even prayed enough to see healing?*

There is no way to know what caused Noah's eye and speech problems. Perhaps they were spiritual attacks. Perhaps they were unrelated. Perhaps they just happened. What I do know is this: God was faithful to my son.

Since he was a newborn, I have prayed the same prayer over him every night. *Lord, let Noah's life be marked with great, great joy. As he grows, I pray that he will know You, love You, love Your word, and speak Your word to other people.* Noah's life is, in fact, marked with great, great joy. This boy who lost his words can rarely be silenced now.

In recent years, I have added one line to this nightly prayer. *Multiply the blessings You've already done in his life.* Some nights I stop to remind him about the blessings God did in his life way back then. Most nights he prays the same words out loud as I pray for him.

Thankfully, Noah does not remember much from those early experiences, and the trauma associated with them has been softened with time. He does know, though, that God has been faithful to him. He has his very own story of God's faithfulness in his life. It is not one I would have chosen for him as we were living through it, but it is the one that God allowed. And He wrote it before we ever stepped foot on the first airplane.

—*Nancy Haney*

Chapter 16

DO IT SCARED

A cockroach scurried up the hospital wall, a baby cockroach but still a cockroach. I sighed. "Do you know what someone would do in the U.S. if there was a cockroach in the room where they were about to give birth?" I asked my husband. "Probably sue the hospital." And this, this was the nice hospital, the private hospital. Not the hospital across the road where, at times, women ended up giving birth in the hallway when not enough beds were available. *Were there cockroaches in the stable when Mary gave birth?* I wondered. Stables aren't exactly known for being sterile environments.

This was my third time giving birth in Papua New Guinea, a country not known for having the best medical care. My firstborn nearly died when after an extremely long labor he inhaled meconium into his lungs. His gray coloring and shallow breathing concerned my mom but did not seem to concern the midwife who was casually chatting away as she stitched me up after performing an episiotomy during delivery. My mom, who used to work as an

OB nurse, ended up suctioning my little guy's tiny lungs, and when the on-call doctor finally came, he started an IV. All the while I laid there alone in the hospital room wondering why no one was coming to give me an update but having no way to get up and check on things. My baby had been put on oxygen. When they tried to take him off again so I could attempt to nurse him, he struggled to breath on his own.

Although he was just hours old, I was told that my son needed to be transferred to the hospital across the street. The hospital where I gave birth did not have a full intensive care unit for newborns, and my son needed immediate care. As I rode, cradling my newborn in the back of the ambulance, the oxygen tank he was connected to emptied and apparently there wasn't a spare tank. *What kind of ambulance doesn't have a spare tank?* I screamed internally. Thankfully the trip was brief, and within minutes he received life-giving care at the hospital I had been trying to avoid due to hearing too many horror stories from people whose children had died in that very hospital.

"Trust Me." I felt God whisper. I didn't want to trust. I wanted my baby. I wanted to hold him, take him home. I wanted to watch his chest rise and fall. But what choice was there? In those unimaginable moments when I did not know if my son would survive, I questioned if it had been the right decision to give birth in a third-world country. I already loved my sweet baby so much, and there is a very real risk living in a country without access to the latest medical care. My new mama heart felt at times that it was asking too much to trust in such circumstances. Did Mary feel that way too?

My daughter's birth was thankfully much less stressful. Everything had gone by the book, no complications, and my midwife had been wonderful. Still I was grateful to have my mom with me for the birth. Now, this third time around, it was just my husband and me. COVID-19 was making it difficult to travel, and I had told my parents not to try and come.

I had felt so optimistic checking into the hospital. Contractions were strong—consistently six to seven minutes apart. I was two weeks past my due date and sooooo ready to finally hold my sweet girl. The doctor had told me that if she wasn't here by Friday he wanted to induce. On Wednesday night light bleeding told me that labor was finally starting. We called some friends to come and spend the night with the older two kids, and I went to bed to attempt to rest up as much as possible. By 3 A.M. contractions were strong enough that I could no longer sleep through them. By 5 A.M. we headed to the hospital. I had dilated to four centimeters by that point, so the midwife admitted me. *This is perfect timing, I thought. The baby should be here by the time the other kids finish school for the day.*

The birthing unit felt familiar now. The private room that cost extra still had a shared bathroom. There was a broken lock on the bathroom door. Expectant mothers were still told to bring their own toilet paper, sanitary pads, diapers, wipes, crib coverings and toiletries. The inflatable gray birthing ball was so deflated it wasn't usable. I guess Mary didn't have a proper birthing ball either. The room had no extra bed for my husband to sleep on and definitely no birthing hot tub. There was a small TV, but it only played one channel of commercials.

Even though contractions had been steadily progressing, within hours of checking into the hospital, the contractions slowed instead of increasing. They went from usually six minutes apart to as far as fifteen minutes apart. The midwife seemed annoyed when she wheeled in her birthing cart but instead of being ready to give birth, I hadn't dilated past four centimeters. I got the impression that I needed to hurry up and have this baby so they could clear me out to make room for the next expectant mother. "You're too relaxed," she told me. "Try walking around."

So I paced back and forth in that cramped room as the hours slowly ticked by. I tried squats, walking, more squats, more walking. Reluctantly, I finally agreed to let the midwife break my water. It helped some, but progress was still slow. A full eight hours passed. The first midwife gave up on me. She stopped even bothering to check in on my "progress." The midwife who had originally checked me in started her shift again. She mentioned starting a Pitocin drip if by midnight the pace did not pick up more, but she was not pushy as the last midwife had been.

The hours dragged; the pain steadily increased (no option for an epidural here) and it felt like too much. I was done—physically, mentally, emotionally depleted. But more than anything I was terrified. Should I have let the midwife break my water sooner?

Up the Mountain with Isaac

Was I going to need a C-section? Was my baby okay? I just wanted to see her—watch her chest rise as it filled with oxygen and hear that sweet first cry.

I have heard courage defined as being scared and doing it anyway. I don't see myself as an overly courageous person. I do tend to lean towards fear, especially when it comes to the safety of my kids. But I'm still here, still walking out each day, still trusting. Some things you just have to do in spite of the fear.

I have seen too much brokenness and even evil in this world to naïvely think everything is always going to be okay. Sometimes things are very much not okay. At just eight-years-old I saw my twin sister's lifeless form lying on my parent's bed. The doctor speculated that her sudden passing might have been caused by respiratory complications due to malaria. Losing my twin was crushing, and yet as she laid there, her pale blue lips wore the sweetest smile I have ever seen. Right before she closed her eyes for the final time, she told my dad she heard singing. He told her it was just the medicine she was taking. I know my sister is in a better place, and I saw God's presence firsthand as our family walked through the most difficult experience we have ever faced. I learned so much as an eight-year-old, but one lesson that was branded on my brain is that life is fragile. There are no guarantees this side of heaven that everything will be okay.

In that tiny birthing room, just barely big enough to hold the hospital bed and an extra chair, I felt fear rising. "I can't do this," I said through tears. And there God met me. "Yes, you can," the midwife told me and wrapped me in a hug. "Speak positively to your baby." Her calmness calmed me.

Finally, around 3:00 A.M. I had dilated enough to push. I pushed so hard that I tore to the point of needing stitches, but I didn't care. I needed to see my baby. I needed to know she was okay. She came out quickly. As my midwife held her up, I could see my daughter's skin was a ghostly gray. My heart skipped a beat. There was no cry. The umbilical cord had wrapped itself around her neck three times. Quickly the midwife unwrapped the tangled cord and began to gently but firmly rub my daughter's tiny chest with her fingers. Then there it was—a cry, breath sucked into tiny lungs. My sweet girl was alive.

"She's okay; she's okay. I'm so happy. Oh, she's all right." I kept saying over and over. By that point my head was pounding. The room felt like it was spinning. The words echoed in my ears almost as if someone else was saying them. Tears piled up in the corners of my eyes, but they were tears of utter joy and pure relief. It was over. I had walked through it, and my baby was here now lying on my chest. God had met me and provided just the right midwife in that slightly rundown hospital room far away from my family.

I flicked a baby cockroach off the metal frame cradling the bassinet that had been wheeled next to the hospital bed. I stared at my sweet girl swaddled tightly in a warm blanket. Her daddy had chosen her first name, Abigail, which means "a father's joy or delight." I had picked her middle name, Jane, which means "God is gracious."

Up the Mountain with Isaac

He had been so gracious. There are no guarantees in this broken life. We don't deserve a life free from pain or even free from cockroaches. Sometimes we are asked to walk through very hard things and that is honestly scary. But we are not asked to walk through anything alone. He meets us there in the manure-filled stable, in the third-world hospital room. He is there. So we can trust, so we can rest. We can do it, even do it scared at times while resting in the One whose perfect love casts out fear.

—*Ruth Potinu*

Chapter 17

FAITHFULNESS ALONE

"If only I knew that this would just last a season," I sighed in exasperation to my friend, "then I could contentedly serve with joy." Though this statement could easily be said about a variety of situations, I was referring to my state of singleness on the mission field.

Serving globally as a single missionary was never what I had in mind. Since the time I was an eleven-year-old little girl who gave herself to follow God on the mission field, I took for granted that this calling would include serving cross-culturally with a godly husband and raising our children in whichever new culture we found ourselves. I prepared at a Bible college where friends met their future spouses, many of whom are now serving cross-culturally with their families. I served for a year on the mission field and then returned to my home country for another year at a different Bible institute, yet I still went back to the mission field single.

The evening before the aforementioned conversation with my friend, I stood in my kitchen debating what to prepare for supper. As I walked to the sink, I caught a glimpse of myself in the reflection of the window and imagined this same scene but with a baby in one arm and a toddler at my feet, asking for a snack or drink of water. This thought weaseled its way into my meal preparation and left me with a tear or two in my eyes. Would this image in my mind ever become reality? Would I marry and have kids of my own or did choosing to follow God on the mission field mean giving up this dream indefinitely? I convinced myself that if I only knew the timeline of this sacrifice, if I only knew that it would one day end, then I could serve fully and unhindered.

As I shared my frustration and desire with another friend, I confided that I often wrestle with God's intention for singleness. In Genesis, He explicitly states that it is not good for man to be alone and then creates a woman so that they can form one flesh and create their own family. Later, in the New Testament, Paul makes a claim for why singleness is better for the Lord's work if one can accept it.

To me, these teachings have always been a source of confoundment and even frustration. On one hand, I have prayed many times for contentment in my status as a single person, asking God to help me see this current stage as a gift with which to serve Him rather than as a punishment or difficulty I must endure. On the other hand, I wrestle with not seeing marriage as God's obvious best—singleness as something He can use, but marriage as the better of the two.

However, in that conversation with my friend, she stated something profound that I had never before considered. Together we read Genesis 2 where God says that it is not good for man to be alone, so He created woman. She stated here that what was not good in this passage was not singleness itself but rather isolation.

It is true that it is not good for us to be alone; we see this throughout Scripture. It is why God's perfect design for the believer takes place within the Body of Christ. But within the boundaries of it not being good that we are alone, there is room for both singleness and marriage in Christ's Church. This is why Paul could say that, from his perspective, singleness was better. He was not contradicting the God-given order in Genesis 1 but was rather writing within the context of an audience that was already in the Body of Christ. Therefore, whether single or married, they were not alone but living, serving, and loving within the community of believers.

This simple yet profound understanding has helped me to reframe my view of singleness on the mission field. I am single, but I am not alone. Whether for a season or for life, my identity is not in my marital status but in who I am as a daughter of the King, living and serving in a family that encourages, challenges, supports, and prays for me. On the days when I most feel alone or doubt that singleness could somehow be as God-given and purposeful as marriage, I am thankful for this truth. I see and appreciate the Body of Christ in a way that I may not if I were married; I am learning to give thanks to God for not leaving me alone but putting me in His family.

The reality is that we all—whether single or married—are walking by faith in this journey of obedience. We are not guaranteed how long certain seasons will last or if certain sacrifices are ones God is asking us to make without giving an end date. As someone older than the majority of my friends and family who have gotten married but still considered "young" by more seasoned colleagues, I do not know if my giving up marriage to serve God is permanent or whether it will only last a season. What I do know is that, whether permanent or temporary, marriage is a desire that I have had to give to God for this current step of obedience.

When I finished college, a well-meaning elder from church told me that it would be understandable if I wanted to stay in the United States for a little while longer in order to find a husband before I left for another country. He reminded me that young adult groups at churches are good places to make such connections, and such groups would be much more difficult to find on the mission field. Though well-intentioned, this suggestion left me feeling a little uneasy. I was well aware of the implications of leaving for the mission field directly after college without a husband or prospect on the horizon, but I was also deeply convinced that this was the next step of obedience God was asking me to take. To delay obedience in turn for my desire of a family was something I was not willing to do.

So, armed with stories of single missionary women much more courageous than me—Amy Carmichael, Gladys Aylward, and others—I graduated college, finished preparations, and boarded a plane. Now several years later, I am in my second term and still learning how to daily submit my desire for marriage to the God who has called me and has been faithful up to this point in my life. He is a good Father, and I know I can trust His plans and timing to be for my good and His glory, even when that is difficult to see.

Some days it is more difficult to submit than others, like the day standing in the kitchen or the day when I shared my frustration with my friend. Nights are often the loneliest, when I long for someone with whom to review the day. I tend to be keenly aware of my singleness when big changes are coming, and I have no one with whom to discuss the possibilities, challenges, and excitement. And sometimes, when friends or teammates are talking about marriage, children, and family life, I realize that I do not fully relate to what they are saying. Nonetheless, I take another step forward. It is true that I do not know the length of this season or the depth of this sacrifice that I am being asked to make, but God has been teaching me that singleness can actually be a gift from Him as well.

Singleness means that I do not have someone by my side in bed at night with whom to review the day, but it also means that friends invite me over in the evenings for an impromptu meal or even to stay the night because they know that I am alone in a culture different than my own. I have some of the most meaningful relationships and conversations forged during late evenings, a time when if I had a husband and kids I would be in my house with them instead of sharing with neighbors and friends.

When big changes come, it is true that I do not have a partner with whom to walk through all the details, but it is precisely in this that I see the mercy, faithfulness, and love of God. Sometimes I see it through teammates or friends from my host country who set aside hours and days of their time to help me move to another town or install household appliances, even though it is not in their job description. Sometimes I see it when I do have to make the decisions myself and am terrified of the next step, only to see God provide in every little detail. Regardless, I always see it in the way God draws me to increasing dependence on Him, even in the times of loneliness and transition.

And when friends and teammates talk about experiences with which I cannot relate, I realize that I also have experiences with which they cannot relate. I have come to understand that it is in this space of difference that we both have something to offer the other. It is in diversity that the Body of Christ has its greatest chance to shine.

So, yes, being single—especially in a culture different than my own—has its challenges. Some nights are filled with cries for companionship, and sometimes it feels like the courage it requires to be faithfully single in this setting is too much to ask. I have fallen asleep with tears in my eyes as I ask God once again how long this sacrifice of singleness will last. Is it a season or is it for life? But even in the questions and the longing, there is an intrinsic beauty to this call: the beauty of trusting Christ when I am not enough, the beauty of knowing my belonging in His Body, regardless of marital status, and the beauty of seeing God's present faithfulness in my singleness.

—Shirley Anne Jacobs

Collateral Damage

Part Two

Collateral Damage

"Can you thank me for trusting you with this experience even if I never tell you why?"

Without even knowing who said these words or the context of this sentence, it is powerful. I'm sitting here asking myself who in this world would I be able to give a "Yes" to, if they asked me this question. My conclusion is that that number, my dear friends, is a single digit.

The question is not "Will you trust me to take care of you during this experience?"

The question is not "Will you trust me to take care of you during this experience even if I never tell you why?"

The question IS... "Will you THANK me for trusting YOU with this experience even if I never tell you why?"

The night Helen Roseveare gave her life to Christ, the leader of the conference handed her a Bible and wrote Philippians 3:10 in the front. It was the first Bible she had ever owned, and I can't imagine he knew the significance the words he pressed into her hands that night would have on the young woman who stood before him.

I want to know Christ—yes, to know the power of his resurrection and participation in his sufferings (NIV).

In her later years, Dr. Roseveare alluded to the impact this verse and Philippians 1:29 had on shaping her view of the most traumatic time in her life.

> *For you have been given not only the privilege of trusting in Christ but also the privilege of suffering for him (NLT).*

From the very first moments with her Savior, He had been forming in her a foundational idea of the privilege of suffering. And when the moment came, it was to these verses her mind went.

When her teeth were kicked out by rebels that forced themselves into her home; when they severely beat the local friend who tried to protect her; when they eventually raped her twice and took her away against her will, she remembered the question being uttered to her heart by the only One she could imagine answering "Yes" to. The Lord asked, "Helen, can you thank Me for trusting you with this experience even if I never tell you why?"

It was then that Helen was quieted by the idea that the God she trusted with her whole heart was also trusting her.

"Lord, I can't imagine in this moment that someone would ever be blessed by this but if You're asking me to trust You, I say yes."

Helen felt peace settle over her as the Lord laid out His request. "All I want from you is the loan of your body. They aren't fighting you, they are fighting Me."

It didn't stop the pain, the humiliation, the cruelty. It was all there. But suddenly she wasn't alone. She was in it with Him and for Him.

"There was a moment that I knew he was there with me. The rebels weren't really the ones in control. They were very small in comparison to the overwhelming presence of God."[8]

The women in the following section have realized this question being asked of them. There is not one of us who escapes the call to enter and serve in enemy territory without experiencing some collateral damage. It is in how we view our suffering and the One who asked or allowed it that our testimony holds its power.

It doesn't stop us from doing everything we can to be wise and minimize the risk for unnecessary collateral damage. It doesn't stop us and those we love from asking the hard questions.

Like the women in this section, we may still wrestle with this question that was asked of Helen. I pray that we too may know the Father in such a way that we can answer as she did:

"Why did a God of love allow a missionary to suffer? Well, I never felt the need to ask that question. He is our Master, our Friend, our Savior, our Lord, our King. He has the right to anything. I had given my life to him so instead of asking 'why,' I asked 'why not'? I have truly come to believe that it was a privilege! The Lord of all of the universe asked something of me. And so as I look at it, I see it as a privilege. A privilege to be given the opportunity to serve him or to suffer."[9]

—*Denise Beck*

Chapter 18

A NEW NAME

I remember sitting in the Atlanta airport in September 2016, filled with anticipation and excitement, looking down at the word *courage* inscribed on the Giving Key my best friend had given me as a goodbye gift. *Courage* was a word the Lord had put on my heart during the months of preparation, planning, and support-raising to move overseas. Here I was, about to move halfway across the world to be a missionary, so naturally I needed courage to trust God in the face of the unknown. Little did I know I would need courage for far more than that. I would need to face my eating disorder and say, "I no longer need you."

Let me start from the beginning. I grew up in a strong Christian home in the United States with loving parents who taught me about God and the Bible. At six years old, I put my faith in Jesus Christ and began a relationship with Him.

As I grew up, my heart was tender towards God, and I longed to know Him and obey Him. However, I came to believe that the way to be a good Christian was to be good and do all the right things.

Throughout middle and high school, I was actively involved in my church youth group. Like most middle school kids, I desperately wanted to be liked and accepted by my peers. However, I was homeschooled. Add on a couple of traumatic experiences with mean girls, and I came to believe that different meant *weird*. I was not enough. I was lacking. There was something wrong with me.

Enter shame.

In high school, these feelings of inadequacy—of not being enough—were reinforced over and over. I did not understand my identity as God's dearly beloved child, so I desperately tried to be accepted by others. I sought other people's approval through my body image and my performance. It was only a matter of time before I translated these feelings to God as well. Shame made me believe that I had to spiritually perform and do everything right in order to be accepted by God.

During my junior year of high school, I went on a "diet." While it started out harmlessly and only lasted a couple of months, the damage was done. I saw how controlling my food and exercise made me feel good about myself and gave me the approval I so desperately craved. Somewhere along the way, this developed into an eating disorder. I had no idea how much it would enslave me.

In college, the eating disorder spilled over into other spaces. I strove for perfection in all areas of my life—schoolwork, body image, involvement on campus, and ministry. I got involved with a campus ministry, and before long, I was doing it all—leading Bible studies, going on summer mission projects. But inwardly, I was in bondage. I felt powerless to get out of the rules and habits I had developed for myself, and I was suffocating under the weight of trying to be perfect.

For three years, I tried to fight the eating disorder on my own with "God's help." I was the resolver. I went to counseling, I sought accountability, and I met with a nutritionist to gain weight. While my heart longed for and cried out to God for freedom, I couldn't fully give up control. It was still serving a purpose, helping me cope with feelings of shame and inadequacy.

After graduating from college, I felt the Lord call me to serve Him overseas. I decided to move to Thailand, where I taught missionary kids and assisted with ministry on a college campus. I genuinely loved God and loved cross-cultural ministry, but it was more guilt-driven than love-driven.

However, during my initial interview with the mission organization, they strongly recommended that I go back to counseling before I went on the mission field. I was devastated. Was this going to keep me from doing missions work? From serving God? From doing what I thought He had called me to?

After a few more months of counseling, my counselor gave me the "stamp of approval," and I started support-raising. There I was off to Thailand feeling pretty good about myself. The food and culture in Thailand are so different than in America, so I anticipated my eating and body image struggles wouldn't be an issue.

Fast forward to December. Within only a few short months of being in Thailand, the eating disorder reared its ugly head again. I was stripped of my comfort and control, placed into a new culture, language, and community, and experiencing spiritual warfare (our enemy hates it when we step out in faith to follow Christ).

On the outside, I was thriving. I was adjusting well to the culture, excelling in my teaching role and building friendships with Thai people. I had jumped fully into the ministry, and I was loving it.

But inwardly, I was a wreck. I lost a lot of weight, but in an Asian culture where being thin is the norm, no one thought much about it. I was desperately striving to do it all in ministry, putting immense pressure on myself to be perfect at everything. I said "Yes" to every ministry opportunity, and I had no idea what Sabbath rest actually looked like. I was absolutely exhausted, holding on for dear life to some semblance of control.

But without the comforts of home, family, friends, or other distractions back in the States, I couldn't escape. I couldn't ignore the Holy Spirit speaking inside me. Like Jacob wrestling with the Divine, I was one-on-one with God—left alone with Him to grapple with the lies, sin, and shame I had become ruled by.

The choice was before me: Either continue down the path I was on or go down a new road. One led to destruction, the other to life. But the one leading to life looked much harder—it was narrow, steep, and full of bushes and thorns. Going down that path would be hard, maybe even painful. I would have to come face-to-face with the things I'd stuffed and buried for years. But the view at the end would be worth every single scrape and bruise.

I cried out to God. *Will You deliver me from this bondage? Can You?* My soul ached for freedom. I longed to serve God with my whole being. I didn't want anything to hold me back.

There in my small bedroom in Thailand with the faded orange curtains and the creaky floors, God began the process of pulling back the layers of my cold, unbelieving heart and speaking words of love and delight over me.

During this time, I remember reading the story of the invalid man who had been sitting by the pool for thirty-eight years. I broke down crying. I was just like this man. I didn't believe Jesus could really heal me and free me from this struggle. Like the man at the pool, it had become so much a part of me that I didn't know who I was without it. I had become known for being thin and skinny. How could I give that up? I had relied on my rules and habits to feel secure and in control. How could I give those up? The condemning voices in my head were comfortable and familiar. *What would it be like without those?*

I could feel Jesus asking me the same question that He asked the invalid man: "Do you want to be healed?" "Oh yes, Jesus!" I replied. "Yes, yes, yes, a hundred times yes!"

Over the next two years, God did a deep work of healing and freedom inside of me. The turning point was truly understanding my identity as a child of God. The writings of Christian author

Neil T. Anderson were instrumental in this process. As I read *Victory Over the Darkness*, I felt like scales were falling from my eyes. Was I really a child of God, seated in heaven with Christ, looking down on Satan, a defeated foe? Did I really have the power and resources to fight sin and overcome bondage since I am in Christ?

For the first time, the Gospel I knew since I was a kid began to take deep root in my heart. Nothing, even my sin and mistakes, can separate me from God's love (Romans 8:38-39). I have been adopted as God's child and brought into His family (Ephesians 1:5). I am raised up and seated with Christ in the heavenly places in Christ Jesus, meaning Satan has no power over me (Ephesians 2:6). I am alive in Him (Colossians 2:13). There is no condemnation for me since I am in Christ Jesus (Romans 8:1).

Knowing that I was loved and accepted by God gave me the courage to walk in the light, openly acknowledging my sin. I went through *The Steps to Freedom in Christ*, a prayer and repentance process. I repented of sin, renounced deep-seated lies that I had come to believe because of my sin, forgave those who had hurt me in my past, and declared the truth about my Father God.

The lies and shame that had ruled my life for so long were replaced with liberating Gospel truth. But complete transformation didn't happen overnight. For months and months, I wrestled with God. I quickly learned that my struggles wouldn't immediately go away, nor would the lies magically disappear. But the difference was that I was choosing, by faith, to believe what

God says is true. I no longer felt defeated.

In God's kindness, He provided multiple Christian women in Thailand to walk through this healing journey with me. In particular, an older, godly Thai woman, a Thai friend my exact age, and a loving, supportive roommate. For two years, we shared our hearts together, cried together, and prayed together. These women are still some of my dearest friends today.

I would love to say that from that time on, my life has been a walk in the park. Far from it. Coming back from the mission field and adjusting back to my home culture was excruciating. I grieved the loss of purpose and identity I had being a missionary. I missed my friends, the food, my church, everything.

Back in America with no idea of what was next, I felt like a failure. The grief and pain triggered old feelings of shame and lies from the accuser. I struggled to live out the truth that I had learned in Thailand, to embody the new identity God had bestowed on me. In times of weakness and temptation, I gave in.

But our Abba Father is faithful, loving, and kind. He didn't let me go. He carried me through this season, and He is still carrying me. As Jacob was changed forever after his wrestling encounter with God, I was changed forever by my wrestling encounter with God on the mission field. Jacob left with a limp and a new name, a new identity. I, too, left with a limp—a story to remind me of God's faithfulness. And I had been given a new name—Fully Accepted and Delighted in by God.

Collateral Damage

"And you shall be called by a **new name** that the mouth of the Lord will give. You shall be a **crown of beauty** in the hand of the Lord, and a **royal diadem** in the hand of your God....You shall be called My Delight Is in Her, and your land Married; **for the Lord delights in you**, and your land shall be married" (Isaiah 62:2-4, ESV, emphasis added).

—Abby Batson

Chapter 19

HANGING LAUNDRY AND ENOUGH

Like all good missionaries, we left our passport country with a clear plan for how God was going to use us in our area of service. We had heard of the need, responded in faith, and sold everything we had to move and go.

We decided to say "No" to one more Christmas in the States and leave before the holidays toward what awaited us. It made sense, it helped our team out, it gave us time to settle in our location, and it seemed a small sacrifice to get started with our new life in the best possible way. I remember the frantic packing of last-minute items, the excitement as we loaded our four children onto an airline, and the trepidation at the long flight that awaited us. I like to prepare, and we left with a solid plan. We were heading into Kenya just long enough to get a quick orientation before moving to our North African home.

The plane landed, and almost immediately our plans began to disappear. Denied visas, closed borders, the realization that no one would be allowed to enter the country we had yearned to call home. Then the holidays hit. We were stranded in a big city we had never planned to live in, all offices had shut down for the holidays, and we found ourselves alone sitting in a tiny apartment on Christmas Day.

There was no home to anticipate moving to, no plan for the future, and no reason that I could think of for being in an unknown place instead of celebrating Christmas with our family. I found myself grasping for normalcy as I tried to make yogurt from scratch or roll out tortillas in a country I had never intended to live in, and a feeling of overwhelm crept in.

Years of planning had landed our family of six in a little flat in a large city with nowhere to live, unknown ministry to anticipate, and buckets of laundry.

Lest you think I am exaggerating, we had four children under six and two in cloth diapers and then to top it all off a prayer letter was due.

Christmas passed, and as we ushered in the new year with our young kids, the struggle intensified. I had no idea what the future for our little clan would hold; it felt like a failed new year. The empty prayer letter template mocked me; what would I tell everyone that had sacrificed for our journey: that I was barely keeping up with laundry and that we were homeless?

I desperately tried to cling to what I could predict. We would probably be studying a language, somewhere, for some amount of time. The litany of unknown in that sentence brought me little solace. Then another wave of despair washed over me. Decisions can take weeks to be made, and the guest house had a limited time they would allow us to stay. The future stared at me like a blank canvas void of possibilities.

Not surprisingly, laundry taunted me from a heap in the corner, and I trudged to the back porch. There were not enough clips in the guesthouse to hang everything, so I balanced on a stool trying to squeeze all the clothing onto a few small lines, overlapping and flipping it, hoping it would somehow dry and not crash to the ground to be rewashed. As I teetered on the stool, it wobbled precariously, and I cried out in frustration as I tumbled to the ground. I still remember how the cold, dirty floor felt as I sat in the back room trying to wring out clothes to dry and tears trailed down my cheeks. How could I trust God when all the plans had failed, when there was nothing in the future that I could even anticipate trusting Him about except the imminence of more laundry?

It was in that rather pitiful moment that I heard God speak; it was a quiet clear thought trickling into my subconscious as the laundry dripped overhead. "Abuk, if I brought you halfway around the world to hang laundry in this city, is this enough.... am I enough?"

I sat there with clips in my mouth, the partially dry laundry dripping on my head and the cold hard floor beneath me. The question was too big to answer, so I hung a few more clothes and returned to my family.

Collateral Damage

As the days turned into weeks the unknowns kept coming, and I discovered that my favorite time of day was hanging clothes out to dry. Laundry cannot go long without smelling in this part of the world, and if we got behind, there was nowhere to hang clothes. So, every day, twice a day, I found myself hanging laundry to dry.

The room I was in was little—no glass windows, just stucco patterning that allows a breeze, squeals from children, or lots of rain indoors. It is an inconvenient room of the home, and often the children did not follow me there. But over the weeks that room became my prayer room. They weren't eloquent prayers, or verses God gave me. Just a simple task of hanging laundry. Often as I hung the clothes and diapers God would meet me by asking me the same questions. "Is this enough, Abuk? Am I enough? If I brought you halfway around the world to hang laundry here would it be enough, am I enough?"

I would cry, and at times my soul would protest. I would hang the laundry and curse under my breath as the stool rocked back and forth precariously. I would mumble under my breath because the reality I felt was that I did not move halfway around the world with my four children to hang laundry, I came to change the world, to share the Gospel, to reach the least reached. I am pretty sure our prayer cards hanging up in people's rooms did not encourage them to pray that we would hang laundry well. The prayer letter template was still blank, and as the frustration mounted at the unknowns and failed plans continued, something miraculous would happen. It would be time to hang laundry once again.

Quietly the Holy Spirit would prompt, "What if I brought you out here to homeschool, cook, clean, disciple the children, and clean some more?" Tears would run down my cheeks. I would protest: "Of course, Lord, You are enough, but I didn't come to hang laundry!" Sometimes the questions would begin to crowd in, "What are we doing here? How will we learn language? Why did the visas fail? Did I really move all this way for this?" Then, once again, something amazing would happen. It would be time to hang another load of laundry.

At one point the wringer broke on the laundry machine, so I would spend even more time and wring each piece by hand. Over and over again this question would dance in my mind, *Is this enough Abuk...am I enough?*

It took probably twelve loads of laundry before I could squeak out, "Yes, Lord, it is enough; You are enough!" And then in the same breath I'd have to cry, "Help my unbelief; God meet me here."

In many ways that little laundry room became holy ground to me. Those cement walls and the broken washing machine, too few clips and the drips that danced on my head as I worked. That laundry room became a place that allowed me to challenge the deep fear I had—that my life would be summed up not in changing the world or wild successes, but in hanging laundry and knowing God is enough. I needed laundry to hear God gently whisper to me that His worth in me was found not in what was written in the prayer letter, not in sharing the Gospel with the least reached, not even in changing the world. He brought me to that laundry room in Nairobi to whisper to me that He is enough, that if my whole overseas story was about knowing Him more, it would be enough.

As I type this, we are celebrating ten years of ministry in East Africa, and one thing is abundantly clear: what we came to do, accomplish, and succeed in had little to do with why God brought us overseas. You see, I am convinced that God brought me halfway around the world to whisper in a laundry room that He was enough. To teach me, not just others, more of who He is. And that is enough because He is enough.

I still love hanging laundry. Sometimes I hang it in my backyard, sometimes on the back porch. Sometimes I even hang it during home assignments when dryers are available because I need to remember that wherever I am and whatever I am doing it is enough because He is enough.

—*Abuk*

Chapter 20

ON BEING A DIFFERENCE MAKER

"I still don't get it," I said to my husband as we sat in the living room, decompressing from the day. The familiar sounds of the jungle settled around us for the night. Although late, my mind was full. My body felt heavy from the news of the day: More children displaced, more needs unmet, more suffering without an end in sight. "God is for us, right? He is true to His Word. He stakes claim to the orphan and widow. He defends the weak and powerless. So why is it so difficult and seemingly hopeless? Why so much evil and resistance?"

The rhetorical questions spilling out of me were an overflow of desperate cries for justice in the midst of injustice swirling around us, threatening to drown us.

As a kid, I dreamed of being a difference maker. I wanted to go to far away places and heal wounds and preach truth and love hard.

Collateral Damage

The desire grew as I read stories of our missionary forefathers. I craved their resolve to face trials with unshakable faith and confront the enemy with boldness. The task looked easier back when I could close the pages and roll over in my warm bed, clinging to the triumphant ending, casually dismissing the trials that led up to it.

I was one daydream away from skipping through fields of daisies, Bible in hand, with a slew of new converts hot on my heels. Missionary work was easier before we lived it. Before we had hurt so deeply. Before childlike dreams were crushed and replaced with the harsh realities of a broken world in need of True Love, not showcase Christianity.

I somehow overlooked the hardship in those heroic stories I read over and over as a child. It's easy to think of Noah standing in the sunshine with a dove and a rainbow and a big grin on his bearded face (like on all those coloring sheets in Sunday School) and forget that he also listened as all of humanity drowned outside the walls of a boat he had built with his own hands. Those were dark days leading up to the rainbow.

We would call him a difference maker, but I doubt he felt like much of one at the time.

Sitting together that night, we not only grappled with the needs mounting around us, but we also mourned the loss of support from the people who had commissioned us to this land far from home. Our sending church had known us most of our lives. They said they were with us and for us, yet in what felt like an instant, their backs turned, and we were alone. We felt abandoned.

Our church disagreed with a ministry choice we made. Policy (not Scripture) took precedence over orphans, the marginalized, and the good taking place in the name of Jesus because of a cultural disagreement.

In the following weeks, I received emails from people within that church body making clear their disappointment with our decision, even questioning our hearts. People who barely knew us and couldn't tell you a single name of a person with whom we labored or a child we were fighting for said things about us that had no basis of fact. To them we were another lost cause because of a difference of opinion.

It was another blow on the heels of many trials. We felt kicked while we were already down.

The strangest part, perhaps, is I actually didn't blame them.

It took that dissolution for me to understand that similar to my church family, in some ways I was unwittingly a fair-weather fan of missions during those early days with my well-intended but whitewashed ideas of what ministry was "supposed" to be. Perhaps my church and I were after the romance of it all: the adventure and incredible stories we could share from our life in the Amazon jungle, but not the real, blood, sweat, and tears day-to-day battle. I learned through years on the field that mission work looks a lot more cut and dry before reality is sprinkled on top. Our church didn't understand. When it was hard, they remained silent. When it was devastating, they were absent. But when it broke their rules and made them uncomfortable, they were quick to turn away for the sake of policy. They were fair-weather fans. Quite honestly, had God not divinely orchestrated our circumstances the way He had, I may very well have walked away too in those early days.

But it's too late to walk away now. I know too much. Those fairy-tale days are long gone.

We've sheltered friends and neighbors being taken advantage of because they were poor or uneducated. We have cared for children exposed to sexually explicit environments and abuse from birth. My heart has broken each time the victim became the victimizer.

I see poverty and recognize that it has very little to do with a financial state and so much to do with a vicious cycle that runs generations deep. I have seen the men passed out on the roads every morning and the women with their bodies exposed staggering down the street. The depravity of man. People hopeless without Christ.

I have looked into the empty eyes of an orphan, and it changed me.

I have watched an institution called "church" use the holy name of Jesus Christ for its own gain. I have seen them falsely accuse faithful, humble servants of God. I have seen them condemn and vomit hate on the very ones we are called to love. I have observed "pastors" build their kingdoms, preach a false gospel of comfort and prosperity, and lead so many down the same path of deception.

I have seen injustice. But more than that, I have felt it deeply.

It is devastating when we finally step outside of ourselves, our preconceived ideas, and our comforts to bend down low, truly seeing the brokenness not only in this world, but also in ourselves.

When we are removed from the suffering of the world, it is easy for policy to trump people. Not so when we kneel down in the midst of that suffering.

And oh the beauty that is to be found in that place!

I have witnessed miraculous redemption. I have seen children rescued from hopelessness and bellies filled. I have seen souls redeemed, love abound, Truth proclaimed, and bonds broken. I have seen transformation and confession, unity and freedom.

I have also watched a Body called Church come together as one in a place of deep darkness, despite differences of language, culture, ethnicity, and rejoice in a Savior who knows and cares and sees us. I have seen emotional wounds healed and bodies mended. I have wept with those who weep and rejoiced with those who rejoice.

I have seen True Love, and it is a radical, transforming power.

"I don't know why it's this way, really," my husband responded thoughtfully, snapping me back to the present. "But I know that I would much rather walk these deep valleys now and suffer with our brothers and sisters. Because from my experience, the deeper the valley, the greater the joy and the deeper the relationship with our Father. And that? That's worth every hardship."

Collateral Damage

I ponder his words, running my fingers along the design in the rug, listening to the crickets sing their evening tune. Then it occurs to me: This is what it looks like to be a difference maker.

This is, in fact, what I have actually dreamed of my whole life and just didn't know it. Hard. Overwhelming. Incomprehensible. Debilitating. Lonely. It's *supposed* to leave me face down in my closet weeping because I can't breathe under the weight of it all; begging God to draw near, to defend His name, to bring justice and mercy.

Being a difference maker looks a lot like confessing I can't handle it on my own.

It was never intended to be easy, with comfortable buildings and fancy programs and convenient, mediocre commitments to check off a man-made list. It's not ABC or 123. It's not rules and restrictions. Being a difference maker does not equate with being passively passionate about the newest bandwagon brigade on social media. It is not building our kingdom here, fattening our hearts for the day of slaughter, as James describes it.

It actually looks more like dying. It looks like enduring. It looks like sacrifice and surrender, defending the poor and powerless. Being a difference maker means welcoming the lost into our homes and lives. It is opening our doors and hearts, even when it inconveniences us.

It looks like the opposite of everything that makes sense to the world and even to ourselves.

Personally I have never seen any of these transformations take place in the midst of comfort and ease. I can't seem to find an example in Scripture either. It's always in the brokenness and the longing where the real change begins because it is in that space we are driven to our knees and emptied of ourselves.

To be cut off by those we consider brothers and sisters was a painful experience, yet there is a big part of me that is grateful for the lessons that it taught, namely that I must constantly lean directly on Jesus. Yes, we can enjoy the adventure in the mysteries of far away places, but it does not neutralize the sacrifice and pain involved in serving in a lost world. We must not allow adventure (or the lack thereof), discouragement, cultural differences, or man-made rules to distract us from caring for those to whom we are called.

I've met some real-life difference makers. I call many of them my closest friends. They don't look much like we might expect. Many are uneducated and unrefined by the world's standards. They are simple and weak, poor and broken. They aren't eloquent, and they don't own much. They make mistakes and get scared. But they've given everything for the sake of the Gospel because they believe so deeply in its power.

And more often than not, they are a little lonely on the journey. Outcast and shunned by the ones they love.

Being a difference maker is not quite as pretty as I imagined in the early days. And for the life of me I can't seem to fit it inside of a neat little box.

Collateral Damage

And yet I still long to be a difference maker myself because difference makers are some of the most beautiful people I've ever met.

And that's because they look a lot like Jesus.

—*Ashley Whittemore*

Chapter 21

THE COURAGE TO HOLD ON

There is a bedroom window in China that looks out from a fifth-floor apartment down to a tiled courtyard below, where bundled-up grandmas gossip and peel chestnuts in the winter. In the spring, old men bring out their songbirds in wooden cages to put on display and smoke pipes. Children jump in rain puddles and chase stray dogs. The window in China that looked down on the courtyard was *my* bedroom window; it is a good thing it had bars.

When my son was ten months old, we moved from Seattle to a bustling university town in southern China. Though struggling with what I called "mild depression," I convinced my husband that the move would be good for me. I told myself I could handle anything—a new language, a new culture, a new adventure. We would study Chinese and then, according to plan, move to the countryside where we would do mother-tongue education and community development work. I convinced myself the move would make me better—that it would take the postpartum depression away and stamp out the bad memories surrounding the traumatic birth of my son ten months earlier in America.

But living in a Chinese city was not like living in a Kenyan village where I had spent my first, three-year term overseas. I missed open spaces; I missed baobab trees and the sunburnt dirt path that led from my home to my neighbor's compound. I missed the soft, rolling Bantu language, and the warm cups of masala chai. Here I was in a city that writhed in smog and smoke under a gray sky. Alleys, courtyards, and markets teemed with people, and yet I felt so isolated. Everywhere I went with my son people stared, commented, and crowded around us. The damp air chilled my desire to get up and move. My confidence, energy, and patience waned. I lost interest in eating, and I laid down on my bed every chance I could get, but I never really slept. Sleep only brought terror. In my dreams, I saw the doctor crouch down in between my legs. I saw my friends in Africa eating without me. I saw myself floating away on gray clouds, and I would wake up with my heart racing.

Looking out my fifth-floor window, I felt trapped. The bars on the bedroom window were there for my protection, yet made me feel like a prisoner in a place where I didn't belong. My plan wasn't working—the move didn't make me better; it made me worse. The postpartum depression was not lifting, and I had no resources or people who could help me through it (or so I thought). It was only a matter of weeks after our move that I began to spend a lot of time staring out our fifth-story bedroom window. I wasn't looking at anything in particular, just "out." While my husband was at his language class and our little boy was taking his afternoon nap, I would wander over to that barred window and stand for two minutes, ten minutes, sometimes longer. Thoughts raced through my head that scared me: *Would you really? If only those bars weren't there.* I would snap myself "out of it," but then find myself staring out the window once more, dizzy, looking down, then quickly turning away.

The days wore on. I resented the noise, the weather, my slow language progress, and the fact that I didn't serve any purpose... at least not yet. My identity as a nurse, an educator, and a trained linguist got lost in the adjustment to motherhood and a new culture. Before the baby I believed I had things to offer, but now I wasn't so sure. My resentment toward everything and everyone turned into anger. The anger made me feel ashamed, which made me question my spiritual maturity, which made me feel like a failure, which made me feel like maybe I wasn't of much value to anyone for that matter... so why go on living?

One day a neighbor in our building passed away, and his funeral tent was set up in the courtyard—his coffin lay inside the tent, directly five floors below our bedroom window. For days, people huddled around the red tent, playing music, talking, and eating. Firecrackers went off like erratic gunshots at all hours of the day and night. I paced and fretted during that week of mourning. I would wake up at night and walk over to the window, slide it open and listen to the recording of the monks chanting; their foreboding drones reverberated throughout the courtyard. I gripped the dusty, gray bars with my hands and squeezed. I still wanted my husband and little one. Did they want me? Certainly not like this. I leaned my head against the bars and cried. Looking down through the tent, I told the dead man: *I wish I was like you.*

It might sound dramatic but I can only tell you it is true. Misery is like being buried alive—suffocating and terrifying. I lied every day—to myself, to my husband, and to my colleagues. I was afraid to tell the truth because I was sure I would be judged and misunderstood. Maybe I would be sent home, deemed a total failure.

If I could go back, I would tell the woman at the window that she would get better sooner than she could imagine, that the lies and pain would no longer find a home in her heart. I would pull her fingers away from the bars and gently turn her towards my chest and kiss her cheeks. I would rock her wasted body and let her cry freely. I would tell the woman at the window that she would soon find her footing. And I would tell her about the warm glow of the future, about a little girl who would grow inside her the next year and miraculously cancel out the trauma of her older brother's birth. I would say her name, her God-names: Autumn the Counselor, Nurse, Goat-herder, Mother. I would tell her: *Trust me, you are courageous and can do all things through Christ who strengthens you.*

It was not long after the funeral that my language tutor came to our apartment with an excited look on her face. Smiling, she eagerly handed me a piece of paper with three Chinese characters and their romanized spelling. The English interpretation was spelled out below: *Dream Elegance Autumn.* "Your name," she told me. "This is the Chinese name I have chosen for you, *Meng Wan Qiu*; it is from classic poetry. This name means you are like a soft, dreamy breeze on an autumn day. It means you are the colors of autumn, like dancing leaves in a dream." I stared at her, stunned. I had a new name. I hadn't even asked for one! It sounded way more elegant and poetic than my scrappy self deserved, but I thanked her and sat down at the table to practice writing and saying it while my son slept in his crib. I wrote 梦婉秋 over and over again: *Dream Elegance Autumn.*

When I heard my name it was like God-talk spilling over me, like sunlight saturating a frosty meadow. It was God saying, "I've been here all the time. At the window, in the street, by your side." How strange that I could hear God now in my new name. All along in my depression, I had read Scripture, played worship music, and prayed. Nothing seemed to penetrate my despair. I was lost in an ashen world, a no-name in a foreign land. And then someone said, "You are Dream Elegant Autumn," and I was me again, but different. I suddenly felt courageous. I finally felt seen.

Something shifted—a few months after watching the funeral and receiving my Chinese name, the loneliness and sadness began to subside. The weather changed, and sunlight poured through my bedroom window. I had a handle on the language and began to make local friends. I felt enough courage to share "some" of my struggles with my husband and a few friends whom I trusted— they listened to me and affirmed me. I gathered with new friends at the university fountain to chat while our toddlers played under cherry blossom trees. I began to find opportunities to use my nursing skills in the city and in nearby villages. I still struggled at times, but slowly, slowly, the gray shadows retreated, and my window visits ceased.

In January 2007, my daughter was born in a low-lit hospital room in Chiang Mai, Thailand. The Thai nurses hummed softly and spoke in whispers as I leaned against my husband for support. A doula rubbed my lower back and prayed quietly, sometimes humming along with the nurses who prepared the bed. My doctor stood against the wall and waited patiently until she knew I was ready. She touched my knee and said, "Now is the time. Push, *kah*." I nodded and knew this experience would be different than my first; I had complete peace and confidence from the Lord.

I can't explain it, but somehow, my daughter's birth redeemed the last of the trauma and remnants of depression I had experienced between leaving Africa and moving to East Asia. It was simply a miracle. In the weeks following my daughter's birth, I couldn't believe I didn't feel depressed. In my mind I kept looking over my shoulder, expecting a dark, lurking foe to *tap, tap, tap*, and sneer, *"Here I am."* Instead, I returned to our city in China with a sense of renewed hope and determination grounded in Christ, not in what I thought others expected of me.

There are always the "should haves." I don't want anyone to think postpartum depression is resolved through a new name or a change in the weather. I *should have* gotten help. I *should have* been honest. I *should have* been on medication. I *should have* told my husband I wasn't fine. I *should have* had some therapy to deal with my son's birth and our departure from Kenya where I kept my first pregnancy a secret out of respect for the culture. There are a hundred *should haves.*

It wasn't until years after the birth of my son, during a counseling session, that I finally opened up about the severity of postpartum depression—the panic attacks and suicidal ideations. When I told my husband about the secret "window visits," he broke down in tears. He was devastated, not because I'd done anything wrong, but because he never got the chance to "be let in," to walk my depression with me. But I was so ashamed. Deep down inside I was worried that I would be judged by people in my church, by my family and friends, and by God. But I was reading the Psalms all wrong; God wasn't mad at me for being in the pit. God was in the pit with me. I *should have* seen this, but I didn't at the time. That's where grace abounds.

For all my mistakes, especially as a nurse who *should* have known better, I've found grace for myself. Grace in the form of being open—sharing my story, counseling new mothers in the clinic where I work, and speaking up about mental health care. There is a freedom that comes with being honest about these things, and I often find it helps someone else who is struggling. I wish I would have handled my postpartum depression differently, and I'm sorry for that. I lost my way and didn't know how to get to where I wanted to be. I just knew to step back and not to do the one thing that would hurt the ones I loved. I thank God for the bars on my window and the courage to live.

—Autumn

Chapter 22

LORD, HELP MY UNBELIEF

My family moved to Germany for the second time when my four kids were between the ages of six months and five years old. We didn't move with an organization and didn't work in the church full time, but my husband and I always considered ourselves missionaries, working in the church in different parts of the world since we were married. With this move, I was full-on ready for sharing Jesus and creating a home and environment where people could feel loved and experience the hands and feet of Christ.

Sight unseen, we moved into a house in a village about forty-five minutes away from the church we wanted to be part of. What is *forty-five minutes?* I thought. I could still build a community around me like we had in our previous country; we had a house with two extra rooms for guests, so I was set and ready. I sent emails asking friends and family to commit one day a week to praying for our little village of 1,800 people. I sent updates weekly, and we had people stay at our house three or four weekends a month. Most of the guests were old friends or family, but sometimes we had people we had never met before who just needed a place to stay. It was my ideal set-up for mission work.

The first six months I just ran myself ragged. In my mind I had to have things perfectly clean, so I would stay up until midnight cleaning. My husband's commute to Hamburg was over an hour one way so he often just stayed in the city to do his work or training in the church. He was away at least three nights a week, so sometimes the kids didn't see him for days on end. The weekends were filled with guests, whom we thoroughly enjoyed, but which didn't leave any margins for family time. Mondays I did laundry and cleaning; Thursdays I prepared for the next load of visitors. Not only that, my German wasn't very good as it had been five years since my language classes. I took my eldest child into kindergarten and struggled through cultural understanding. I often used the wrong form of "you," sometimes did not understand what was going on around me, and frequently could not find that one item at the grocery store.

I kind of prayed and read my Bible regularly, and my kids seemed to be thriving. But I had no friends close by, no community, and this German village would not accept me. Instead of coming over for the women's brunches I had planned, they didn't even respond to my invitations; not to mention, they would often yell at me over the fence that my children were too loud! Going to church became a big production of me sitting in the church basement with the kids and watching them there instead of at home. Sometimes my husband could watch them, which left me to listen to a sermon I couldn't fully understand.

These circumstances were not the only factors leading to my downward spiral, but they set the scene for what was coming. I am positive a spiritual battle raged behind my struggles.

My husband and I started noticing something might be off with me, but we didn't know what. I was unable to read or pray and relied solely on worship music for some kind of "spirituality." I was exhausted. Thoughts one cannot say out loud started rolling in...depression set in. Not just depression—I wasn't sure there was a God at all or if my life made sense or had any meaning anymore. What got me through each day were the guests I knew were coming and my five beautiful family members. The kids remembered to read the Bible since that was a daily habit, and I made sure their teeth were brushed. Those were my main daily goals. My sweet husband always took care of me, but being in the midst of it, he wasn't sure what was going on either.

I couldn't bring myself to say out loud that maybe there wasn't a god. Maybe this universe was created and whoever made it stepped back to let us be. I knew something must have set the universe in motion, but I didn't think I had a specific place or reason to be here. I just needed to keep going for the kids. *Can this be it? All those people who died for the faith for nothing? Didn't C. S. Lewis say that even if in the end it all turned out to be fake, it was worth it anyway? I will have lived morally and nobly as a Christian, even if*

Collateral Damage

Jesus didn't really die on the cross for my sins. Is that enough?

Those were the days before all the cool apps to keep in touch with people, and I used to *talk on the phone* to my family. My sister was the one to notice what was going on. She asked the right questions—poignant questions you never want to have to ask your little sister. My sister is my safe place, so I answered honestly. She gently suggested I pursue counseling. Having taken counseling courses, I readily said "Yes." I had long been a proponent that everyone should receive counseling, whether in a crisis or not.

I will never forget that first counseling session. I sat on my bed and burst into tears as soon as I saw the counselor's face on my screen. She asked how I was, and I couldn't get through one sentence. The first thing she told me to do was to go to bed earlier and leave the dishes in the sink. That seemed strange and oversimplified—how could that help me if I don't believe in the Creator God anymore? But as I typically do, I readily complied, and by our next session a few days later, I had slowly, slowly started feeling better.

It took lots of counseling and a couple of years for the fog to lift, although it's a fog I fight regularly now. I read the Bible even when I didn't believe it. I prayed even when in the back of my mind I had this nagging thought or feeling I was praying to nothing. I went to church. I read books about doubt and books by people who thought Christianity was bonkers. I read articles by women who have left the faith, then I read things by people who seriously doubted and yet kept the faith. Do you know the unbelievable amount of doubt major preachers and women of God have fought with? I started to realize that fighting with my faith and belief means that my faith actually exists—it is a living and active faith, not an absence of faith. I am not some robot who just believed and am on an upward projection toward heaven. My faith is moving and fluid and alive. Even small faith is faith.

Just glimpse in the Psalms to read of men who were confused and depressed and crushed; they couldn't connect their circumstances with a sovereign and good God. Reading the Psalms gave me permission to ask God the questions I had and to know it is okay—He's big enough to handle us.

It's hard to pinpoint exactly what brought me from a heart on fire to a heart of doubt. It's equally hard to pinpoint exactly when the fog dissipated.

The life of a woman in missions is often a transient one. A couple years after first realizing I was in the deep darkness of depression coupled with my crisis of faith, we moved again. This time we moved within walking distance of our new church plant and closer to friends, but we were also met with all sorts of new challenges. Now we had a house that we were renovating ourselves, and my husband was doing ministry and working full-time outside of church all at the same time. But I still met with my counselor, and we were prepared for the potential dangers that lay ahead.

Being in missions comes with a specific spiritual battle, and there is nothing the enemy would like more than to make us feel ashamed or less-than for doubting our faith. God put plenty of examples of doubters in the Bible so that we would know we aren't alone. He also answered those doubters and loved them. Just as He will answer you and still loves you.

Now my family's circumstances are better, and we are in full-time ministry. We have more time as a family and as a couple, yet I still fight and struggle with my faith. I still sometimes wonder. In these moments I cry out, *Lord, help my unbelief.* And you know? He does. Instead of seeing faith and salvation as only a one-way street of sanctification, I now see it as a big, rocky hike of challenges and victories. Questioning your belief doesn't mean you are not saved. In fact, through my questioning I have a greater understanding and a greater conviction that Jesus is our Savior. I have a deeper need to understand why I believe what I believe, and I am not shocked when other women who have long trusted Jesus start questioning. I am completely sure that they will be okay. Just as Paul reminded us that He who began a good work in you, will carry it onto completion until the day of Christ (Philippians 1:6). Going through this fire of faith has given me a greater confidence in God's power, love, and sovereignty. He will carry us through until the end. There will be highs and lows and questions, but that doesn't change our standing before Him for the One who calls us is faithful (I Thessalonians 5:24).

—*Caitlin Lieder*

Chapter 23

WHY SNACKRIFICE?

Grocery stores overseas seem to be the backdrop of so many vividly memorable moments! The first grocery shopping trip that I remember was when my roommate and I had been on the field for about three months. We were in the height of culture shock and transitional chaos. We were shopping at the nearest big chain grocery store, which carried a variety of imported foods. Usually we steered clear of the imports in our efforts to stick to our grocery budget. That day, however, as we walked through the aisles, a box of crackers caught our eyes. It was a box of Wheat Thins, something both of us loved. We stood there for a few minutes, agonizing over the cost of the Wheat Thins and whether it was good stewardship of our finances to splurge on a box of overpriced, imported crackers. Then we picked up a box off the shelf and turned it over. The back of the box said, "Why snackrifice?" We laughed at ourselves and bought the Wheat Thins.

Collateral Damage

Another day, in the same store, our problem was a bag of bagels and a tub of cream cheese. Different food, same dilemma—was it okay to treat ourselves? Both of us had raised our financial support to be on the field, and we felt the weight of stewardship and accountability to our donors. We bought the bagels and cream cheese that day, but we often resisted what we saw as temptation to splurge on small treats. After all, we were missionaries, and everyone knows that missionaries sacrifice comfort and ease of life in order to serve Jesus.

Fast forward a few years, and my new husband and I were working through the same dilemma. This time, though, it reached beyond the grocery store walls. My husband's ministry role took us to beautiful beaches around the world, and we occasionally added on a few nights of vacation to the end of a work trip or splurged on a nice date night dinner while we were traveling. We struggled not only with what purchases were acceptable uses of our funds but also what was okay to share with supporters. We felt the need to justify our spending, making sure people knew that the ministry paid for our flights or that we used frequent flyer miles to book the nice hotel or that we had been saving for a few years to take a vacation in the country of and around the dates of a ministry conference. We don't usually share pictures from our "splurge" moments, even if they aren't actually splurges because it takes too much explaining. Those aren't the stories and pictures that end up in newsletters or blog posts. Stewardship is hard enough when you're "earning" your paycheck, and even more complicated when your paycheck comes from other people's tithes and gifts.

Recently, we had to call all our supporters to let them know about my husband's change in organizations. He is leaving the ministry we have been working with, for which we fundraise all our support, and taking a position of leadership for a new university here on the field. His new role is a salaried position, not support-based. I will remain with our current ministry. We expected some of our donors to let us know that they would be ending their financial commitments to us since we were moving from working full-time as a couple to just me working part-time for the ministry. Every donor we talked to, though, echoed the same sentiments: "We believe in what you are doing. We trust that you are doing what God has called you to do, and we trust that you are stewarding our gifts well. We would love to continue supporting you financially."

Over the years, and again in those recent donor calls, I have learned that our donors give because they have confidence that we will steward their resources well. That understanding makes me feel the weight of using their gifts in the most God-honoring way, but it also frees me to discern what that God-honoring way is. I have also come to accept that it's okay to be a human who needs culture breaks, occasional imported treats, and regular rest and vacations. And as I have grown in my understanding of accountability and stewardship, I have grown in my confidence in making decisions. Often what brings a healthy perspective back into the situation for me is thinking about the people I'm trying to be accountable to—my donors. If I had called them back when I was standing in the grocery store agonizing over a bag of bagels, I am 100% sure they all would have told me to buy the bagels!

A pivotal moment in my growth in this area of balancing stewardship, sacrifice, comfort, and accountability came six years into my time on the field, when I was introduced to the idea of imagined expectations. I realized that I felt many imagined expectations from my supporters and from myself. I had assumed my supporters wanted me to live as frugally as possible so that more of their funds could be used directly for ministry programs. I had assumed they wanted assurance that I was suffering for the Gospel.

Some of the most hurtful words said to me were spoken several months after I arrived on the field. A woman who had lived overseas for a time and then moved back to the U.S. visited my home and commented, "You have screens on your windows and an inverter (backup power)—you're not *real* missionaries." Even though she was joking, the judgment of her words stung for a long time. Were those things frivolous, unnecessary purchases, or were they wise purchases that would allow me to serve better?

I discovered that I subconsciously expected to have a hard life overseas because I had bought into the narrative that someone living comfortably couldn't possibly be a good missionary. I imagined my supporters wanting us to spend all our money on ministry programs and meeting material needs of the people we serve, pouring ourselves out until we were empty.

To my surprise, I realized that not a single person had ever voiced any of those expectations. On the contrary, I had supporters who would send extra money so that my husband and I could go on a date. I had supporters encouraging us to live in a way that felt comfortable and sustainable. I had a sending organization that helped us create a budget that provided for our living expenses, while also accounting for ministry funds and discretionary money for us to give to others.

Once I realized most of the expectations I felt around stewardship and sacrifice were imagined, I had to change my mindset. I had to start asking God how He would have us live and how He would have us spend our money. I had to stop comparing our house, grocery budget, vacation style, and activity choices to those of other overseas workers I knew. I had to go back to the basic principle of finding my identity and value in my relationship with God rather than how much I was sacrificing for the sake of my calling.

God has been teaching me that just because He asks me to do something, doesn't mean it will be hard. And just because something is hard, doesn't mean it's what God wants me to do. Way back at the beginning, "snackrificing" would have been the hard choice, but as silly as it seems, I think God wanted us to buy the Wheat Thins! On a more serious note, sometimes God wants us to take a vacation. Sometimes He wants us to get more house help or a back-up generator or a more reliable car.

Collateral Damage

On the flip side, there are many moments in this overseas life when God does ask us to sacrifice. We sacrifice physical presence with our families, especially at major milestones. We sacrifice self-sufficiency as we learn a new language and a new culture. We sacrifice many of the comforts of life in our passport countries. And sometimes we sacrifice even bigger things—dreams of marriage, professional ambitions, friendships that fade with the miles and years.

There are also many moments when God calls us to make smaller sacrifices as we steward our money and time—giving to friends who were in an accident and need to pay hospital bills, opening our home to share meals with others, setting aside a task I hoped to accomplish so that I can spend time investing in a relationship.

So where does all that leave me? I continue to walk the tightrope of stewarding our resources well, rejecting the idolatry of suffering that so often permeates overseas communities, but also rejecting the idolatry of comfort and ease. I continue to put aside the imagined expectations I thought my supporters had and embrace their true expectations to seek God's will and follow it. And I continue to work to steward money and time in a way that glorifies God by balancing comfort and sacrifice.

—*Emily Miller*

Chapter 24

THE LIES OF SEXUAL HARASSMENT

It was a rare event for me to be home alone, but I was happy to have the house to myself. I shut my doors up tight before putting on my workout clothes, filling up my water bottle at the dispenser and pulling out my weights. It was the middle of the afternoon in hot and sweaty Indonesia, and I was thrilled to exercise in my shorts and tank top to let off some of the daily stress that had built up in my body.

I didn't wear shorts outside the house or inside the house with the doors open. I kept myself covered as much as possible, constantly aware of the skin I was exposing. Now I could roam around the house in my comfy clothes and exercise to my heart's content. I was safe behind those solid wood doors and my windows were covered with black-out curtains. No one would complain. I was safe.

In the middle of my workout my husband called me, interrupting me. He informed me that our handyman would be stopping by the house soon. He needed to pick up our neighbor's house keys as there was an urgent issue with the neighbor's electricity. No one wants a defrosted refrigerator while on a visa trip. I had known this man for three years; he was the neighborhood handyman. He was in and out of our house weekly, cleaning our water tank, fixing roof tiles, or scraping maggots from my ceiling. He was from the countryside and taught us Indonesian culture, being in our home since day one in this new country of ours.

I paused my workout, annoyed at the interruption, cracked open the door and passed him the key. I shut the door again and continued on with my workout, finishing it in a good, stress relieving sweat. He knocked again, and I opened the door wide. Customarily I would offer him water and bring it to him on our porch. There were two chairs outside under our overhang where he could refresh and rehydrate.

As he followed me inside the house, without invitation, my body sounded an alarm. He knew that I was home alone and that it was not appropriate to enter my home while my husband was gone. Many men in the community wouldn't risk breaching our outer gate if they knew my husband wasn't home. I got him a glass of water and he sat at the table in our entryway, making himself at home. He started talking innocently about exercise and running, and I stood across the room, as far from him as possible. He shifted conversation quickly and began talking about how the neighbors would assume that he and I were engaged in sexual activity because we were alone in my home. He explained how I shouldn't have let him inside the house because now the whole neighborhood would be talking about it. He moved closer to me, invading my physical space, and his comments grew even more personal and explicit. He made comments about my body, how beautiful it was and how it blew his mind. He smirked, he laughed, he enjoyed my discomfort, using hand gestures to emphasize his meaning.

When will he leave? Instincts took over, my face flushed, it was hard to breathe, and I was trembling. I kept a smile on my face and my stance as calm and relaxed as I could. I pretended I couldn't understand. I was scared to escalate the situation or encourage the situation to continue. I wanted it to end. I wanted him out of my home. I let him say his piece. I let him look at me and harass me, and I didn't push back. I didn't want increased violence to follow. I couldn't provoke him to anger.

I sighed in relief when he left, expelling the breath I was holding in. I shut and locked my doors. I wept. My body shaking and burning, I curled in on myself. I cried behind the wooden doors that I thought protected me, feeling exposed and vulnerable within the walls of my fortress. "I am not safe," I thought.

I immediately started to question whether the event occurred in the way that I remembered. Maybe it wasn't that bad? Maybe I'm just sensitive? Maybe I deserved it because I should have known better? I definitely shouldn't have been wearing shorts, that was an invitation to think of me in a sexual way. This was obviously my fault. I was responsible. I was to blame. Self-blame has served me well over the years. In some ways it helps me mitigate the powerlessness I feel to defend myself, and in other ways it makes me smaller, diminishing my capacity to make an impact on the world around me. I become invisible.

God's grace extends intentionally into these deep spaces of our humiliation, especially seeping into the realms of shame that we keep hidden, even from ourselves. Sometimes, within His grace, the Spirit moves in a still, small voice that whispers truth to my soul, bringing comfort, but there are other times the Spirit lights a fire in my belly. A hot, burning fire that heats and infuses steel to my spine. It is a holy anger. It took time to realize that God was speaking to me through anger. It didn't seem a gracious, Christian act to feel disgusted at the sight of this man and yet I did. I was in a country to spread the Good News, and I felt revulsion, fear, and hatred toward the men of my host country. I tried to push the feelings deep, I tried forgiving, I tried letting it go, but God kept letting anger bob back up to the surface.

What this man had done to me was wrong; it was evil and cruel. There is no excuse for it; it was an act of willful dominance intended to shame and disparage me. The shame and fear can become overwhelming at times, and it has irreparably changed the way I interact with myself and my environment.

Experiencing God's anger was a grace because in all of my experiences no one expressed anger on my behalf. I'd become accustomed to flippantly informing those around me that I had been flashed or that a man had run his hands around my body. No one was shocked by my stories or mortified. It fueled my feelings of shame and objectification, all the while leaving me confused. My body told me that I was harmed, but the reactions of people around me informed me that I was not. I could not discern what the truth was. This is why God's anger is so good; it lets me know what is true. God told me that my body was beautiful and good. Every curve, every movement, every color was created by the most accomplished artist there is. In fact, it could even be considered the temple of God that houses the very beauty and glory of the One who created it. It is holy and, therefore, worthy of respect and ought to be held in the highest regard.

He told me that these men had lied to me when they declared me an object with their lips and their hands. The power in the action is held in what it projects. The act itself does not have to leave physical scars; the judgment that is communicated can last a lifetime if it is not counteracted with the truth. These lies are covert lies. They imply that what is communicated through our experiences is truth. But God says, "No." God hates acts of sexual harassment and assault. He loathes it, and He detests it because He knows the truth of who we are. We are God's workmanship, His prized possession, His Bride, and He does not condone any action that diminishes those truths.

God hates liars and deceivers who convey to His daughters that they are less than valuable. "There are six things the Lord hates, seven that are detestable to him: haughty eyes, a lying tongue, hands that shed innocent blood, a heart that devises wicked schemes, feet that are quick to rush into evil, a false witness who pours out lies and a person who stirs up conflict in the community" (Proverbs 6:16-19, NIV).

The world is not always a safe place, and there is no utopia. We know this. We are women of the world, and we accept that there is no way to protect ourselves from every form of harm or victimization that humanity has to offer. However, we can band together and be the harbingers of truth for our sisters. We can help reduce the shame and be the voice of God, restoring their humanity and breathing light back into their souls.

God does not diminish our experiences, and neither should we. Downplaying our trauma may help us cope in the short term, but it is detrimental to our health and life, and it forces us to stay steeped in the lie we won't acknowledge. Only the truth sets us free. Sexual assault tells us that we are objects. God tells us that we are precious. We are told that we are dirty. God tells us that we are pure. We are told that we are powerless. God says we are powerful, and He is all-powerful. We are told we are victims. God says we are armored, and we will not be destroyed. We are told we are worthless. God says we are priceless. We are told we are broken. God says we are perfect.

No one has the right to lie to God's sacred women. We are holy. We are God's, and He will do battle for us. So let's also fight for each other. Let's do battle against the lies that sexual harassment and sexual assault perpetuate and speak God's unchangeable truth.

—*Joy Smalley*

Chapter 25

WHEN RELATIONSHIPS BREAK

For months, my teammate and I felt burnout chasing us. After finally hitting our stride in ministry and setting up long-awaited training sessions, we were tired and struggling with parts of our work that didn't feel quite right. We knew something needed to change.

We received visitors from our leadership team, and they sat with us for hours. They asked questions and listened to our stories, digging deeper to help us process the past few months and bringing up ideas we hadn't even considered. We were also informed that new organizational policies were coming impacting the work we had been doing, but also giving us direction we needed. Firmly, but gently, those leaders pointed out some things we needed to let go.

It felt right. It felt like time, and in many ways it was a relief. It meant hard conversations with our local partners, but we also knew this could result in more freedom for both of us and create space for

Collateral Damage

God to work in a new way.

Our team leader had retired the year before and returned to her passport country, but she was still very much a part of the local ministry. She had invested decades into the work in this rural area when no one else was brave enough to live there. She traveled for miles in taxis crammed with people, crossed borders, and endured the heat and mud. Her friends in the village still messaged her and sent her pictures, knowing how deeply she cared.

We sent a quick email letting her know this new direction and then made a trip to the village. We sat with our local friends, and they were so gracious as they heard the changes coming and brainstormed with us about ways to move forward. The meeting went so much better than we were expecting.

So when we opened up an email from our former team leader, my teammate and I both looked at each other in shock. Instead of understanding, there were questions about our decisions and accusations about how we were handling the situation.

I wish I could say that a few emails or phone calls cleared things up and we moved on. We weighed our words carefully, begging God for wisdom in our responses. But each new email from her sent us spiraling. The situation was sensitive, and we didn't want to compound the hurt by sharing information broadly, so it felt like we were carrying a heavy burden alone as we kept the details to ourselves.

Then another email arrived from a couple in one of our supporting churches. They wanted to understand the circumstances and felt a video chat would be the best format. Finally we felt like someone truly wanted to understand our hearts, to know how to walk with us in the situation that seemed to be going from bad to worse.

We sat through the questions, the one-sided information this couple had received from our former team leader. They listed Scripture passages to demonstrate our mistakes and admitted they thought we were villains for the decisions we had been making. The words stung.

I had never felt so alone or betrayed by people I cared about, who cared about me. I wrestled through long, sleepless nights and endless conversations with my teammate. We went back over the steps we had taken, the emails we had sent, and the firm love we had tried to incorporate.

We were already in a precarious place from the exhaustion of the previous months. "God, what are You doing?" we asked over and over. He seemed like the only one to turn to when I wasn't sure whom else I could trust.

But there in the broken pieces of relationships and ministry, He met me. I came across a song on YouTube called "Your Love Defends Me" by Matt Maher. The lyrics were like gentle rain straight to my parched soul. I hit replay over and over so I could listen to these words that reminded me no matter what, God was my refuge.

I needed a defender. My betrayed heart needed a lawyer, someone who would buffer me against the accusations and confusion. And I found that in Jesus.

He knew the motivation in our hearts, the reasons we had made the decisions that we did. He knew our heartache over the broken relationships, the burdens we were carrying close. God brought two trustworthy people within our organization that we could share this journey with. They stepped up to defend us too, to seek resolution when my teammate and I couldn't see a way out.

I came to the field with a grand vision and high expectations about what team life would be like. There were sweet moments along the way, but also many times when I failed to be a good teammate. Life overseas brings all of our imperfections and struggles right up to the surface, spilling over on the people who are closest to us. Our insecurities, even the way our identities become entangled in the success and failure of ministry, can impact our teammates and partners.

My teammate and I made mistakes; we are human too. I look back at those months of hurt and betrayal, and I also see the unity between the two of us as we carried the weight of it all between us. There was a deeper friendship forged through the trials. When I was tempted to respond to emails with snarky comments or harsh words, she was firm and reminded me of the boundaries we needed to put in place. When everything felt out of control and hopeless, I would make a run to the import store for chocolate or stop for iced coffees. We held each other up, prayed endlessly on the hard tile floor of our home, and spoke truth when it was needed.

We have walked through the pain of relationships not restored but forgiveness given, surrendering our right to be fully understood. The road hasn't been easy, and it's still hard to look back at what became the end of a season overseas.

Sometimes it feels easier to go it alone. Life would be so much less messy without investing in our teammates and partners, wouldn't it? Despite the pain of these experiences, I also know the value of vulnerability and walking through life with others. God can bring beauty from ashes, lessons in the pain, and, above all, we can trust Him each step of the way.

—*Kara May*

Chapter 26

WHEN DEEP BREATHS AREN'T ENOUGH

I leave my house to take my daughter to school. I take a big gulp of chamomile tea. I hit play on the worship playlist on my phone and set it on the dash. Everyone is buckled. Everyone is safe. I am okay.

The traffic is relentless. Not crowded and stagnant like a parking lot, but more like a fast-paced cross between bumper cars and dodgeball. I wince every time I pass a large truck. Is there room for us both on this narrow road? Will I hit a moto taxi if I try to move over?

Deep breath.

I close my eyes briefly as I pass the intersection where a sideswipe shattered the side mirror into mine and my husband's faces as we drove to dinner at a friend's house. I see where we pulled over, only to be tailed and harassed by someone who witnessed the incident and swore we were at fault. We had to speed on back roads to lose him in traffic. My heart rate climbs as

I remember staring back, looking for headlights, watching him get lost in the crowd. The relief when we got safely into a friend's compound and the gate locked behind us. How I tried to steady my breath as I picked glass up off the seats and dabbed my husband's face with a towel.

Deep breath.

I make it to the main intersection and turn, remembering when I had been T-boned there a few weeks before, my first accident with my children in the car. After getting out and doing my due diligence, I returned to the vehicle to see my five-year-old daughter sobbing because the people around the car wouldn't stop staring at her. I hadn't been able to hear her screams for me over the traffic and commotion of the crowd. Her face is burned in my memory. I promise myself I'll be more aware next time. I won't let her be scared like that again.

Deep breath.

I turn onto the next road, trying to focus on the newly revealed green of the city that comes after a fresh rain. Instead, I am flooded with images of the dead man I passed on this road months before, splayed on his back in the middle of the street after being hit while on his bicycle. I can't drive through this valley without seeing his face, without seeing the crowd that gathered but didn't touch, didn't help. Then again, I didn't stop. Confusion, resentment, and regret stir in my heart.

Deep breath.

Collateral Damage

I drop my daughter off at school and turn around to repeat this liturgy of trauma over again on my way home. I blast the worship music; I take another sip of tea; I take an herbal pill to help me be calm. *I didn't even have caffeine this morning,* I think to myself. *Maybe I need to go for a run. When will I have time for that? And with the people staring, following, kids yelling for money, is it even worth it? Can the endorphins outrun the stress?*

Deep breath.

As I park in front of my gate, I see the large pile of rocks in the construction zone next to my home. I hear the muffled sounds of the woman who was raped behind them in the middle of the night earlier in the summer. I didn't know what the sounds were, maybe an animal or someone getting sick, so I didn't go to help. I went back to sleep. I found out what those sounds were the next morning, my knees going weak as our houseworker explained what had happened. "I heard it happening," I whispered. "I didn't know." I am haunted by my lack of action, lack of awareness. I pull the car into the drive and shut the gate behind me.

Deep breath.

An hour later, my two-year-old son refuses to take his nap, screaming uncontrollably, though he is safe in my arms. The loudness, the closeness of his cries overwhelms my senses, puts me on high alert. I taste the bitter adrenaline, cognitively knowing I am safe though my body says otherwise. His screams transport me to his bout with malaria a year before, riddled with headaches and high fevers and confusion. He was constantly screaming. I was so helpless. I remember thinking to myself: *Am I a good mother? How could I choose to live in a place where this could happen to my child? How could I let this happen to him?* My thoughts run wild again, uncontrolled despite my great efforts. *Is it happening again? Is that why he's screaming now?*

I set him on the carpet as the all-too-familiar crushing warmth of a panic attack begins to set in. I make a frantic call to my husband to come home before I start to hyperventilate. Every time he leaves the house to work, I worry this will happen. More often than not, these days, it does. He may as well stay home. I wish I could handle myself so he could get work done. I'm hurting our family's ministry.

He arrives fifteen minutes later to our son sitting sleepily beside me on the floor, while I lay panting and sobbing in a helpless pile next to him. He tells me to go to sleep; he will watch the baby. My racing mind keeps me from sleeping. I feel so guilty, so out of control, so sad, so helpless.

It was in this difficult season that I shared this story with a mentor from our organization. I ended by saying, "This is my yoke. For our ministry to be successful, my life is going to be very hard. I just have to figure out how to survive it. I have taken this on. I love my family's ministry and have accepted my fate. I won't ever feel better. I'll always struggle. It's my sacrifice."

My mentor looked at me directly and said, "I can't accept that." My husband agreed. "You either need to change what your life looks like here and get help or leave the field. I won't let you live like this. You can't survive, neither can your family, neither can your ministry. It's time to call in the big guns and make some changes or call it quits."

In the coming weeks, we planned a long trip back to the U.S. to rest, reflect, heal, and regroup. After many hours of therapy, including several sessions of EMDR (a type of therapy specifically for processing trauma), agreeing to make gigantic shifts in what our life looked like in Rwanda, and the prayer and support of community across the globe, we returned to our host country. We moved to a different house, which removed a lot of those daily triggers. We raised more money to allow ourselves to make a few carefully calculated quality of life changes. We learned to rest and play and heal, instead of glorifying running on empty for months on end. We decided to continually check in and reevaluate, constantly ask ourselves what needs to be tweaked and changed to keep us healthy. We consider our kids in this as well.

Slowly, we found health. Slowly, I became stable.

Now I not only feel at home in my host country, but I've found my own ministry and community here. I've found the life I knew in my heart Christ was calling me to. I just stood in my own way for a while. I wish I'd gotten the help I needed so much sooner.

While my mental health still becomes shaky in certain seasons and I struggle with panic and depression from time to time, I know that I have tools at my disposal to make this the exception, not the norm. I expect that will always be the case. But in this space, in this season, I have peace.

Living as a support-raising expat (or even self-funded or employed) often comes with a tremendous amount of "You're so amazing" and "God bless you for what you do" and "You must love it over there." We deny ourselves pleasures and comforts for the sake of our work. And often we fail to take care of ourselves well, for fear that a self care or mental health line-item in the budget will reveal weakness or self-centeredness and distract from our ministry.

Living with mental health challenges while overseas is brave. We have to find new coping mechanisms, new therapists, new medications (or bring a suitcaseful), new routines, and regimens to support our health. But we do it because we are called. And we know that the Lord provides all that we need.

I no longer think my yoke is to struggle through the life God called my family to. Will it be hard? Absolutely. Will I need to lean on His grace? Without a doubt. Should I wallow in mental health struggles and call it ministry and a path to holiness? No, friends. This is not what Christ desires of us.

Maybe you struggled with mental health before you went to the field. Maybe your challenges have developed as you've lived overseas. Wherever you find yourself, I pray that you would reach out and find the support and help you need to live well where you are. Christ is our peace, and He will provide what we need to do the work He has called us to do.

—*Karli Von Herbulis*

Chapter 27

NO LACK

One of the first pieces of art I bought for my new apartment in China was a slender painting with Psalm 23:1 drawn in beautifully delicate characters along the side. I couldn't read any Chinese yet, but when the artist at the expat Christmas market told me what they said, I couldn't resist buying it and bringing it home to hang as a promise over my new season overseas.

I moved to China when I was twenty-two, fresh out of college. I came to join a team of missionaries, and my role specifically was to share the Gospel and disciple college students. My initial term was two years, and it seemed like forever as I laid awake at night those first few weeks, wondering how I was ever going to adjust.

The Lord is my Shepherd; I have no lack.

These words often came to mind in the days that followed, a whirlwind of language learning and cultural adaptation that consistently left me feeling like I lacked everything.

Intelligence for language learning? Lacking. Energy for one

more new cultural adjustment? Lacking. Optimism that China would ever feel like home? Some days, also lacking.

Yet little by little, the ripples of initial culture shock gradually grew smaller. Eating with chopsticks, speaking another language, navigating life in a megacity—all the things that seemed so overwhelming and scary became the things I cherished. I came to see that life overseas could be as rich and abundant as life in the States, and I began to love it. Before I knew it, I'd made it through a whole year in China.

The Lord is my Shepherd; I have no lack.

This took on a new meaning for me as I saw the Lord growing and shaping me into someone I knew I could never be on my own. I grew to love my city deeply, as well as my life and ministry there.

So after much prayer and consideration, I decided a few months before the end of my first term to continue serving with my team. I'd never felt more peace about anything. The spiritual needs in our city were overwhelming, and I was so excited for the chance to keep walking alongside the Chinese churches our team partnered with as we loved and served our communities.

I'd never been someone who really had a concrete career path or plan before moving overseas, and that had never bothered me. But I finally felt like I could see my future taking shape, and I couldn't wait to get started.

Then, just two weeks after I committed to long term ministry with my team, all my plans unraveled overnight.

Collateral Damage

My team leader was denied entry into the country when he tried to return from the U.S. A ten-year season of ministry for his family came to an end in an airport immigration office.

Their departure had a ripple effect on our whole team. The clear path forward I thought the Lord had given me became entangled in many unanswered questions. Would our team leader's family be okay? Would the rest of our team be able to stay together? Was I still sure I wanted to return to China? What was I so sure I had been called to?

The Lord is my Shepherd; I have no lack.

Now it felt like the verse was mocking me. Every time I passed it in my apartment, I felt numb. It felt like I'd been shepherded right off a cliff, and now I was free falling with no idea when I'd sense firm ground under my feet again.

During the last few months of my first term, I retreated into myself with no idea how to face the decisions or uncertainty that lay ahead. I had no idea how to trust my own discernment of God's leading again. I had no idea what was next for me.

Slowly it became clear that whatever was next for me, it wasn't life in this city I'd come to love. It wouldn't be possible for our team to carry forward with our ministry; it wouldn't even really be possible for me to return to it once my visa expired. I grieved the loss of this dream deeply, more confused than ever.

The Lord is my Shepherd; I have no lack.

I remember looking at those words as I took the painting down to pack it, struggling to trust that life in Christ had no lack when it felt like I was losing everything. I'd lost the person I was before moving to China, and now I'd lost the future I'd hoped to have in China.

The painting went into a suitcase and then into a box in my parent's basement as I adjusted back to life in America. Slowly but surely, the ripples of shock over our team's sudden transition grew smaller, just as the ripples of culture shock had two years earlier.

I began to unwind from the sadness and stress and emotional exhaustion I hadn't even realized I was feeling. Time with family and friends was incredibly healing. I began to feel the ground under my feet again.

The Lord is my Shepherd; I have no lack.

In this season of healing, God kindly and gently reminded me of how He had shepherded me all the way through the ups and downs and joys and losses of my first two years overseas. He gave me the peace and confidence to trust Him again, to trust His initial leading for my life was still true even if my next season overseas didn't look quite like I expected.

It didn't take away the hurt of my broken dreams or the grief I felt at losing a home I had come to love so deeply. But it did help me understand that deep emotions and even deep pain don't have to exclude deep trust in God.

Loss, change, transition and hurt are just parts of life. There's nothing we can do to avoid them. We can, however, embrace them and give them back to God instead of letting them stay buried in our hearts to become walls of bitterness and fear.

Collateral Damage

As I learned to do this, God helped me look toward the future with hope again. I accepted a new university ministry role in Taiwan, and amazingly the rest of my teammates also found wonderful roles that suited their gifts and talents not only also in Taiwan, but even in the same city as me. Though we were all starting over, we were starting over together, which was a wonderful gift of grace.

The Lord is my Shepherd; I have no lack.

I put the painting in my suitcase as I packed for Taiwan, humbled at the way God had blessed me and provided for me even as I doubted and questioned His promise to shepherd me. I wanted the painting with me in Taiwan as a marker of His faithfulness.

Though COVID-19 delayed and complicated my transition, I've been in Taiwan almost a year now. The painting was one of the first things I unpacked, and it hangs right beside my desk. This new season has been both harder and sweeter than I expected, especially as I've struggled through the final levels of Mandarin learning to pass the fluency tests my job requires.

Just last week my small group at my Taiwanese church asked me to pick a Scripture and share with them why it mattered to me. Without hesitation, I picked Psalm 23:1.

The Lord is my Shepherd; I have no lack.

It was such a sweet, full-circle moment to read and share what this verse means to me in Mandarin with my Taiwanese brothers and sisters, something I could have never imagined doing when I first bought the painting and hung it up in China.

I could never have imagined all the valleys the Lord would shepherd me through either. Or the gentleness with which He would lead me beside quiet waters and restore my soul when those valleys felt like the shadow of death.

I don't know what the future holds in this next season overseas. If the last few years have taught me anything, it's that I don't even know what tomorrow holds. But one thing I'm absolutely confident in is that with Christ as my Shepherd, life is always abundant. No matter what I gain, lose, grieve, or rejoice in, I have no lack.

If I ever doubt again, I've got the memories to prove it and the painting to remind me (and I can even read it for myself now).

—*Kathryn Hall*

Chapter 28

TODAY IS ABOUT HOPE

I knew the instant my bedroom door opened in the middle of the night and the intruder walked toward me that my dream was shattered—scattered like pieces of broken glass on a tile floor. For two months I lived the dream I had pursued for seven years—cross-cultural ministry in South Africa. Those seven years had been filled with completing college, applying with an organization, serving in a different country, and raising support. Now, after finally arriving in South Africa with a three-year visa, my dream was in pieces.

But my thoughts in the following moments weren't on my broken dream, they were on survival. By the time the intruder reached me and smothered my mouth, I barely had time to put my chin down to prevent him from choking me. Within a few minutes I realized there were three men inside of my home. And during the course of the home invasion, they stole most of my clothing, random household items, and anything electronic. Then one of the men raped me. And finally they kidnapped me, tied me to a bush in a brush area near my housing complex, and left me for dead. As I lay there, I was able to remove the gag from my mouth and the blindfold from my eyes, but untying myself from the bush proved to be much harder. At one point I gave up, told God I was done, and asked Him to please take me to heaven. I couldn't see how I would free myself; I was tired of fighting for survival. Yet in the next moment, I thought about how I couldn't do that to my family or my teammates. How long would it take my teammates to find me? How would my family find out? So I kept fighting. And thankfully God gave me the strength to free myself and walk back to the housing complex where I lived to find help.

In spite of all the trauma being inflicted on me, I had hope in those terrifying moments. Hope because I knew God was with me. I was a child of the Creator of the universe. A child whose Heavenly Father is all-powerful and just. It was His Word that filled my mind as I fought for survival. In the days before the home invasion I had read and meditated on Psalm 56:3. "When I am afraid, I put my trust in you" (NIV). I repeated these words in my head over and over and over that night. And in that verse I found comfort and hope. God was in control. I could still trust Him, even when "the worst" was happening to me.

The day after my home invasion I stood in front of a mirror as I applied concealer and said to myself, *Today is about hope.* I didn't know what hope after trauma looked like. I didn't even know what the day would hold, but I knew in the deepest part of my being that there had to be hope. God had not and would not abandon me. And because of this, hope existed.

The initial days were filled with glimmers of hope. I found hope in God's justice when the men who broke into my home were caught by the police and many of my belongings were found. There was hope in a recovered laptop and car. And a quick surge of hope came when the man who raped me died while in police custody. Hope appeared when I stepped on U.S. soil and for the first time in weeks felt brave enough to walk alone into a shop, where I purchased a bottle of water. And there it was again as I drove to counseling each week and sat in church each Sunday. It was there as I played with my then two-year-old niece who knew nothing about what I had survived, just that I was around to play with her and buy her toys. When I searched for hope each day, I found it. On the days when the tears fell without stopping and as I walked through the soul-wrenching process of forgiveness, I never stopped searching for hope.

Hope grew brighter and stronger when I moved back overseas just over a year later. God led me back to Portugal, a place I had thought was just a stopping point a few years earlier on my journey to South Africa. But here I was again, boarding a plane to Lisbon. Hope was giving me the strength to look at the shattered pieces of my dream and to see them beginning to be shaped into a similar but different dream. I was independent in a foreign country again—another surge of hope!

Hope often came in the form of people during that time. God provided an incredible roommate, who became a dear friend, with a listening ear and understanding heart. When the days were long and life threatened to overwhelm me, teammates showed generous compassion and helped lighten my load. Hope surfaced as I found purpose once more in preparing lesson plans, teaching, and investing in the lives of my students. I wasn't healed, but I was healing. And I could tell the darkness was fading and hope was strengthening.

I spent two years in Portugal; two years filled with the ups and downs of recovering from trauma. And then God led me to yet another country and ministry. It was in Ireland that I lived alone again. I still struggled with fear and the emotional turmoil that follows trauma, but it was there that hope blossomed. It blossomed in the independence of morning walks and bus rides. And in the comfort of chats over coffee and visits from friends. Writing words that my heart and mind had been processing brought hope. And as I began to tell my story, my hope grew as my words gave others hope in their dark and difficult valleys.

And then, once again, I boarded an airplane. This time to the United States where I quietly released my dream, the one I had lived for ten years, of cross-cultural ministry. Yet even as I traveled across the ocean again, hope was with me, slowly growing after a month of communication with a guy I would be meeting in person in a few short days. Hope that maybe, just maybe, my dream of marriage—the one I thought I had given up when I moved overseas in my early twenties, the one I was certain was gone after I was raped—would be realized. Turns out that he was "the one." And we began married life together thirteen months after our first date. One dream replaced another, and hope bloomed. And continues to bloom as we navigate marriage, life, and ministry together. Hope has thrived in spite of the difficult circumstances we have encountered since we said, "I do."

When I spoke the words, *Today is about hope,* that August morning in South Africa, I didn't fully understand all of the hope God would give me as I healed. All I knew at that moment was that I needed to cling to the God of Hope. So I did. Over the years, God used people, places, and circumstances to weave hope into my life as I adjusted to life after trauma. But certain, lasting hope, the hope that results from suffering, came as I clung to my Heavenly Father and His promises through each counseling session, each international flight, and each new situation.

I held on stubbornly to His promises: He will never leave me or forsake me, He is a very present help in times of trouble, He will strengthen and uphold me, He will fulfill His purpose for me, and He will work all things for good to those who love Him. I immersed myself in His Word, filling my mind with His promises day after day and night after night. And the hope that blossomed in me is deeper and more sure than it would have been without rape, kidnapping, and a shattered dream. Each time I face a new trial—cancer, chronic health problems, financial instability—I am reminded of what God has brought me through already. God hasn't changed. The trials have changed, but God is still the same—always with me, all-powerful, all-knowing, faithful, loving, and good.

My dream was shattered in a most traumatic fashion, like a sudden, violent hurling of a glass to the ground. On occasion I still find a sliver of glass that's been hiding for years. I don't know where or when I will find them, but as I come across them, I take them to the One who restores my soul. My Heavenly Father put my shattered dream back together. Piece by piece He shaped and formed it into a different, yet equally beautiful, dream. A dream which has taught me how to hold on tight when life falls apart; a dream in which I can say like Job, "My ears had heard of you but now my eyes have seen you" (42:5, NIV). A dream filled with hope because of the God of Hope.

—Laura Bowling

Chapter 29

HE WILL SUSTAIN US

The howling wind woke me up, an occurrence I had grown accustomed to since my husband and I chose the top floor of our three-story house as our bedroom. When we moved in, we had been dazzled by the large window with the breath-taking view overlooking our new city, not considering how loudly the wind would whip against that same window.

I slipped out of bed, trying not to wake my sleeping husband, shivering involuntarily as the early-morning chill hit me as soon as I left the warmth of the heavy quilt and comforter. The ever-present cold was not something that I had grown accustomed to yet, despite eighteen months of living in our host country. I was trying to sneak quietly into the bathroom when I noticed that my attempt at stealth had failed. My husband was stirring, turning on his bedside lamp and moving his body to sit on the edge of the bed.

I sat down on the bed next to him, putting my hand gently on his shoulder. "How did you sleep last night, babe?" A glance at his face gave me a pretty good gauge of what the answer would be, but I wanted to hear him say it.

"Not great." He mumbled, darting his half-open eyes in my direction.

"Did you have trouble falling asleep or staying asleep?" I asked, once again able to make a decent guess, having felt the tossing and turning on and off through the night, but still wanting to hear about his experience.

"Both. I just couldn't shut my brain off. And then, I had a bad dream."

"Oh. I am sorry. What did you dream about?"

"My funeral."

"Your... What?"

"Well, I dreamed that I went to a funeral. And I couldn't figure out who was dead at first. Then I realized that it was me."

"Babe." I whispered, turning my body to face his and pulling him into my arms. Something was wrong. I knew it. "There is something you're not telling me. What is it?"

He took a deep breath, tears filled his eyes as he spoke, his voice barely above a whisper. "I have been having suicidal thoughts. And thinking about self-harm. Yesterday, I had to leave the room because all I could think about was cutting myself with the scissors that were sitting on the other side of the table."

The tears fell after that, and I just held him. Relieved to finally understand, scared to know the depth to which he had been hurting.

Collateral Damage

There had been signs. The difficulty sleeping. A daily beer or two with dinner for a guy who usually only had one or two on the weekend. A quicker temper. Complaining about things that normally brought him joy. Low energy that caused the work that he loved to feel more like a drudgery instead of a pleasure. Being frustrated and overwhelmed. Feeling anxious and paranoid, like everyone was against him.

And yet, putting two and two together is never as easy as it seems. Yes, the signs can be there, but sometimes, in the absence of open, honest conversation, understanding remains just out of reach. I listened as he shared how many months he had been feeling this way, how he hadn't told me because he didn't want to worry me, and how he thought it would be too big of a burden with everything else going on.

"You are not a burden. You are my husband. I want to be in this with you. But I can't be in it if you don't let me in."

He nodded and whispered, "I'm sorry that I didn't tell you."

"Babe, it's okay. I'm not upset. I am just thankful to finally understand what is going on. I love you. You are not alone. We'll get through this together."

And we did. Disclosure was the first step. We sought out trusted friends in our passport country for counsel and support. We knew that we couldn't walk this alone, and we had to let people in. We needed people who loved us to know what we were going through, to pray, to ask questions, to listen, and to help us think through what our next steps needed to be.

We sought professional help. Mental health services are notoriously difficult to access in many places around the world, and our host country is no different. It felt like stepping into a hedge maze and having no idea which direction to turn. And yet, we knew that we had to try. The intersection of body, brain, mind, emotions, and trauma meant that all the help that we pursued had to be multi-faceted, one leading to another and each complementing the other. Counseling appointments were scheduled. Supplements were ordered. Psychiatrist appointments were scheduled. Medication was delivered. Psychologist appointments were scheduled. Each step was an important part of the healing process in the midst of the mental, emotional, spiritual, and relational complexity that is anxiety and depression. We found that there is no quick, easy road to healing. There is only one day at a time, moment by moment.

And so we took things step by step. Living with anxiety and depression severely limits the ability to plan, to dream, and to set goals. The focus becomes getting to the next moment, or as an understanding friend put it, doing the next right thing. Whether the next right thing was taking a shower or meeting a neighbor for coffee, it often took every bit of energy available to get to the next right thing. We had to learn to be content with and even grateful for the tiny victories of simply doing the next right thing.

We began to speak openly to our children about all of Daddy's appointments, letting them know what they were for and how they would help. We read books with our kids about how depression and anxiety affects the brain and how it affects relationships. We watched YouTube videos about the importance of caring for your mental health. They had noticed the changes in their dad, but they hadn't been able to make sense of them. "Children are excellent observers and terrible interpreters,"[10] to be sure. We wanted them to understand that it was not their fault that Daddy was struggling nor was it their responsibility to make Daddy feel better. We wanted them to know that Daddy's brain, mind, heart, and soul needed some help and that doctors and counselors and friends and family were giving Daddy the help that he needed.

We practiced gratitude. This was hard for my husband while his depression was at its worst, but our children and I found it life-giving to write down three things that we were thankful for every day. It invited us to seek out, look for, and name the good in the midst of everything that was hard and sad. And it encouraged us to see the ways that God was working, providing for us, helping us, giving us moments of joy, even in the middle of great difficulty.

We had rituals and routines that brought us joy. Putting things in place that we enjoyed but also didn't have to think about was crucial on the days when energy was so low that it seemed impossible to muster up strength for anything, much less something fun. Tuesday was Taco Tuesday. Friday was (frozen) Pizza and Movie Night. Sunday was talking to grandparents. Thursday was Game Night. Family read-aloud was every weeknight, and we intentionally chose fiction books that let us all live in an imaginary world for a short time. Depression and anxiety steal not only the ability to enjoy things but also the desire and energy to plan for fun. Having those things in place was crucial for the days when it would have been out of reach otherwise.

We have now passed the one year mark—which means that it has been one full year since the lowest point when suicidal ideation and thoughts of self-harm made me worried about leaving my husband alone. I am so thankful for that. By God's grace, we have been able to access effective treatment in our host country, allowing us to stay and continue to serve with adjusted roles while pursuing healing. The smiles and laughter have returned to my husband's eyes, and the dad jokes have made a comeback with all the groaning and eye-rolling that accompanies them. It feels so much more normal.

And, at the same time, our bodies remember. There are still days when our bodies recall the hurt and the trauma, the grief and the loss that we were living with one year ago, and those are the days when just getting through the day feels like swimming through molasses. We get to the end of the day exhausted, even though nothing "too taxing" really happened that day. We try to be kind to ourselves on those days—we try to give ourselves time to feel it, journal about it, pray about it, and share it with God, with one another, with trusted friends. We have learned that it is easier to bear when it is witnessed, acknowledged, and accepted, rather than resisted or ignored.

Collateral Damage

It is possible that depression and anxiety might always be present in our lives to some extent. There will continue to be days when it is barely noticeable, and there will continue to be days when it will knock us off our feet. One thing that is certain is that it will continue to be unpredictable, which means understanding and accepting it as it comes will be vital.

That is the thing about anxiety and depression—it is an invitation to acknowledge our very humanity. The weakness that is carried about in our very bodies, in our very brains, reminds us that we are dependent and needy. As with any limitation, we have choices: We can resist it, resent it, and push it away until it grows too big or overwhelming to ignore. Or, we can accept it, attend to it, and allow it to give us a deeper experience of the presence of Christ, who promises that His "grace is sufficient for [us]." (2 Corinthians 12:9, NIV)

It is this very presence of Jesus and His sufficient grace that has sustained us thus far. Our Savior who experienced in His very being the darkest moments of the soul and body has been near to us in our own moments of darkness; He has not left us or forsaken us, just as He promised. And we have every reason to hope and believe that He will sustain us to the end.

—*Libby Wilkes*

Chapter 30

THE POWER OF RAW COURAGE AND SMALL BEGINNINGS

When my husband arrived home for lunch, I yelled, "I refuse to unpack one more thing. Coming here was a mistake, and we are leaving."

Dave knew I was serious, and my crisis plunged him into his own crisis. I could see it in his eyes, his neck muscles, his ragged breathing. "You are emotional and irrational, and I refuse to discuss this until New Year's."

He paused. "We can't leave now. Classes start in a few days, and people are counting on me to teach their kids. We made a two-year commitment. If you insist on leaving, we can—at the end of the school year. But we're not talking about it until the new year."

It was mid-August. I couldn't think. Or speak. Or even move. *I can't do this*, I cried.

A few days earlier, Dave and I and our kids, ages four and six, had arrived at a missions center in the middle of nowhere in Colombia. We Seattleites were accustomed to cool weather, so the equatorial heat sapped our energy. Sweat-drenched clothes stuck to our bodies—a new experience for us. The air was heavy, thick with stench. Was it rot? It made me sick to my stomach.

A dinky commissary was our only source of food. Hand-hewn wooden shelves held just a few canned goods. In a chest freezer I found two pieces of meat, and the miniature produce display was almost empty. I did buy an old loaf of bread and small plastic bags of powdered milk, flour, coffee, rolled oats, and rice. Heartsick, I cried out to God, "How can I feed my children nutritious meals?"

Dave, thrilled at getting to teach missionaries' kids, spent his days setting up his classroom, and our kids enjoyed playing in the yard with new friends. Meanwhile, I felt an urgency to get our family settled before I began my job in the administration office, but that would prove to require raw courage and resolve beyond anything I'd experienced before.

Besides unpacking, I had to adequately stock our kitchen, and that required frequent hikes to and from the commissary—frequent because we could bring home only what we could carry in our arms. Our fellow missionaries had motorbikes, but we didn't. Both coming and going, we climbed steep hills under cruel sun, and by the time we arrived home, we felt sick with queasy stomachs, aching heads, and eyes throbbing from the sun's glare. Our clothes clung to our dripping bodies. I would give the kids a drink, settle them to rest in their bedrooms, and I'd collapse across my bed. I hadn't expected living here would require so much dogged effort.

Until we had sufficient food in the house, we ate noon meals in the dining hall, located next to the commissary. That meant more battles up those hills under a merciless sun, making us sick and disheartened. I wished I could wake up to find it was a bad dream. But this was no dream.

Even though I was exhausted from our month-long journey from Seattle, sleeping at night was a challenge. We had no fan to take the edge off the heat. Mosquitoes dive-bombed our ears. Bats clattered in the attic. Cockroaches ran across our faces. Tossing and sweating, I begged God, "Please don't let me give up tomorrow. Make me a fighter. Give me courage."

"Courage doesn't always roar," writes author and artist Mary Anne Radmacher. "Sometimes courage is the quiet voice at the end of the day saying, 'I will try again tomorrow.'" And so, each day, battling nausea and perspiration, I tried again, rummaging through luggage, finding silverware tucked in Dave's tennis shoes, dishes wrapped in shirts, drinking glasses protected by towels, a saucepan full of socks.

Little by little the commissary's inventory grew, and our cupboards and refrigerator looked less bare. I was inching closer to accomplishing the longing of my heart, getting my family settled and well fed, and one morning we turned a corner—we had bread and canned tuna so we could eat lunch at home instead of hiking those killer hills to the dining hall. My heart soared.

But then—*but then!*—a man knocked on our door and told me to remove everything from the kitchen so he could spray for insects. After my hard-won progress, it was all undone.

I was undone too.

I yelled at God, "You got this all wrong. What could You have been thinking to send us here?"

And then I screamed at Dave that we were leaving.

And then he put his foot down and said we were not leaving.

And then I plotted to run away, hiking through Central America, Mexico, California, Oregon, and Washington, finally arriving at home in Seattle. But, deep down, I knew I'd never attempt that. I was stuck here.

But one day in early December, it dawned on me that I had fallen in love with living here, my job, and my colleagues. With a start, I realized the end of the school year was rapidly approaching. *No way,* I told myself. *There's no way I'm leaving in six months and returning to the States.*

How did that change of heart happen? Only God knows the whole answer, but here's what I can tell you.

Although God had seemed distant and sometimes silent, He never abandoned me (Hebrews 13:5). As I stumbled through my wilderness, He whispered, "You have never been this way before (Joshua 3:4). Don't be afraid. I am your God, and I'm with you. I'll help you" (Isaiah 41:10, 13).

When God heard the harsh words I roared at my husband, when I felt ashamed, when I regretted my immaturity, He lavished His forgiveness on me. He stood in my corner cheering me on, "I'll teach you how to live here" (Psalm 32:8).

When I fell into bed, dismayed over my clumsy, lurching attempts and my slow progress, I awoke the next day to God's mercies, new every morning (Lamentations 3:22-23).

While I fought to take one step and then one more, He held me close—I, the brokenhearted one, the crushed-spirit one, the fighting-not-to-lose-hope one (Psalm 34:18)—and He promised, "I'll give you sufficient strength to make it through each day" (Deuteronomy 33:25).

I have come to recognize a few things about that first week. God told Zechariah, "Do not despise these small beginnings" (Zechariah 4:10, NLT). In other words, "People should not think that small beginnings are unimportant" (NCV). Those words are true, but you and I are impatient, irritated with fits and starts and slow progress. We want instant results, and we want God to answer in big ways—as if with windstorms and earthquakes and fire—but often He speaks in a hushed voice (1 Kings 19:11-13), urging us not to turn our noses up at the subtle ways He helps us make small yet significant beginnings.

Take, for example, six short words spoken by Karen who had invited us to join Ron and their sons for dinner on our first evening. She drove to our house on her Honda 90 motorbike, squeezed my little girl on the seat between the two of us, and we headed out. By then Ron had arrived on his motorbike, and Dave and our son hopped on with him.

Our mission center sat on a cluster of short but steep hills, and as Karen drove up, down, and around them, we clung to her.

Suddenly she came to a stop at the foot of one hill. "I need to drive up our steepest hill now. Hold on tight—and don't wiggle!"

I gazed up. Steep? She wasn't kidding. And it was strewn with loose rocks. *She's really going to try that hill,* I asked myself, *with three of us on this puny putt-putt bike?*

Yes, she was.

Sit still, I ordered myself—I was afraid to even blink—and we made it to the top without a glitch. But if my daughter and I had panicked, if we had squirmed, or tried to jump off, we could've caused a serious accident. Karen's six little words, "Hold on tight—and don't wiggle!" made all the difference.

Karen's words were packed with wisdom for me. Breathless and disoriented, I had somersaulted into an alien corner of South America. Learning to live there was like a steep climb scattered with sharp stones that could make me slip and fall. Karen's words echo Bible teachings urging us to hold tight to God instead of waffling and wiggling—emotionally, physically, mentally, and spiritually (James 1:2-8), teachings urging us to stand firm and unshakable (Ephesians 6:14, Psalm 16:8) instead of panicking or making rash decisions. Karen's six words, a small beginning—the stuff of living well.

My neighbor Ruth showed me how to make another small beginning. She stepped into my kitchen carrying matches. "I've come to show you how to light your stove." The matches were half the size of wooden matches in the U.S. The stick part was short and flimsy—string, I think—coated in paraffin. Ruth struck half a dozen matches before one caught fire, but she never grew impatient. She just kept trying. Watching her was like a parable teaching me how to tackle life on the mission field. After that, each time I struck a match, Ruth's example inspired me to resist grumbling and never to give up. She gifted me with a small beginning packed with a big lesson on patient endurance (Colossians 1:11).

My next lesson came from Lois. She and Ron invited us to dinner a few days after we arrived. By then, I'd had plenty of time to stress over adequately feeding my kids, given our commissary's skimpy supplies, but stepping into their home left me speechless. Their dinner table was covered with bowl after bowl of food—it looked like a Thanksgiving feast. But how did Lois do that? I blurted out, "Where did you find all this food?"

"At the commissary," she smiled. "I've learned to be creative with what we have here." That was an *Aha!* moment for me. From then on, I thrived on the challenge to think innovatively about our family's meals, to be resourceful—and even a little adventurous— and the four of us enjoyed the outcome. That was another small beginning, yet so big for me.

Small beginnings. Baby steps. Seemingly insignificant encounters and conversations. God tells us not to turn our noses up at them because in them He offers us ways to make progress, to mature personally and spiritually, and to accomplish in us and our circumstances what might have seemed impossible.

Collateral Damage

God doesn't promise instant reversals, rapid success, or immediate ease in living. Acclimating, learning, and growing take time, but making courageous, tenacious, faith-filled small beginnings can lead to big successes.

By the way, we didn't leave at the end of that school year. In December, when I realized I loved living and working there, I longed to tell Dave I didn't want to leave, but he'd said he refused to talk about it until New Year's, and I was just stubborn enough to refuse to talk until New Year's too.

December was a long month. Hardly able to contain my joy, several times I almost let slip my secret change of heart. I put up a good fight throughout the month but, a few days before January 1, I could wait no longer. Wrapping my arms around Dave and grinning, I looked into his eyes, and they twinkled as if he knew what I was going to say. "There's no way I'm leaving in May," I said. "Can we stay another year?"

We did. And we stayed another year after that too. I had accused God of getting it all wrong when He sent us there, but I was mistaken. Those were the best years of our lives.

—*Linda K. Thomas*

Chapter 31

PANIC ATTACKS AND ANGELS

The first time I had a panic attack I was five thousand feet above ground.

We were in the mission Cessna, heading back to our jungle home after a break. The weather wasn't exactly brilliant, with a heavy layer of cloud beneath, solid gray above, and us sandwiched in the middle. Every now and then we'd get a peep of the misty green mountains far below.

Our pilot was a German fellow, an exceptionally skilled and intuitive flier. Nothing much fazed him, and he was always willing to give things a try, within the confines of "reasonable risk," of course. I trusted him. I trusted all our mission pilots, knowing they were some of the most experienced, well-trained pilots in the world.

But trusting our pilots didn't mean I enjoyed flying in the tiny modified planes, touching down on our miniscule airstrip powering uphill if landing, or racing downhill on takeoff before swooping up at the last minute over the village roofs and cheerfully waving people.

That particular morning we'd risen before dawn as usual for a flight day. I never slept well the night before a flight, ears straining for the sound of rain which might mean a canceled flight the next day. Or wondering if I'd forgotten anything, which I usually had, and if what I'd forgotten was vital as it would be several months before we next flew out to town.

It had been a good break, but "break" was a relative term meaning more "change from one's normal circumstances" than "restful, restorative, refreshing time away." The kids always loved spending time with the other expat MKs who lived in town. Normally they were on their own in the village or out with their tribal friends in the forest. Breaks in town for my husband and me, though, meant wading through long lists of things to do and buy to get us through the next extended time in the mountains, far away from shops and doctors, hardware supplies and hairdressers. We were exhausted.

So it was that I hoisted myself aboard the plane and strapped in that early cloudy morning, mentally and emotionally preparing myself for the weeks ahead. As always, I forced myself to relax my breathing and pray as the pilot went through his checklist, did a final turn in his seat with a smile to make sure we were all okay and said a hearty, "Okaaaay, we're off then!" He revved up the engine to full capacity before releasing the brake, and we hurtled down the runway and up into the skies.

Once we're in the air, it's actually not too bad. I mean, what can go wrong from here, right? Kind of *que sera sera*; whatever will be will be; all in Your hands, Lord; not like I can do anything about it now anyway. So I'd look out the window at patchwork rice paddies which never ceased to intrigue before they gave way to denuded foothills cleared of their valuable timber, then the mass of dense virgin forest covering a vast mountain range.

I closed my eyes for a while, thinking how it never got easier even after all these years flying in and out of our mountain village home where we worked with an indigenous group of people, translating the Bible and discipling the growing church. I'd always been a scaredy-cat, my vivid imagination conjuring up the worst of scenarios.

On the very first flight into the village many years before I'd held my baby tight to my chest, praying my children wouldn't sense my fear. I didn't want them to grow up scared of everything as I was. Now the children were older. They knew of my fear. As the plane fired up and that initial roar became deafening, they'd turn and give me a grin or reach over and squeeze my hand. I'd be touched, but feel equally quite useless as a brave mother role model.

Until, that is, one day when my husband no doubt tired of my self-loathing said, "But hon, the fact of the matter is, yes, you're afraid, but it's now been twelve years and every single time you still GET IN THE PLANE. I appreciate that."

Oh. Yes. I guess he was right.

So I kept getting in and strapping in, consciously relaxing my breathing, asking God not to let my fear carry over to my children, choosing to trust Him. In the very early days the Lord gave me a vision of sorts. My heart was thudding with the pain of fear as we dashed down the airstrip building speed then lifting off. *O God, O God, O God,* I silently cried, not a blasphemous oath or meaningless idiom but a heartfelt call to the Creator of the Universe who holds all things in His mighty hands. Suddenly, without any warning, I had a picture of two large angels complete with massive wings and flowing robes. One was on the right of the plane, and one was on the left. They were effortlessly flying alongside the plane, one hand touching a wing each. As I looked, the one nearest me turned and smiled. And I smiled back.

Whether it was real or whether it was simply a beautiful reminder from my Father God that He was indeed there and there were whole realms all around which I'd never comprehend, my heart instantly slowed its thudding, and I was at peace.

I still never enjoyed flying in small planes on marginal airstrips. But it was part of the job, and it had to be done. And I had a Father watching over us and angels I could easily picture escorting us on our way.

So back to that one particular cloudy day. I had remembered the angels. I'd practiced my breathing, and as we continued to fly, now several minutes longer than I knew was normal—we should be right over our village by now, but all I could see was cloud—I once again entrusted our journey to the Father and reached for my daughter's small hand in the seat next to me. She, at least, wasn't in the least perturbed. She'd grown up flying in small planes. It was life and fun.

The minutes stretched out, and I could see my husband who was up front and the pilot talking through their headsets, straining to look out the window, pointing every now and then.

We circled round and then circled again. My heart began its steady thump—thump—thump. I could feel it beginning to ache.

My husband leaned back and shouted, "He's going to try going higher and over to the west to see if there are any holes, okay!"

I clenched my jaw and nodded a vague smile. I knew the deal. We'd found miracle holes in the clouds before and been able to safely land.

Up and up and up we went, round and round and round.

Breathe, I scolded myself, just breathe. *Don't be a ninny, you've done this before. Breathe, relax, trust, trust, trust. You can do this. You CAN do this, girl!*

I closed my eyes, my head beginning to spin. *Think of something else*, I commanded. But the busyness of the last few weeks rattled in my brain making crazy thoughts. *Did I remember to get butter? I don't know. Oh no. How will I bake? DID I BUY BUTTER?!!!! I'm such a bad mother. Where are the angels, God?!*

And all of a sudden it was too much.

I cannot do this. We're going to crash. I'm going to die. I think I'm having a heart attack.

Collateral Damage

My head became lighter and lighter. Was I going to pass out? My heart pounded, hard and fast now. I couldn't talk myself out of it. And that made me even more afraid. I've always been able to talk myself out of things. *Now get a grip, girl! That's the spirit.*

But no.

Not this time.

I could feel myself as if on the edge of a deep, black hole. I was still conscious, but I felt like I was falling. Tumbling down, down, down, down.

Without a doubt I must be having some very serious attack, most likely a stroke or heart issue. The fact I was in my early forties and otherwise extremely healthy simply didn't come into it. I was going to die.

I never like making a fuss, but this time I knew I had to. After all, if my children were going to be left motherless the least I could do was say goodbye from a hospital bed without the thunderous racket of a plane's engine at five thousand feet.

I reached out and clenched my husband's shoulder. He whirled around, knowing I rarely tried to communicate in the plane.

Seeing my ashen face and hearing my shouted, "Enough! I don't feel well," he gripped my hand in a quick squeeze, then spoke into his mic. The pilot turned and gave me a smile and a thumbs up, and we leaned into a long, slow turn back to base.

I knew we'd be up for the cost of the long, aborted flight, and tears stung my tightly closed eyes. I felt so stupid, so frail and silly. But my head was floaty, and I was still sinking into that strange bottomless void.

Not for the first time I questioned God. *Really, God, you made ME a tribal missionary? Me who has grown up in privilege and comfort. Me with no perceivable great gifting or skill or talent. Me who is so easily exhausted and sees danger around every corner. Why, God? Are you SURE?*

And not for the first time I felt His kind, knowing smile. There were no words, no flashes of inspiration or angels this time. Just a quiet, deep knowledge that He was there. That He knew exactly what He was doing. And even if I was about to die, it was going to be okay.

I quivered a deep breath. And rested.

Later, much later, we discovered what I'd actually experienced was a panic attack. There were at least a dozen more full-on panic attacks, thankfully none of them in the deafening confines of an airplane, but all of them brutal and leaving me drained and bewildered.

When I finally worked out what they were—after ruling out all sorts of potential health hazards ranging from ECGs to check out my heart to an MRI to be sure it wasn't brain cancer or I wasn't in imminent danger of an aneurism—I was incredibly relieved. A panic attack! I read all I could about them and marveled to see my symptoms lining right up.

Somehow finding out what they were made all the difference. In time it became longer and longer between attacks. To this day I still start to experience them—that floaty feeling and gazing into the deep, black abyss as I teeter on the edge. But now I can laugh and back away. *Oh, how interesting, a panic attack wants to come. I wonder what's behind it this time?*

Sometimes over the years with my many battles God has sent help through common sense. Sometimes He has simply smiled and let me know He sees, He knows, He cares. Other times it's advice from others or online searches or helpful books or articles which explain things.

There are, of course, still times when I can't sense Him at all. Those are the times I have to simply trust His truth, what He's shown me in the light, believing Him in the dark. And get on into that plane.

And sometimes, just sometimes, He allows me to see angels with beautiful smiles to glimpse the realms unknown.

But always, always, He is there.

—*Lynne Castelijn*

Chapter 32

BE TRANSFORMED

My body was rigid with tension as I lay in the sweltering heat of another Pakistani spring. It was Easter 1995, and we had just dedicated our baby, Curtis, in the little church there. At forty, I still felt like a baby myself as I struggled to raise two sons, build a marriage, and be a missionary in the unforgiving environment of the West Punjab.

In Pakistan, nothing was standard or straightforward. Or easy.

Making meals was an obstacle course of sanitizing vegetables, sifting flour for unwanted objects like bugs or pieces of string, pressure cooking tough buffalo meat, and rationing luxury items such as cheese. Cookbooks from home were practically useless with their one-can-of-mushroom-soup recipes. And after all the work of wrestling meal ingredients to the ground, things still didn't taste like "home."

When the electricity was not being randomly turned on and off by the authorities, seasonal dust storms inevitably disrupted the power. In the dead of night, we would be plunged into a world of heat and mosquitos as ceiling fans ground to a halt. We were forced to drag portable beds and zombie-like children outside to "sleep" under mosquito nets. If the dust storm was too severe, we simply lay in our sweat inside under a sheet, praying for the electricity to return.

Self-diagnosing and treating our illnesses were standard. A reliable hospital was a three-hour drive away on wicked, dusty roads. We thought long and hard before making that trip. I remember the drama of trying to decode the small print Urdu language instructions on a medicine bottle in the middle of the night with a feverish, listless baby in my arms. Trying to be a good mother but feeling like a dangerous one.

Communication was a daily challenge. Whether it was with a stubborn toddler, a husband with problems of his own, an Urdu-speaking cook with ideas of his own, or a Muslim acquaintance playing coy with me out of fear and mistrust. For a person who prizes communication, it sometimes felt like a wasteland punctuated by the odd desert flower.

Perhaps nothing tested our love/hate relationship with Pakistan as much as the adoption of our two sons. Both boys had been born to unmarried Muslim girls. We now joke that I got the babies, and my husband did the labor. And labor he did, from the hospital to offices to the court to the embassy. Pleading, filling out forms, creating forms, waiting, paying fees, collecting documents, driving untold miles. Being told "No. Wait. I can't help you. I won't help you." Meanwhile, at home, I mothered the boys and fought off fears that some zealous Islamic leader, some capricious official, or someone else would ultimately take the boys away from us.

I worked so hard to make sense of that world. *How do I do the right thing in a culture that is not black and white? How do I show compassion without creating dependency? What made a joke offensive? Whom could I trust to be a real friend?* I longed to be understood. To feel "normal." To look competent.

Underneath all the tangible irritants lay the real culprit—the battle for the ownership of my mind. The competition was stiff.

Satan accused and suggested. *What if you don't keep believing in Christ? Is there enough fruit in your life? You're a liar—a failure.*

People opined and expected. "Well, I personally feel that you..."

And finally, years of sermons and Bible studies, often contradictory, vied with each other for my convictions.

The battle seemed a little unfair. I was literally learning how to use my sword and shield amidst a relentless hail of arrows. There was no "pause" button and no end in sight. It was personal. Lonely. And humiliating. How I longed for someone wise enough to help me unravel life's perplexities.

As I lay in bed sleepless on that sultry spring night in 1995, beside a husband who had no idea how to help me, my mind whirred like an out-of-date computer trying to keep up. Irrational fears, false guilt, and exaggerated responses plagued me. *I think so and so is mad at me. Maybe I shouldn't have said or done such and such. Why can't I relax? I feel so unstable. Do others see me as a basket case?*

Collateral Damage

Will my husband grow weary of my struggles? Will the mission send us home?

I had come to Pakistan to "change the world for Christ." But I was the one who needed to change. *How?* I asked myself in the darkness. *How do I change?*

Suddenly, Psalm 27 came to mind: "The Lord is my light and my salvation." Whoosh. My mind gratefully escaped its stuffy confines and latched onto those life-giving words. "Whom shall I fear?" (verse 1, ESV) I was like a prisoner, suddenly realizing the door of my cell was open. *Oh, God, I don't have to live like this.* Faith came alive. *I am not alone in this darkness. Somehow You will give me the light of understanding. You will save me from what I cannot even identify. And when You are all this to me, whom shall I fear?*

I had veered into the Truth. I had discovered the nuclear option for which none of my enemies had an answer. As I basked in the passage, the silence on the battlefield was deafening.

My arms, my back, my neck relaxed onto the mattress. A coolness replaced the sweating. My heartbeat slowed. Hope emerged. Transformation trickled in. I slept.

In the days and weeks that followed, I committed all of Psalm 27 to memory. If a few thoughts could transform a sleepless night, imagine what the whole psalm could do? I added Psalm 23 and over several years went on to memorize entire books of the Bible. It became my preferred devotional method. Consume, memorize, meditate, be transformed. Rinse and repeat—full-strength doses of God's Truth for my weakness, ignorance, and confusion.

I was a ravenous, needy woman. Insatiable. I memorized the Word. I noticed pronouns. I comforted myself in the night. I pondered to understand. I quoted life-giving words to friends. I compared Scripture with Scripture. I relished context. I rehearsed as I drove, washed dishes, or walked. I put on spiritual weight. I used my brain and put my feelings in their place. I clung to Jesus in the Word so very aware of my weaknesses and the power of my enemies.

Over twenty-five years later, baby Curtis is now a full-bearded, married man.

The mission did not "send us home." In fact, after our evacuation from Pakistan after 9/11, they redeployed us to India, where we served for over fourteen years.

My husband did grow weary of my struggles (Who wouldn't?), but he faithfully loved me and gave me grace to grow. He still does.

By God's enabling, I am winning the battle to own my mind. I stand guard daily. No longer a prisoner of Satan's lies. No more tossed here and there by the expectations, opinions, and theologies of others.

I am being transformed by His Word.

> Do not conform to the pattern of this world, but be transformed by the renewing of your mind. Then you will be able to test and approve what God's will is—his good, pleasing and perfect will. (Romans 12:2, NIV)

—Nancy Rempel

Chapter 33

JESUS OR ALLAH?

From the moment I surrendered my life to Christ and felt the call to be a cross-cultural worker, I knew that I wanted to go to the Muslim world. My heart longed to be on the field among unreached Muslim people. When I finally had the opportunity to move to a Muslim majority country in Southeast Asia, my heart was overflowing with joy and excitement. Little did I know that soon after arriving in my new home, I would begin one of the most challenging and exhausting battles I had ever faced since beginning my walk with Jesus.

I very quickly fell in love with the people, the culture, and the country. Daily I would hear the call to prayer sound and watch as neighbors and new friends would stop what they were doing to pray. I admired and saw beauty in the genuine devotion these people had to their religion. I would often have conversations about Islam and about Jesus with taxi drivers, friends, and random people I would meet as I ran errands. Between the beauty I saw in the culture of religion and the conversations I would have with devote Muslim people, I began to question and wrestle with the truth. I never thought that when I moved to a Muslim country for the sole purpose of sharing the love of Jesus I would question which god was the one true God or that I would find myself with the unwelcome desire to convert to Islam.

This desire and questioning silently ate away at my heart. I longed for understanding and truth. Was Jesus truly the Son of God and Savior of the world? Or was He just a prophet and messenger of Allah? Was salvation a gift of grace through Jesus, or was salvation given to those who strived their whole lives to do good works and to live a good Muslim life? I wanted answers, but I was afraid to ask for help. What would people think of me if I told them that I was questioning my faith and that I was questioning who Jesus was, especially since I had experienced Jesus in many tangible ways since giving my life to Him? Was He the Jesus that I had given my life to? Or was He just a prophet? I spent countless hours studying Islam and comparing it to Christianity. And the more I studied Islam, the stronger my interest and desire to convert grew.

I was at a crossroads. Doubts and questions from my childhood started to come back up. Having grown up in a legalistic Christian family, I fought and questioned the validity of the Gospel for years, having seen many contradictions with what I was being taught about grace and what I saw being lived out at home. I thought that if I became a Muslim, I would no longer have to deal with these contradictions and questions because my salvation would be based on my own works, and Islam sets clear rules as to how to obtain it and how to be a "good Muslim."

Some days the desire and pull towards Islam was so strong, I would find myself walking to the nearest mosque, with the intentions of going inside, taking the Shahada and renouncing my faith in Jesus. But once I got to the mosque, I could never bring myself to go inside. Instead I would sit outside nearby or pace back and forth for long periods of time. I would look at the mosque and hope that someone would come outside and talk to me and convince me to convert, but every time someone came out, it was like I was invisible, and they walked right past me. I know now that the Holy Spirit was protecting me, and it was Him who was stopping me from entering the mosques. But at the time I felt I was drowning, alone and lost in a sea of confusion. I longed for answers, and I was afraid that I would end up choosing to follow the wrong God.

For the year and a half that I was living there, I found little peace or resolution to my questions and doubts. When the time came to head back to America, I felt I was being uprooted from a place that I now felt more at home in than I ever did in America, and I felt I would never be able to get answers to my yet unresolved crisis of faith. At first, during my re-entry, the doubts I had been struggling with seemed to quiet and subside. I was back on my university's campus, and I distracted myself with homework, class and re-entry sessions with our member care team.

I felt a small level of relief, being able to focus on finishing school and enjoying my last few months with friends before we graduated. I even began to forget about my desire to convert and my questions about whether I truly believed in Jesus or not. But just a couple short months after we returned to America, we were kicked off campus and sent home due to the pandemic. Heartbroken, I packed up my dorm room and moved back to live with my parents in Colorado where I would finish my senior year online, away from my friends and community. As I began settling into my parents' place, all the doubts and questions about my faith came back like a flash flood with no warning. I was again faced with the desire and temptation to leave Jesus for Islam.

Finally, the weight of it all had gotten to be too much to bear alone. My spirit could no longer bear the weight of confusion, uncertainty and doubts, I was tired and hurting from the spiritual chains that had trapped me for the past two years. I finally got the courage to call one of my good friends from school, and after a few minutes of small talk, I told her that I needed help and prayer with something. I told her about everything and about how I was so lost and ashamed that I did not know what to believe. Sharing these things that I had carried in secret for so long lifted a huge burden off my shoulders. I was met with grace, compassion, and love. She did not condemn me for my questions. Instead she listened, asked questions to help me process, and then she prayed over me.

After talking and praying with my friend for a couple of hours, I sat in my car and began to think about the day that I had given my life to Christ when I was a freshman and how the Holy Spirit met me right where I was in that moment of my life. He met me in my sin, doubt and uncertainty. I was tired of my spirit being restless and absent of the peace that I had felt when I first believed. I cried out to the Lord; I told Him everything that I had been wrestling with for so long. I told Him that I hated that I had the desire and temptation to follow Islam and that I was so lost and confused. I confessed how I was having an easier time understanding and believing what I had learned about the god of Islam and that I was having a hard time believing in Jesus as God and not just a prophet.

After this, I asked the Lord for answers; I asked Him why I felt so drawn to Islam and why it made sense to me. As I waited on the Lord, I began to understand that one of the biggest reasons I was drawn to Islam is because it preaches works-based salvation, and growing up I had come to believe that it was my works, not the grace of God that saved me. I was still living under the law of sin and death and not under the new covenant of grace through the death and resurrection of Jesus Christ. He revealed that I still did not fully believe in His grace. And that God could be so loving that He would have grace on me and accept me based on His death on the cross and not based on my good works.

Then the Lord reminded me of testimonies that I had heard from people who left Islam to follow Jesus and how Jesus came to them in dreams and visions and revealed to them that He was "the way, the truth, and the life. No one comes to the Father except through Me" (John 14:6, NKJV). With these things that the Lord had shown me about my doubts and questioning, I asked Him for confidence and a renewed faith that He was the God of the Bible and that Jesus truly was the Savior. For a while, I sat there in silence. I felt peace but did not receive an answer from the Lord and began to question if I was just going crazy. Then the Lord gave me a vision. He showed me one of the largest mosques I had ever seen, and then as I was standing in front of the mosque, I looked up to see a bright and heavenly light that was shining over and blocking my view of the mosque. I looked at the light to see where it was coming from, and I saw the cross of Jesus. The light was surrounding the cross, and I completely forgot about the mosque being there.

As I looked at the cross in awe, I heard the still, small voice of Jesus say to me, "Beloved, I am who I say I am." I cannot begin to describe the depth of peace and the warmth of the light that I had and saw in the vision, but I can now say without a shadow of a doubt that Jesus truly is the Son of God and that the way to the Father is only through Him. And when the enemy tries to tempt me or confuse me with lies about what the truth is, I can remember and proclaim the truth that the Gospel of Jesus Christ is my salvation, and I can boldly proclaim the Good News to the unreached.

—*Sarah Bliss*

Chapter 34

GOD'S GOT YOU

Breathe. Just breathe. God's got you, Stephanie.

I lay there in the examination room that day scared. I literally thought I was dying. The increased palpitations of the heart, the needle-like sensations consuming my body, the breathlessness and the impending feeling of doom—they all came on so suddenly. I was exhausted, and my mind went wandering down the fear-winding road of "what-ifs" waiting on the results of the EKG.

I tried to calm myself, to convince my mind of the words that had been written on my heart—that God will never leave me or forsake me, that He's got me. After all, I'd left mother, father, sister, and brother to join my husband in his homeland to tell others about the love of Jesus. I envisioned the faces of my two children, both under the age of four at the time, and the thought of not being there for them overwhelmed me.

"God, You can't leave me here. Don't let me die young like my daddy did," I murmured to heaven.

The seconds turned into minutes and the minutes into half an hour. My palms were clammy and my cheeks tear-stained. I could peripherally see a pair of brown dress loafers stopped on the other side of the curtain and heard the whispering of my name as the doctor exchanged notes with the nurse. Then he came in.

"Hi, Mrs. Clarke, how are you feeling now?" He continued to ask me questions, most of them centered on the demands of life. I couldn't tell if he was even listening, but he nodded his head with seemingly great concern.

"All of the tests that we did on your heart show that everything is fine. I am going to refer you to a psychiatrist and suggest that you take some time off of work to get some rest."

Um, a psychiatrist? He handed me a medical excuse to present to my employer, as I also worked a secular job to help supplement our income. At the bottom of the paper, it read:

Reason for absence: Generalized Anxiety Disorder.

My heart was still palpitating abnormally, but at that moment, my mind found some solace that it wasn't a heart attack and that I wasn't dying. I had no clue what exactly the diagnosis would entail in the days ahead, but I was just thankful—thankful to be going home to my husband and kids and that there was no need for me to be transferred to the local hospital.

I took the recommended two weeks off from both my job and my ministry responsibilities to focus only on motherhood and rest—if that combination is even possible. Although my subsequent visits to the psychiatrist helped me to begin to understand the physiological triggers of anxiety, I experienced several more attacks in the following weeks, each one worse than the last. I honestly became paralyzed with fear.

Fear of driving, especially on the highway where fast cars and jersey barriers made me feel closed in.

Fear of crowds because I could no longer wear my well-versed façade of being okay.

Fear of being labeled crazy, should I dare confide in anyone about what I was experiencing.

Fear of disappointing God because rather than being anxious for nothing, I was now anxious about pretty much everything.

How could I mother well when I could barely find the energy to get out of bed? How could I manage well when I could barely focus on the tasks that solicited my attention at home? How could I do ministry well when I could barely feel God in the midst of my trial? Maybe I just wasn't cut out to be an overseas worker. After all, I had no formal training having not attended Bible college, and I didn't exactly have the emotional support going into my decision to "go into all the world" in the first place. I'd already served nearly a decade, which was five years more than I'd committed to serve. Maybe these attacks were just indicators that it was time to move on. Or maybe they weren't.

I finally confided in a friend of my husband's who also happened to be a local pastor and our neighbor. He came weekly to pray for me. I spoke to my mentor who also happened to be on the missions committee from one of our supporting churches. She arranged for me and my husband to attend a week-long intensive Christian counseling retreat that would successfully expose the roots of the anxiety and would teach me how to deal with those deep issues. And I beseeched God morning, noon, and night on my knees, in my car, at my desk, while grocery shopping—literally everywhere I went. If people were going to label me crazy, let it be because my lips were murmuring the prayers of my heart like that of Hannah.

Ten years have passed since that first attack, and the thorn in the flesh that is my anxiety keeps pointing me to the sufficiency in the faith that is His grace. Grace that has kept me for twenty years as a laborer in these fields. Grace that keeps using the deepest parts of my broken past for good. I never knew mental health would be a part of the journey of serving in an overseas life—but I do now. I know it first-hand. I know the grit it takes to muscle through the heavy days when you are hurting and homesick. It can be hard and holy all at the same time. It can feel friendless yet fulfilling. And rest assured, there will be times that will overwhelm you and times that you will overcome. But know this—you are not alone. You are never alone. God's got you.

He's got you, like He's got me—in the palm of His hand, in the peace of His presence, and in the power of His might. I want to share with you some of the instruments that God has given me along the way in this healing journey. While not medically prescribed, they have each helped me to move past the anxiety and have profoundly grown my faith in Him.

Pray for a mentor.

Pray that God would bring or show you the people in your life that you can reach out to in confidence and without judgment. As an overseas worker, a pastor's wife, and someone who struggles with anxiety, this has become a routine part of my prayer. And what I've found is that God will send valuable resources in the form of mentors and prayer partners who will specifically invest in you with their experience, their wisdom, their time, and their genuine love. He will send different people in different seasons, but all with the same goal—to let you know that He is for you.

Seek out His word.

At the advice of one of my mentors, I compiled a list of what she liked to call "Survival Verses." These are go-to verses that personally speak to the situations that I battle in my mind. I keep a list in my wallet, hang them on my fridge, and hide them in my heart. Each verse serves to remind me of God's promises when I feel an attack coming on. Declaring them and putting them on repeat literally quells my anxiety and quiets my fears, bringing them under His authority and bringing me within His peace. Here is an example of just a few of them:

> *Fear not, for I am with you; be not dismayed, for I am your God; I will strengthen you, I will help you, I will uphold you with my righteous right hand. (Isaiah 41:10, ESV)*

Humble yourselves, therefore, under the mighty hand of God so that at the proper time he may exalt you, casting all your anxieties on him, because he cares for you. (1 Peter 5:6-7, ESV)

When anxiety was great within me, your consolation brought me joy. (Psalm 94:19, NIV)

I sought the Lord, and he answered me; he delivered me from all my fears. (Psalm 34:4, NIV)

But blessed is the one who trusts in the Lord, whose confidence is in him. They will be like a tree planted by the water that sends out its roots by the stream. It does not fear when heat comes; its leaves are always green. It has no worries in a year of drought and never fails to bear fruit. (Jeremiah 17:7-8, NIV)

There is no situation that God's Word cannot deliver you from. Speak to your situation from His Word and then walk in your victory.

Seek out Christian counseling.

I wouldn't exactly say that my visits to the psychiatrist were wasteful. As mentioned previously, she was very thorough in explaining the triggers physiologically. However, it wasn't until I received counseling from a Christian clinical psychologist that I began to understand what was triggering me emotionally. His methods did more than just put a band-aid over the wounds. They encouraged me to use the Word of God to heal from the inside out. Good counsel is important, but when dealing with the battlefield that is the mind, godly counsel is imperative.

At the right time, share your story.

This one I was a little nervous about. At the time of my panic attacks, the culture in which I serve did not view a mental illness like anxiety as an illness at all. It was simply perceived as weakness. And if that wasn't intimidating enough, a visit to the psychiatrist was a sure sign that you were crazy.

It would be a few years after that initial attack, but I shared my story. It was an unplanned and unscripted moment. I was leading worship that Sunday and could feel the heaviest of burdens to just be vulnerable—vulnerable before the congregation, vulnerable before the Lord. Up to this point, only a few members of the congregation even knew I was struggling. As the musicians played between songs, the tears began to fall. I looked up and eyed people within the congregation that I thought may judge me the least for what I was about to say. My mouth opened, uttering words raw with the realities of mental health disorders and ripe with thanksgiving for God's ever-present help in times of trouble.

I didn't want to share my story. I didn't want anyone to know. But that day, it wasn't up to me. The Holy Spirit compelled me to share it. What was up to me was that I be obedient in doing so.

After the service was finished, three women came up to me and thanked me. Two were visitors to the church and said they'd been struggling with anxiety disorder in silence. The other said she'd been diagnosed as bipolar. Each said that they were skeptical to share with anyone simply because mental illness was not exactly considered culturally acceptable. But acceptable or not, that day something changed for me. I realized God was using my story to help erase the stigma and to give others hope of a deliverance found only in Him. So at the right time, at the Holy Spirit's prompting, share your story.

Rejoice. Pray. Give thanks. Repeat.

Paul's instructions in 1 Thessalonians 5:16-18 have honestly been an antidote to my anxiety and a weapon of warfare in the battle for my mind. Remembering to do each continually invites the presence of God into my most anxious moments. Scripture tells me that in the presence of God there is the fullness of joy and where there is His joy, anxiety cannot exist. Where there is His peace, worry cannot remain. Where there is gratitude, downheartedness cannot prevail. So each day, in each battle, choose to rejoice, to pray, to give thanks, and then repeat.

Lastly, remember to breathe. Just breathe. Because God's got you too!

—*Stephanie Prater-Clarke*

Chapter 35

SELF-CARE, SABBATH, SURVIVAL, AND SUCCESS

I took a deep breath and scribbled my name on the code of conduct for the sending organization that was placing me in China, then grabbed another Kleenex out of the now almost empty box of tissues. I had been putting off completing this paperwork as it felt so overwhelming and so final. It didn't help that the last page of the packet provided details about accidental death and dismemberment and what would happen with my body should I die while in China. I was 93% sure that I wouldn't die in China, and I had been trying to convince my parents about how God would protect me overseas. Why did this sending company have to remind both me and my parents that I might not return from the field in one piece? Would I be able to thrive or even just survive the experience of living abroad?

Spoiler alert: I have spent fifteen years in China and have never needed to refer again to the death and dismemberment page of the code of conduct. Surprisingly, the line from the code of conduct that has given me the most trouble over the years is one that I barely noticed as I was first pouring over the document: "All staff members are required to take a twenty-four hour Sabbath every week."

I had only been in China for a few weeks when a teammate had to bring this requirement to my attention. With teaching English, unpacking, learning Chinese, getting to know the city, and making new friends, neither death and dismemberment nor Sabbath rest were on my mind. As my teammates and I were discussing our plans for the upcoming week, I shared about all that I was going to be doing. "Other than teaching my classes, I have plans to meet up with some of my students, I have found a Chinese tutor to meet with me three times a week, I want to finish buying some household items for my apartment, and the school has asked me to help out with some extracurricular English events." I felt important, accomplished, and energetic thinking of all that I was going to do for God in China.

"What day are you taking a Sabbath this week?" my supervisor questioned.

"Actually, with all that I have to do, I don't think I can rest this week. Maybe next week I'll take some time to Sabbath," I innocently replied.

I was expecting my teammates to nod in understanding and agreement, sharing stories of their own busyness and reminding me that we will have plenty of time to rest once we get to heaven.

Collateral Damage

Instead, my teammates staged an intervention, much like we would do if someone told us they were planning on disobeying one of the other Ten Commandments.

"I'm feeling lonely so I've decided to commit adultery this Friday."

"I have fallen on tough times but don't worry, I have a plan to steal some food from a grocery store tomorrow."

I find myself shocked and alarmed by these two statements of planned sin, yet I was unmoved by my own plan to sin and not keep the Sabbath. My teammates though, were not okay with my lack of commitment to rest.

One teammate said he would come over and spend three hours cleaning my apartment, which really got my attention since his own apartment looked like it hadn't been cleaned in a number of months. Another teammate offered to get a babysitter for her children so that she could teach my classes for me while I took time to Sabbath. A third teammate volunteered to cook me meals and set up a food train so that I wouldn't need to prepare food and could spend time resting instead.

The news that I was going to skip Sabbath seemed catastrophic to my teammates, and their responses reminded me of what we offer to do for others when they are diagnosed with cancer or someone in their family passes away.

Apparently the organization I joined was actually serious about Sabbathing, and they were going to hold me accountable to it since I had already given my consent by signing the code of conduct. I had dabbled in Sabbath before coming to China, but now resting was serious, and I could no longer get away with using busyness as my excuse.

In protest, I reminded my teammates of how unforeseen events come up, and sometimes our meticulously planned and protected Sabbaths are canceled anyway.

"Yes, but you can't plan to sin. You work hard to protect your rest and then you ask God to give you grace when things don't work out. But don't give up on the practice of rest just because you can't do it perfectly," my teammate wisely responded.

As it became clear that I was going to have to rest, I attempted to understand why resting felt so hard. I was tired, still getting over jet lag, and loved the idea of taking time for self-care, but the dark fears underneath these thoughts were lies about self-worth. Who am I if I'm not hard at work to further God's Kingdom? I need to earn favor and acceptance and love by working hard. I can't possibly be doing any more for God so He must be pleased with me because I am so productive, right?

It sounds ridiculous, but I think I was scared to stop and rest. If I took a Sabbath, then I would have to listen to all the places of pain in my heart. I would have to face the sadness of missing my best friend's wedding and the birth of my niece. I would have to figure out who I was without hiding behind busyness, productivity, and success. I could no longer define myself by my work, and instead I would have to cling to my identity as a child of God. Rest seemed like a lot of hard work.

Collateral Damage

But my teammates left me with no other choice. They actually made a game out of guessing whether or not I rested for the full twenty-four hours each week. At our weekly team meetings, my four teammates would each guess if I had fully Sabbathed. We played this game for six months, and the four of them guessed correctly EVERY. SINGLE. TIME. They got so good at it that they would know within five seconds of my arrival whether or not I had Sabbathed well. They would look into my eyes and know instantly whether or not I had spent time listening to God speak His love over me.

I was starting to see why resting was serious and how my commitment to self-care had a huge impact not just on me but on others too. If my teammates could tell whether or not I was practicing self-care, my students and family and friends probably could too.

I remember talking about this with a close Chinese friend and explaining to her about the importance of rest and how God actually commands us to take a Sabbath day every week.

"Your God invites you to rest? All the gods I have heard about are demanding and harsh. You are so lucky to follow a God who takes such good care of you and who wants to spend time with you every week. Can you tell me more about Him?"

Yes, I will continue to tell others about Him. And yes, I am so blessed to have this kind of God.

I can now say with confidence that fifteen years of life in China would not have been possible without the self-care practice of Sabbath. To be honest though, Sabbaths are still a struggle for me. After getting married and then having a baby, I'm still figuring out my new balance with Sabbath since I can't take a break from breastfeeding, changing diapers, or being a mom. But for me, one of the most important things about Sabbath is how it teaches me to stop worshiping the idols of success and productivity. And to be honest, changing diapers is not part of what makes me feel successful and productive.

As I balance the demands of motherhood with my calling as a missionary, I experience an identity crisis as old lies about self-worth resurface. Sabbath gives me the space to rework my identity and to remember who I am, and as a new mom, this is just what I need. While spending the day with my one-year old doesn't make me feel productive, successful or accomplished, I don't think there is anything else I would rather do with my time.

And yet rest is still hard for me, busyness continues to be an easy excuse to turn to, and I am no longer surrounded by those Sabbath loving teammates. Instead, I find myself staging interventions with the new missionaries who also didn't realize that our company is actually serious about self-care and Sabbath. Maybe we should make our code of conduct more explicit.

"All staff members are required to take a twenty-four hour Sabbath every week."

"ALL staff members are REQUIRED to take a TWENTY-FOUR HOUR Sabbath EVERY week. Literally. It's one of the Ten Commandments. God says you must do this. This is not optional. We will hold you accountable to rest. Get over yourself and start practicing self-care."

I'm so glad that my teammates intervened during my first month overseas and called me out on my sin of Sabbath avoidance. I discovered that even more than death and dismemberment, I feared rest and what I would find in my exposed heart once busyness and productivity were stripped away. I now know that success is directly correlated with Sabbath, and it's not an exaggeration to claim that my survival and success in China is because of Sabbath and self-care. I'm so thankful that I signed that code of conduct, having no idea that it would save my life.

—*Tricia Chen*

We're Going There

Part Three

We're Going There

If you have ever studied missions history, you know that William Carey is often referred to as the "father of modern missions." He pioneered work in India at a time when many others were not even going.

The story you may not know, the one that doesn't usually make it into the history books, is that of William's wife, Dorothy Carey.

Dorothy's life was hard. She was illiterate and considered past marriageable age when she met William in 1781 through the devoted Puritan circles of her family. William's work as a shoemaker and journeyman pastor was not lucrative, but Dorothy soldiered on, trying to do the best she could for her family. She buried two babies and barely left the borders of her small town.

When William felt God's call to India, Dorothy didn't. At the time she was pregnant with their fourth child and flat-out refused to go. Her husband was determined and would have gone to serve without her, but following the birth of her baby, Dorothy left everything behind to follow her husband.

There are many details we don't know about Dorothy and William's story, but we do know that the rigors and stresses of life overseas were very difficult, and Dorothy's heart and mind paid the price. Sickness plagued the entire family, and after a year of life in India, their five-year old son died. Dorothy broke.

She was described as "wholly deranged."[11] She suffered for thirteen years before she died in 1807. History has not been kind to Dorothy, and often she is hidden in the shadows of the greatness ascribed to her husband. She has been called dull and weak-minded, unsuited as William's wife and an impediment to the work of the Gospel.

William kept Dorothy's condition hidden from all but a few close team members and even their families back home. Because her mental illness led to violent outbursts, she was kept at home, sometimes locked in her room and away from her children.

Centuries removed from the Carey family's work and life in India, we don't have the luxury of sitting with Dorothy over a cup of tea to listen and understand. We can't do anything about her pain and heartache, can't try to understand what happened to her mind.

Instead, let's look around at our sisters who have given up everything for the sake of the Gospel. How many women suffer on the mission field in silence today? How many don't ask for help, don't share the depths of their fears or suffering or struggles? How many stories aren't told?

It is hard to share the nitty gritty, not-very-pretty parts of any of our lives. It is vulnerable, and for those who sign on the dotted line for Kingdom service, opening up can have consequences. Will I be sent home? Will my church stop supporting me?

But as hard as it is to be honest, we need those stories. There can be a temptation to put missionaries on a pedestal—they are sacrificing for Jesus, an example for all. The pressure to live up to this life on the pedestal is a difficult weight to bear. What if we just declared, "Let's go there?" Instead of remaining silent, allowing shame or fear to take control, let's get honest about mental health on the field. Let's talk about temptation for women (and men). Let's admit that addiction, abuse, and abandonment can happen even on the mission field. I wonder how life could have been different for Dorothy and William Carey and their family if someone said to them, "Let's talk about this."

The stories in this section are brave and beautiful. These women have said "Yes" to that call for more honesty, allowing us to see how God met them in temptation, despair, and even failure. May we hold their stories with grace, and may it lead us to more conversations, more openness and more courage right where we are.

—*Sarah Hilkemann*

Chapter 36

SHOCK AND AWE: TEMPTATION AS AN INVITATION TO WORSHIP

When we returned to the States on home assignment, we were met with news of all kinds. Friends were getting married, the church nursery was booming with infants, and our children constantly came home with tales of new experiences. We were stunned, too, by some unwelcome news that hurt and confused our family. A dear pastor friend had fallen into grievous sin. We were heartbroken to view the devastation of his family and the consequences his choices had on the ministry to which he had given his life.

It could happen to anyone. It could happen to me, I thought, remembering my own moments of temptation. Though in each instance the Holy Spirit empowered me to walk away, these weak points caused emotional pain which remained long after the fantasies fizzled out. It has taken much time to process what happened and what the Lord has done in my heart through each testimony of temptation and deliverance. He has taught me to see each moment of temptation as an opportunity—will I worship self by yielding to temptation or will I give God His rightful place in my heart as I surrender fleshly desires in obedience to Him?

Temptation stopped me in my tracks on a cool morning in Kathmandu. After a high-stress morning of getting grumpy kids to school and the littlest one set up with her daytime nanny, I donned exercise attire and exited the gate that surrounded our compound on my way to the gym. I passed a young man, perhaps a few years my junior. His brown skin, far more pigmented than my freckled own, keenly reflected the rays of morning sun. On another day, I may have walked by him without noticing he shared the road with me. But today, my wondering heart and wandering eye drew me to him, and I thought, *He might want to be with me.*

In an instant, images of the most intimate nature flooded in as my mind pieced together Hollywood scenes with my own experiences, replacing the stars with this unknown man and me, two strangers embracing in the darkness. I felt the electricity of forbidden romance once limited to novels and secret hotel rendezvous pulse in my veins. In this fantasy, I allowed this man who knew nothing of my soul to know me in a way only one man ever has before.

I gasped at the audacity of the enemy to hurtle these wicked thoughts across the landscape of my mind and my stupidity to entertain them. I whipped my head back from his gaze to the rocky road my tennis shoes tread. Fear edged out the shock that occupied its space moments before. *How could I think that? What is wrong with me? Of course I wouldn't really have an affair...* would I? I felt like I didn't know myself. I certainly didn't know the definitive answers to any of these questions.

The days following, fear bled into every moment and tampered with what would have been lovely encounters with family and local friends. I questioned everything about myself, my marriage, and the ministry we had built together with the Lord. Could someone like me, someone who fantasized about a stranger I passed on the road, really be used by God? Surely, I had no authority to speak from in spiritual matters if I could stoop this low.

My mind returned to the first time I realized such risky encounters were even a possibility. My husband had hailed a taxi and sent me in the direction of our home after scouring an unfamiliar part of town for a building suitable for a new fellowship. He kissed me and promised to meet me back at the house as soon as his errands were completed. Bumping and jolting its way through Kathmandu traffic the beaten Suzuki inched me closer to home where my AC unit awaited me. As we traveled, the driver and I engaged in conversation. The heavy, wet air collapsed in on me as I rolled the window down, stretching my neck to hear the words floating towards the back seat.

The conversation progressed as it usually does with the questions I am accustomed to answering. I told him where we are from, what we are doing there, and how we wish to make Nepal our home for the rest of our lives. It felt very scripted as I had rehearsed it so many times before. This was the point where others either took the opportunity to talk to me about spiritual things or stare off quietly the rest of the drive, interrupting the silence only to inquire about the next turn.

As we neared my home, he shared with me that his wife lived in a rural village far from Kathmandu. He suggested that like him, I must be lonely and bored as my husband works away from home so much. The weight of the air doubled, and my pulse quickened as I recognized the direction he was steering toward. I couldn't roll the window down enough for the wind to whisk me away from there.

He finally came out and said what was on his mind: "I can give you my number. We can have fun together when your husband is at work." I knew he was not hinting at a walk at a local park or a competitive game of checkers. I was more polite than I should have been while I pretended to not understand his intentions. I said I was busy and that I had many friends. Anyone who knew me at this stage of my ministry knew those things simply were not true. I trusted the Lord would forgive my dishonesty.

In hindsight, it is clear I should have demanded he drop me off where the traffic police stood watch as I had done when another driver went off-route with stories I could see through. That time, I had thrown my fare into the front seat and called my husband to convince the driver to let me out of the cab when my pleas went unheard. This time, in my fuzzied mental state, I allowed this driver to take me right up to my front gate. I am grateful God spared me any harm, and there was no further pursuit after that unsettling encounter.

This recollection brought something into view I didn't see when shame made my ears ring on the side of the road: Temptation is evidence of our humanity, and humanity is synonymous with brokenness. No matter our cultural upbringings or moral convictions, because we teem with the blood of Adam, we are born with our finger on the trigger of sinful action. Like earth's first two inhabitants, we wonder if there is a forbidden fruit whose taste would change things for us, making us feel less empty and alone.

This opportunistic driver was not a monster; he was a human as broken as anyone else. Like me, he was subject to temptation, pre-programmed to take things for himself that please the eye and pleasure the flesh. However, he lacked the power of God to convict, restrain, and redirect in godliness. What a lonely drive home he must have had, alone with his thoughts in an empty cab.

The shock I and other Christ followers experience when temptation arises and our hearts instinctively mull over the pros and cons is evidence of our salvation. The Spirit tells again what we are and who reigns over us—that this temptation when taken is a roadblock to our sanctification. We can rejoice when we are tempted and shocked by our sinfulness because it causes us to remember who we are in Christ and that we are made to embrace grace, not sin.

Left to myself, I would yield to temptation every time and not be shocked for a moment. I would compromise the good gifts of God to snatch at something that temporarily fills my cup but leaves me far more empty than before. I would leave the safety of God's way, choosing illicit relationships and mind-altering drugs because I would have no taste for the sweetest joys known only in Christ. I may no longer get passed without notice on the street but instead receive dirty, knowing looks from those who observe my wretched state.

But He has changed me. He has changed every believer who has called on His name, and He continually refines us. Keeping our eyes on Jesus who walked the path of righteousness perfectly, we can follow Him in joyful obedience. When ministry is hard, life unthinkably tragic, and temptation beckons in a booming voice, we can remain faithful through the power of God. We can allow the temptation to reveal our hidden fears and desires and ask the Lord to remedy each one. We will be free to chase down holiness, trusting that He will strengthen us in our weakness and provide our deepest longings. Because He does what He says He will do.

That day on the dirt road, intrusive and unwanted thoughts entered my mind and wrecked me for days, but my Father redeemed them. He showed me my brokenness and led me to repentance. The holiness of Jesus was the light under which I examined the temptation, turning it over on every side. As I surrendered it to Him, He gave me the legs to flee my fantasy and the love to overwhelm feelings of shame and isolation which threatened to undo me. I became undone instead by His character, by His relentless testimony of grace. Only God can turn wickedness into worship.

Temptation may be evidence of our brokenness, but victory over temptation is evidence that God's power is at war with our brokenness. He tirelessly works to make us new. Deliverance displays the beauty of submission to Christ, following His lead away from worldly passions into deeper intimacy with Him. It is testimony of trust in a good Father whose way is the safest and most delightful path for His children. It tells the world of a love that fills the furthest corners of our souls with the warmth of unmitigated acceptance. Temptation is an invitation into this love as He faithfully draws us out from sources of empty promises and shallow highs to the abundance of life in Him.

That's what the driver who propositioned me in a taxi truly longs for, even if he could never find the words for the mysterious ache within. It's the hope we desire to share with him and others like him wandering the globe without the truth. It's what the fallen pastor needs in the aftermath of his sin and what I need when my heart craves acceptance from perfect strangers.

The good news for all is that the heart of Jesus is tender toward and freely available to each one of us. His grace is so great that we can access it right in the middle of our most shocking moments. As we face all kinds of wickedness in the world and in our own hearts, we can turn away to worship Him. Our awe-inspired song will proclaim, "Our God is an awesome God!"

—Amber Taube

Chapter 37

WONDER WOMAN

Ah yes, the comparison trap. I could write an entire book on the topic purely from personal experience.

Now in my forties, after almost twenty years on the mission field, primarily in a remote location working with a wonderful indigenous people group, I sometimes feel like a little old Yoda sitting in my far away perch becoming wrinkled and wise. "Care what people think, I don't," I say, nodding sagely.

And it's true. Well, sort of. I certainly care way less than ever before what people think of me. I've learned from both bitter and beautiful experiences that things are often not what they seem. As Scripture reminds us about spiritual things we "only see through a glass darkly," so too in this earthly realm I realize I'm rarely privy to the whole story. There's always more going on beneath the surface. What I see—of a person, a ministry, a relationship, a situation—is only a sliver.

I chide myself. How can I possibly judge or compare based on a sliver?

And yet, to my shame, I have.

Many years ago (cue Yoda voice)...there was a stunning missionary lady on the field. I mean, she was virtually a Nicole Kidman look-alike. Missionary men and locals alike could barely resist staring whenever she walked by, golden locks swinging, perfect figure obvious regardless of what she wore. Not only that, she was gifted. In a gazillion ways. She was a well-known cook and despite often not having the right ingredients would whip up a feast on her small jungle stove. I, on the other hand, hated to cook. When I was first married, I kid you not, I had to look up in a recipe book how to boil an egg. Never mind a gourmet feast.

The stunning missionary's ministry efforts always seemed to be at the top of the mission's newsletter or on the front of the quarterly magazine. She effortlessly learned the main language of the country and, so we heard, would share the Gospel fluently with all she met. Once I happened to be in a taxi with her, and it was true. Paying no heed to me in the back seat, she faced the driver and launched into a fluent presentation of the Gospel ending with a challenge to the somewhat bedazzled, astonished man.

She also quickly learned the tribal dialect in the remote area she and her husband worked in. I, on the other hand, was a terrible language learner. Words flew in one ear and straight out the other no matter how many times I revised them. And I had trouble telling taxi drivers where I wanted to go, let alone sharing eternal truths with them.

She developed a health program for women, delivered babies, sewed up wounds, trained local clinic workers, and worked out a system where patients could pawn something for a time if they had no money to pay for medicine. I, on the other hand, looked blankly at the "patients" on our porch and offered Tylenol if they had ten pesos to pay for it.

Not only that, this vibrant lady translated the New Testament into the indigenous dialect, wrote Bible lessons, and then taught them, often in local seminars which she organized and financed from donations from the States. I, on the other hand, um, looked after my children each day and battled to teach them elementary math and how to read.

I only met this Wonder Woman a few times. At first I was filled with awe. She was my role model, and I aspired to be just like her. But the longer we were on the field, the longer I came face-to-face with my own insecurities and inadequacies, both real and imagined. Much of it was to do with fearing my husband's disappointment in the missionary I wasn't.

Surely he'd much prefer a Wonder Woman. Not to mention one who looked like a movie star with flowing fair locks. I had glasses, was shaped like a stick, and had thick, unruly, plain brown hair which I always wore in a messy bun.

The occasional time our paths crossed, I'd squint my eyes in a very un-Yoda like way at Wonder Woman and suspect she was flirting with my husband. And surely he was sighing wishing his wife was more like her.

Jealously was sown and took root.

I fought it valiantly for years, a thorn in the flesh of sorts. I knew it was wrong. I knew God had called me, inadequacies and all, to be where we were on our own little island in our own little village. God had brought my husband and me together, and like it or not, he was stuck with me.

Yet the battle raged. *Why didn't you make me more like Wonder Woman, God?* I'd demand. *Think of all the good things I could do for You. Why, oh why, am I such a failure at language, at medical care, at the whole missionary life?*

Long before the words *introvert* and *extrovert* were common, I knew I struggled with people. I loved people, but they utterly exhausted me. I may even, on occasion, have been heard to mutter after the umpteenth person on the porch that day—"Good grief! Missionary life would be great if it weren't for all the people!"

I mean, what kind of missionary *thinks* those things let alone gives voice to them?

Certainly not Wonder Woman.

The jealousy was eating me up, and I hated the ugliness inside of me. "Lord, You have to help me—please. I cannot go on like this." Putting Wonder Woman off to one side and recognizing the problem in me was, I think, the first step towards healing.

I realized too that I was possibly being unfair, and I deeply believed in giving people a fair chance. So I instructed myself, as prompted by the Spirit, that next time our paths crossed I should make an effort to get to *know* Wonder Woman. I also began to pray for her, although admittedly sometimes my prayers were simply words from the Psalms as my fragile heart still felt intimidated, unsure how she could possibly need my prayers and how does one even pray for a paragon?

Before long it was our field conference. We all crowded around to board the bus for the two-hour journey to the conference grounds. Wonder Woman's husband had offered to go with the truck taking the luggage, and as I herded the children up the bus steps, I noticed her sitting at the front, alone.

"Hon, you take the kids. I have someone I need to sit by," I hissed to my husband.

"Ah, hi, can I sit here?"

She looked up, surprised, then smiled her megawatt smile. I smiled back with a closed mouth, conscious of my crooked teeth. Oh dear. Well, I'd stepped out now, no turning back, *God, You'll have to help me, please!*

The trip was somewhat awkward. But I put any conversational skills I'd ever learned into practice, and in as genuine a manner as I could, I sought to get to know my missionary rival better.

By and by she relaxed. "You know," she confided, "I do struggle."

What?! I tried not to gape.

"Er, how's that?" I asked.

"I really don't have any missionary friends on the field. I don't know why. I can't really relate to anyone much. I guess that's why

I pour myself into our work. At least my local friends accept me as I am."

I made sympathetic noises, my mind reeling with the shock of her confession, yet also quite sure I knew why she didn't have many expat friends. It's hard to relate to a Wonder Woman.

The bus pulled in, and the moments were gone.

"Thanks so much for sitting by me," she said, "I really appreciate it."

I smiled and waved a "Seeya" goodbye. Inside I was full of shame at my jealousy. And sad that my female colleagues on the field seemed in the same boat as me, any interaction with this woman sparking in them powerful feelings of inadequacy too.

I confess. I still didn't really like her. We simply didn't click. We never became best friends or anything. But I continued to at least TRY and be her friend and show care. I sensed an ever so slight loosening of the grip of ugliness inside me.

Many months passed. Maybe it was even some years. Little by little I learned and grew, realizing I was, in fact, exactly who God wanted in our place of ministry at this particular point in time with my own husband. Failings, shortcomings and all, I was just what the local church needed at that time of their growth.

It was such a revelation. Such a relief. They didn't NEED a Wonder Woman who could and would do it all for them. They needed me who couldn't do it, so they would need to take up the mantle of medical and Bible studies and teaching themselves. Oh, it was a glorious relief, and I finally thanked God for all the things

We're Going There

He hadn't made me.

Yet still there was that final root of the obnoxious weed of jealousy. Wonder Woman still preyed on my mind when I was having a bad day. It didn't happen often anymore, but it did happen. And it was still a thorn in the flesh, not drawing me closer to Him but hindering my walk with Jesus.

So one day I had it out with Him. *Why can't I be rid of this jealousy? I know You've made me who I am. Why am I still comparing myself with her? Why do I still feel so inadequate at times? All I'm good for is caring for my five children and looking after my husband so he can have a full on ministry.*

Tears flowed. I wrote and wrote in my journal for pages, seeking to exorcize this remaining fragment of bitterness and self-pity.

Finally, utterly drained, I waited.

And as always, in due time, He came.

Child, you say all you do is care for your children. At this time in your life, that IS your particular ministry for Me.

Then suddenly my eyes were opened, and I realized something I'd never thought of before, obvious though it was.

Wonder Woman had no children.

I'd always been puzzled by this but assumed she'd chosen ministry over family. Until one day I heard a whisper of many miscarriages.

I'd had several miscarriages over the years. But I also had five strong children bursting with health and life.

And just like that compassion flooded my heart, and the final root was ripped up. I had indeed only been seeing a sliver of the whole story. I suspected there was still far, far more to Wonder Woman than I'd ever know. While I looked only at her accomplishments and skills and was filled with envy, she was battling demons of her own I couldn't possibly begin to imagine.

I was ashamed.

Yet also thankful the faithful Father helped me see. There always is more to a person, a situation, a ministry, a life.

Comparing ourselves, as the Good Book says, is not wise.

It's been many years now since I've even thought about Wonder Woman. She was greatly used by God in many peoples' lives in this country. Today people know Christ because of her. Others are walking with Him.

But she is no longer here. She's moved on. Away to other things.

While I remain. In my little Yoda perch. Grateful for the person God's made me to be and continuing to learn to rejoice in others no matter how they appear and to grow in what He has for me now.

—Anonymous

Chapter 38

A STORY OF BETRAYAL
AND OF RENEWAL

I remember a conversation with my nephew and his mom, when he asked "Why." Why was his much beloved uncle engaging in such risky behavior? At the time, my response was that some of us can learn by watching mistakes, while others seem to need to make all the mistakes themselves before they'll learn.

Now after having lived through a failing marriage, I feel my answer was very simplistic. But there's truth in it also. For those of us on the outside, we watch friends or family get ensnared by adultery, and we ask, "How could they be so stupid? How could they fall for that trap?" It's a complex question with complex answers. I have mulled over the steps of the disintegration of my marriage many times, and I will try to share what I have learned through it.

To keep this in the right tone, I will not give full details. I want to share truth but not be salacious, and I have asked God for the words to tell it. So here's my story—my husband and I married right out of college with sweet hopes for a life of serving God together. We both felt called to serve God in church ministry, and possibly even to follow His call to overseas work. Our courtship had included much prayer, seeking God's will, service in churches, and sexual purity. However, we had both had experiences of sexual abuse as children, and we both had low self-esteem and huge needs. We tended toward some spiritual resistance and had not fully surrendered to God's lordship. While we had eagerly looked forward to being married, we were still seeking the thrill of romance and allowed flirtatious behavior in our relationships with the opposite sex. So extramarital "crushes" began, and over a period of about ten years they became more entangling until my husband's first full-blown affair.

By that time our marriage included blowups, tears, arguments, accusations, and we had gone to counseling many times. I was distressed and trying to be a better wife, but I also had done a lot of work to come to wholeness after the wounds of my youth. I knew his "crushes" were getting more intense, but I was shocked when the first sexual affair happened. We had to leave our home and our church, but because my husband was so gifted for ministry, I believed that he could be restored, and I was determined never to divorce.

Unfortunately I did not know how addictive the thrill of illicit sex would be, and we then went through four more affairs, revealed in two more major crises, over a period of twelve years. Finally a voice inside me said, "It's over," and I knew that I would give my husband the divorce he had been asking for. By that time, I felt more devastated by the scandal of being a divorced woman than by losing him. I had been determined never to be divorced, after watching my mother go through it. In fact, I believe I had a judgmental attitude toward divorced women, calling them "failures" in my subconscious mind.

There's so much more that could be said about this twenty-plus year experience and the years following, during which God held me and provided for me. He poured His Scriptures into my mind to give me strength for my new life. They were very hard years for my children and me to recover and heal from the blow to our family. Always I felt that God was teaching me and sanctifying me, and I definitely have been able to comfort others with the comfort that I received from Him. So let me try to give the essential truths that God taught me.

The first is that God is my husband. Isaiah 54:5 says, "For your Maker is your husband—the Lord Almighty is his name—the Holy One of Israel is your Redeemer; he is called the God of all the earth" (NIV). God is the only one who can fill the empty holes in our hearts, and He wants to do it with His great love and tenderness. We must not push away from Him. Wholeness and healing come when we seek Him always and come into His embrace morning and evening.

My rebellious, arrogant spirit kept me from believing this for many years. Instead of believing that total surrender was the best and only way, I tried to fill that void with other things. I know I'm not alone in this; I see so many people doing it around me, both believers and non-believers. We are allowing the evil one to deceive us with his lies, that we are "smarter," that we can play with temptations, that we can hold back some of ourselves against the full claim of God. This leads into my second truth.

We are able to lie to ourselves and then believe the lie. How else would a gifted minister be ensnared by adultery? We all know the boundaries; we know with our brain what the right action is. But we are also able to disconnect between what we excuse as a little flirtation and what any other observer would call risky behavior. Now that I've lived through it, I can see other people crossing the line of safe interactions into unsafe relationships. It really disturbs me to see Christian leaders do this. I know they believe they can control the situation and that what they are doing is harmless, just in fun.

But I also see Christian leaders who are very careful and who always keep a safe tone in their opposite sex relationships. These leaders keep in mind that they are accountable to God and that showing His love to a Christian sister or brother means loving them in a godly way, not in a way that would cause harm, which illicit relationships do. There's no way that luring someone into adultery is showing them love. The starkness of that statement compared to the permissiveness of worldly sexual ideas almost seems incongruous. But it shows how we fall into deception when we feel that we have found "true love" in a new extramarital relationship. As Proverbs 2:18 says, the way to the adulterer's door is the way to death. We must not be deceived by any lie that minimizes the damage or gives special exemptions for our relationships because we're "not like anyone else." The deceiver works overtime to cause as much damage to Christian marriages as he can, and we can clearly see this in current divorce rates.

We must set our boundaries and not allow flirtations. Flirting is not harmless, instead it is very risky. Once you allow any type of "romance" to develop, you cannot just turn off the switch in your brain. You have opened a door to emotional entrapment, and only great mental discipline and time will remove the emotions and the thrill of the chase. This is part of the trap, that once the emotions start you can't turn them off. Therefore, it is so important to have intentional boundaries and keep your emotions for the appropriate recipient—your spouse, or for God, if you are single.

First Corinthians 6:18 tells us, "Flee from sexual immorality. All other sins a person commits are outside the body, but whoever sins sexually sins against their own body" (NIV). This confused me because it seems that any sin separates us from God and, therefore, must affect us inwardly and outwardly. But one way I've come to understand this verse is that because sex is such an intimate action and should only occur in the covenant of marriage, sex outside of marriage causes harm on all levels—emotional, spiritual, mental, and physical. By having a pure relationship with God, we are able to more fully enjoy each other and have a richer sexual relationship. God designed this act for us, so we must do it according to the way He designed it.

Our brains are chemically wired to make soothing behavior easy to repeat. Once our brain identifies that a behavior causes soothing chemicals to release, neural pathways are formed that become habitual, which then require disciplined steps to rewire. We can see this in our tendency to default to any activity or thought pattern that initially felt soothing. If we are not attentive to these behaviors, they will soon become a habit. (An excellent book explaining this is *You Are Not Your Brain* by Jeffrey Schwartz and Rebecca Gladding.)

The addictive behaviors are easy to see—eating, spending, alcohol, leisure activities of many types, and sex or romance. My ex-husband had a love/sex addiction and spent a month in a treatment center. He was supposed to attend an addiction recovery support group after being released. Over time he stopped attending, and the affairs resumed. Because he did not resolutely address the primary addiction, he developed parallel addictions, including alcoholism. Having watched this struggle, I have great sympathy for people trying to become sober from whatever addiction they have. It's a lifelong battle, and it might be said that some people are more prone to become addicts than others. Those of us who are able to recognize and avoid addictions should be thankful and should prayerfully support our family and friends who are trying to become sober. Prayer support is the best we can do; emotional and financial support can be exhausting.

Isaiah 61:1-4 is one of my favorite passages, and I felt God's favor in His work of comforting, bestowing beauty instead of ashes, even restoring the ruins of my life. God ministers to the broken-hearted; He proclaims freedom for the captives and release from darkness for the prisoners. We are a planting of the Lord for the display of His favor. There's so much sweetness and healing in those words—I feel the balm in my soul. God's care is personal and perfect. The question of "Why?" won't be answered in this span of time, but we will understand more when we are with our Heavenly Father and can see more from His perspective. I conclude by saying that I paid a price for my ex-husband's adultery, and my children as well, but I know God has healed, restored, and called me to serve overseas in this second half of my life. He is doing His beautiful ministry through me as I walk beside Him and is teaching me so much about His redemptive, sanctifying love. He truly does work everything for our good.

—*Anonymous*

Chapter 39

RESTORING BEAUTY FROM BROKENNESS

You are not alone, dear friend. We all have places inside of us where it feels safer to hide in the dark than risk revealing what is holding us in a tangle of shame and lies from the enemy of our souls. I know how it feels to carry pain you are terrified to share with anyone. I know the deep ache that results from hiding parts of your soul so deeply that you can be in a room full of people and feel desperately alone. I'm familiar with the confusion and chaos that builds so quickly in our minds when we are afraid to let our true selves be seen and loved. I know the weight of believing that no one could possibly understand my pain.

I always knew when I grew up I wanted to be a good Christian wife, mother, and missionary. Emphasis on *good*: I always wanted to do the right thing, respond the right way, and glorify God in my life. I knew I wasn't perfect, but from the outside looking in, well, let's just say I maintained a good reputation, never mind my pride or struggles with self-sufficiency. Truthfully, if there is any good in me it's because of God's grace, "For it is God who works in you, both to will and to work for his good pleasure" (Philippians 2:13, ESV). I didn't realize how my idealistic dreams and expectations left little room for the reality of brokenness and weakness or for the sometimes slow process of sanctification and redemption.

For me, international travel, transition, packing, unpacking, setting up house, establishing ministry and relationships, and all the other things involved in missionary life felt all-consuming. Somehow the deeper issues of life always seemed to surface in the middle of transitions. Sometimes it felt like I was constantly putting out fires, just dealing with the next urgent thing, all the while telling myself, *Someday I'll take time to process this more deeply. After this [next big change or major crisis], we'll be able to take some time to focus on our marriage. Soon I'll have more time to address these concerns in more depth... but for now I just have to keep on keeping on.*

Without even realizing it, I was packing things away, pretending everything was fine, not understanding that these "little" struggles were not trivial interruptions but were actually making up my life. The emotions I didn't "have time to feel" were getting buried alive. I had no idea how good I had become at "stuffing and pretending" until suddenly my world began to fall apart. I couldn't pretend anymore, to myself or anyone else.

I'll never forget the words of a dear friend as I sat with her in a coffee shop, tears streaming down my face: "It's okay to not be okay. You can let go. God is bigger than your problems. You don't have to try to control things. You don't have to hold it all together.

You can let it all crumble; God is big enough." My heart resonated with the truth she spoke, even though I didn't feel confident in how to walk forward in my brokenness.

This was a turning point. I had finally hit rock bottom, and what I found there was the grace and mercy of God. This "good Christian girl" had nothing more to offer, yet I received the loving, compassionate gaze of my Savior—not because of anything I had done, but simply because of who He is. All of my serving, all of my pretending, all of my trying fell by the wayside as I began to learn what it really means to receive God's unmerited favor (grace).

What was it that finally caused my world to crumble around me? I had struggled with anxiety and depression for years at this point. Clearly, I did not have healthy ways of dealing with real life. And my personal baggage coordinated all too well with my husband's baggage. The Lord had given my husband the courage to confess to me point blank, "I've been looking at pornography."

I was shocked and devastated. How could I have been so oblivious? For a long time, I had minimized any concerns, assuring myself there was no way this could be an issue in our marriage. The truth was staring me in the face, but everything in me wanted to turn away and continue to pretend we were "fine." My mind was spinning. I didn't want to overreact, but I didn't know what to do with this crushing revelation. My illusions of our marriage being healthy and strong were shredded instantly by the reality and gravity of his confession.

We're Going There

Suddenly, the man I thought I knew so well felt like a stranger to me. The one person I knew and loved and trusted the most had hurt me in the deepest way. I felt so helpless and alone. I wanted to scream. But instead, I lay silent as the enemy began to plant lies in the fertile soil of the deep pain in my heart: "You weren't enough for him. You never were beautiful. You are worthless. You are replaceable. You always knew there was something wrong with you." Alongside the lies, the voice of shame was saying, "You can't tell anyone about this because then they will know how bad you both are."

Even in the midst of this overwhelming flood of emotions and thoughts I experienced the comfort of God's presence and truth. I knew, no matter how lonely and hopeless I felt, God was with me and would accomplish His good purposes even through this painful trial. Truth from a testimony I had heard over a decade earlier rang loud and clear in my mind that miserable night: *The only woman a man can enjoy sexually without guilt before God is his wife.* It comforted me to know and continually remind myself that I was the only woman God meant for my husband to enjoy sexually.

Facing personal brokenness on the field as a missionary can be frightening and includes layers of uncertainty. What if we're found out? Will we be sent home? Where can we get help? Dealing with the fallout in our personal lives while facing the possibility of being sent home felt impossible and overwhelming. We kept our struggles pretty quiet, only sharing with a few people. I pulled myself together as quickly as possible and fought hard to regain some sense of normalcy. We knew we had a long, hard road ahead of us.

The early days of our healing journey were wrought with pain and difficult conversations. The only thing that sustained me through that dark valley was God and the Truth of His Word. Immersing myself in Scripture, praying, and meditating on the truth gave me courage and strength to keep moving forward. Often I felt like I was just going through the motions, doing the next thing. I didn't realize it then, but I was grieving the marriage I thought I had, and God was gently removing the idol our marriage had been in my heart.

Our journey of healing, recovery, forgiveness, reconciliation, and rebuilding felt slow and required lots of deep heart work in the presence of the Lord. He was faithful to bring His people alongside us: friends, family members, counselors, and pastors. Some walked with us through a single pivotal conversation and prayer time; others spent countless hours listening to our hearts, caring for our wounds, and praying for each of us and our marriage.

The enemy whispered the lie that sin is too shameful to bring into the light, but God's Word reminded me that His love is full and complete right in the middle of our messy brokenness. He never asked for my performance or perfection, He only asked that I surrender my heart, for my soul to be laid bare before Him in honest humility and sweet dependence.

We're Going There

Healing required the choice to obey God in forgiveness, which opened the door to compassion. I distinctly remember the day I voiced that forgiveness to my husband; a small seed of healing was planted. Living out forgiveness, seeing it blossom and flourish in my heart, has been a journey. You see, I've learned that in order to forgive deeply we must feel deeply, for we can only forgive at the level to which we embrace the pain. It is to that extent that we release the grace and healing in our own hearts that God offers through the gift of forgiveness. To address it and forgive it, we must first acknowledge it and feel it.

Nothing prepared me for the compassion God would put in my heart for my husband's brokenness as I watched him courageously pursue healing and freedom. Through material from Pure Desire Ministries, my husband learned that his battle with pornography was bigger than behavior modification or sin management. It was an addiction, and the only way out was deep heart work with God. I began to see him make radical choices to root out this sinful coping mechanism. The day he chose to openly confess his sin to our pastor marked a milestone in our freedom journey.

Previously I had no concept of the level of deep woundedness that drove him to the snare of pornography. But as I watched him walk with Jesus straight into the darkest valley of his childhood and experience the transforming power of God to bring healing to the deepest, long-standing wounds in his soul, I was broken and humbled by the gift God had given me in this man who is my husband.

Step by step God walked with us on this journey. Each victory gave us more strength; each milestone grew courage in our hearts to take the next step of obedience. The day came when we knew we needed to be transparent with our mission organization. This meant walking directly toward some of our worst fears and trusting God for the outcome. Would we be disqualified for missionary service? Would we have to resign from the organization? I had heard rumors that left fear in my heart, but I clung to the promise of Psalm 37:23-24, "The steps of a man are established by the Lord, when he delights in his way; though he fall, he shall not be cast headlong, for the Lord upholds his hand" (ESV).

Our future felt precarious but one thing we knew for certain: life-altering decisions would be made on our behalf as a result of what we were about to share. Though we entered that meeting with fear and trembling, we came out with peace and joy in our hearts. We felt heard, understood, cared for, and supported in our pursuit of healing. Our mission intentionally came alongside us in the most encouraging ways, allowing us time and space to work through things in our personal lives and marriage. We were not disqualified, kicked out, or told we could not return to the field. Instead, we were loved, cared for, and supported in our journey toward healing and restoration.

The Word of God truly is a lamp to our feet. When we expose our sin to the light in humility and repentance, the power of the cross is made evident in our lives. We learned the freedom and sweet fellowship that come to those who walk in the light as He is in the light (1 John 1:7). We experienced the healing that comes when we confess our sins to one another and pray for one another (James 5:16). This place of surrender and utter dependence on the Lord became the bedrock for true healing and restoration in our marriage.

The Lord has blessed us, brought us through much healing, and given us a deep and beautiful intimacy in our marriage. I choose to continue to fight for the intimacy and unity the Lord designed marriage to carry. This means continually coming before the Lord as the Healer and Restorer of my soul and my marriage. He chose marriage to be the symbol that represents Christ and the Church. Dear sisters, as global women, my prayer is that our marriages continue to grow and exemplify the love, sacrifice, vulnerability, and commitment God meant for marriage to manifest in the world.

I can honestly say I am thankful for this journey the Lord has brought us through. Not only did He set my husband free from the bondage of addiction, He also used it to strip away the pretenses and tear down idols in my heart. Walking through this felt like my whole life was falling apart, crumbling before my very eyes. Yet any identity I had outside of Christ was just an illusion. No wonder it crumbled so easily: God was stripping it away because of His deep love for me. It was costly, it was hard, it was humbling, but it was more than worth it all. God has worked an authenticity and beauty into the fabric of our marriage that we didn't even know was possible. All glory to God "who is able to do far more abundantly than all that we ask or think according to the power at work within us" (Ephesians 3:20-21, ESV).

—*Christina M. Post*

Chapter 40

GOD'S GRACE IN THE DETAILS

My family and I landed in South Africa on January 20, 2020, just two days before Wuhan went into lockdown. When we left China, I didn't pack to move home. I left most of my belongings and all our winter clothes in our small Chinese apartment. The plan was to stay a little longer than my (now) ex-husband and sort out our eldest son's new passport.

After three weeks, he flew back to China as the only passenger on the plane. At this point I was still determined to go back, to keep the promise I made on our wedding day as well as the secret I had kept for years. No one knew about the abuse. At first, my decision not to tell anyone was because I was ashamed. I didn't even want to admit it to myself. Later I made the decision for our safety and in an attempt to protect the people I love, knowing how hard it would be for them to know and not be able to do anything to help me.

With the lockdown, I realized that not only would I go back to an apartment on the sixth floor of a Chinese high-rise, but I would be stuck in there keeping two boys quiet while my increasingly aggressive husband worked online. By the grace of God, I missed the lockdown the first time.

Sometimes when you are in the middle of a situation you cannot see clearly or be objective about what is really going on. What I needed was the perspective gained from being miles away. Instead of having to replay an argument in my head, I could read it in black and white. Everything became so clear when an argument about a decision I made in the best interest of our youngest son (against his wishes) escalated to a point where he told me I had three days to get back to China or my sons would not see their grandparents for the next five to seven years. His comments and threats were so demeaning, and as I read through them, I realized that this was a reflection of our communication the past eight years. I kept apologizing for things I didn't even do wrong, trying to calm him while he just kept on accusing, shifting the blame, and forcing his opinion.

I read our conversation to my parents, and afterwards my mom asked if he ever lifted his hand against me. At this point I realized that I had kept a secret, but I never needed to lie. No one ever asked. I still do not know how to share this information with our missionary friends in Thailand. We planted a church there where he and two other pastors took turns preaching. I could think of no way to explain that just the night before he preached that amazing sermon on love, he hit and kicked me everywhere that would not be visible the next day, even in a dress.

I knew once I started speaking the truth there was no going back. I told my parents what was really going on. My dad told me that it was my decision, but if I stayed, he would help me to get back on my feet financially, illuminating one of the biggest reasons why I would have gone back. After moving to China six months prior to our visit to South Africa, I was financially, emotionally, and socially dependent on my ex-husband.

The next day I went to speak with our pastor who gave me great advice, saying that in a situation like this you have one of three choices. You try to change the circumstances, you accept it, or you walk away. He made it clear that if you decide to walk away from a toxic situation, you don't go back because it will likely get worse. I felt that I had exhausted options one and two, and that all that was left was to walk away.

The afternoon after I came back from visiting the pastor, one of my best friends was waiting at home for me, and that night the only two people who came to my parents' home were their lawyer and his wife. When my phone connected to our Wi-Fi, all of a sudden my WhatsApp account was deactivated and deleted from my phone. My email and all my other social media accounts were hacked. I think he was trying to destroy evidence of the threats, which would have been gone, if I hadn't sent the evidence to my mom the previous day. I made my decision not to go back and to file for divorce with the help of my parents, a dear friend, our pastor, and our lawyer. This felt like a Godsend since I needed support to help me make the right decision.

Our lawyer advised me to file for a restraining order based on the threats and history of violence. He also said that because I was currently unemployed I should seek assistance from Legal Aid instead of using a private lawyer. When I went to Legal Aid the next day to file for divorce, which was also the start of our first lockdown, they showed me the door insisting that they were not taking any new clients and that the courts would also be closed for some time.

I felt like I was at a dead end. At least he was in China, and because of the lockdown he could not physically get to me. This was a comforting thought, since the most dangerous time in an abusive relationship is when the victim decides to leave. This didn't stop him from using every other avenue to get to me, especially through the boys who he insisted on video chatting with daily, only to show no interest in their lives but use the opportunity to tell them over and over that they have a "bad mommy." Being an IT specialist he also declared some sort of cyber war, deleting my website, my book from Amazon, and other online points of connection that he knew were precious.

A week later the sheriff knocked on our door to deliver a thirteen-page long court order filed against me in the High Court. This document insisted that the boys were in danger, that I was abusing and neglecting them, and that they should immediately be removed from my custody. If they could not be sent to China, they should go to live with their paternal grandparents. He also filed a police case against me, and the family violence investigator of our province came to do an investigation. It didn't take the investigator long to realize none of the accusations were true. Although this was one of the worst experiences of my life, the only result was that since there was a case against me and I needed a defense attorney, Legal Aid had to help me. Despite the fact that the case against me was retracted, I was now one of Legal Aid's clients, and I ended up with the amazing lawyer everyone recommended to me. After becoming familiar with my case, she insisted on helping me further and filed for divorce.

In the same week the family violence investigator came to our farm, I suffered a severe back injury. I think my body was giving in from all the emotional stress and drama. I ended up at our local physiotherapist who also became familiar with my story and knew that I was in the process of getting my own licensing back in order to be able to practice as a physiotherapist again. Two months later she made me an offer to open a satellite practice in a smaller town nearby. Our farm is in the middle of the two towns so it was very doable for me to stay with my parents while starting off with a few days a week. In a time where many people were losing their jobs because of COVID-19, I was so grateful for the opportunity to do a job I love again.

My lawyer recommended a good therapist, initially for one of my boys, but I ended up seeing her. What a wonderful gift this turned out to be. I believe therapy saved me years in the healing process. I also made a friend with someone who went through a similar experience, and she taught me that it was okay to be angry. After years of walking on eggshells, I was safe now, and I could find safe ways to work through my anger and all the other emotions I stuffed down for so long.

In August 2020 I started working and decided to take the boys to a small kindergarten in the same town. Around this same time my lawyer managed to set up an ultimatum for my ex-husband stating that he was allowed to speak to the boys, but there were certain things he could not discuss with them. He refused to sign it, claiming that if he could not tell them the truth he would rather not speak to them at all. This was the last time we heard from him.

One of the details that probably contributed to him giving up his initial fight to get the children has to do with an international law called the Hague Convention. This law was made in regards to international cases of child abduction. My husband claimed that I was guilty of "parental abduction" although he left the kids with me and even signed the necessary document for me to travel alone with them. For this law to be effective, both countries had to be on the list of countries who signed the convention. China was one of the very few countries that did not sign it. Thailand, where we lived for seven years prior to our six months in China did sign it, so if the exact same scenario played out while we were living in Thailand, they would have taken the children back to our house there and only then started the investigation.

We're Going There

At the beginning of 2021 I realized that as much as I enjoyed working part-time as a physiotherapist again, I would need to do something else if I ever wanted to be financially independent. I considered writing medical articles or something I could do remotely since I believed it was in the boys' best interest to stay on my parents' farm and give them time to get settled. I discussed this with a friend who used to be a secretary at my boys' school. A week later, the day before the school session started, my youngest boy's teacher quit practically overnight. My friend called me asking if this was something I would be interested in, knowing that I worked as a teacher while we were overseas. I sent in my resume the next day, and less than a week later I was appointed.

I was still stressed during this time because although my ex-husband didn't communicate directly with us anymore, he was sending hateful messages to my lawyer and threatened to come to South Africa and sort everything out on his own. Because he didn't follow the correct procedure, our divorce went through without any drama in April 2021. Because Legal Aid helped me, I had no debt from any of the legal procedures. I started feeling relieved after that, still working through the trauma with my therapist and slowly settling into what felt like a second chance at life.

If someone told me ten years ago I would be a divorced single mom in one of the smallest towns in South Africa working as a physiotherapist and kindergarten teacher, I would have laughed. Now I cannot imagine being anywhere else. I do not regret the experience I gained from living overseas and being in a toxic relationship. Maybe one day I will have the opportunity to help others who find themselves in similar situations. In the meantime, I'm just grateful for my freedom and for the opportunity to be so immersed in a community that really feels like the village I longed for. I truly believe God can use us wherever we are and that we always end up where we need to be, even if it's just for a season.

His love is in the details of the way He guides, protects and provides. When I reflect on the past two years and all the ways I've healed, it gives me peace about the future. Knowing it may not be an easy road ahead, I feel like I can trust that God will be there every step of the way.

—Dorette

Chapter 41

(BROKEN) LOVE STORY

"You just left me!" my fiancé shouts. "In the middle of a city I don't know. You just drove away." Our wedding is supposed to be in just a few days.

Feverish with anger and July's midday heat, we are standing by the road in my parents' suburban neighborhood. Dagi, an Ethiopian who has only touched down in my hometown of Indianapolis a few weeks ago, has had to puzzle out a bus route to return to my parents' home where we are both staying before the wedding. He's just been walking from the bus stop.

By now I am shouting too, my body shaking with screams and desperation. "You told me to!" I recall that moment earlier in the day, after yet another argument, when he dared me to go, and I did. I slipped into the car, trembling with tears, and punched the gas—leaving him stranded downtown, alone.

Suddenly a police car stops, and a window rolls down. "You guys okay?" the officer asks. "Some neighbors were calling about a public disturbance." With a shock of shame, I look around at the homes surrounding us, wondering who called. Perhaps someone our family has been trying to show God's love to over the years. Perhaps that bridge has now been broken.

I am too exasperated to consider what other bridges Dagi and I have broken recently. We are both in ministry. I am a teacher at an international mission school in Addis Ababa, Ethiopia, the city where I met Dagi, the media and communications coordinator and interim youth leader at our church.

For the thousandth time since we landed in America—thrashing in that cauldron of prenuptial stress and culture shock (mine reverse)—I wonder if we should call off the wedding. Even though we have filled out endless stacks of forms for Dagi's fiancé visa. Even though we have already prepared everything from the venue to the vows. Even though, in the deepest reaches of myself, I still love him.

To this day I can't remember what ignited the downtown fight that escalated to the one by the roadside. At the time, we'd been fighting so much all the arguments knotted together. But I do remember a common thread: a serpentine selfishness growing more entangled and engorged the more we engaged in sexual sin.

Our love story unfolded in the sun-glittered streets of Addis Ababa. After lunch with friends one Sunday, Dagi noticed the key I wore around my neck, and even then I had the feeling he would win the one to my heart. I hold our early moments like little jewels in my palm: That first day, how he guided me across the dusty street, delicately pressing the small of my back. How he listened to the heartbeat of the paintings in the café gallery and told me what he heard. How he made me laugh after those Ethio-jazz concerts, in that hidden garden under a scattering of stars. How his eyes silvered with tears once when he spoke about God.

I loved how he didn't treat me like a pastel figurine, as everyone else did who mistook my quietness for fragility. He could see through my "good Christian girl" smile to the beating red life beneath. Perhaps that's where part of the problem started. On the outside, I was a Bible-scrubbed missionary. And it wasn't all façade; I truly did desire to know and love God. In the fraught journey of coming to Ethiopia, God had shown me His perfect provision, His shepherding. In preparation for leaving, we would talk for hours over countless walks. But I must have believed the illusion that I was too good to fall. That I, who wore the label of "missionary," could not tame the scaly dragon of my own sexual desire.

I was reluctant to kiss him at first. Perhaps I was toying with the idea of saving my first kiss until my wedding day, as I heard good Christian single people did. At night after dates we would stand in the shadow of the church that neighbored the missionary compound, and he would brush his lips over my face and neck. I would revel in the sensation of being desired, as the prickles of my own desire awakened, but I did not kiss back. Until one night. In the dark of the parked car, I couldn't think of any more reasons to protect myself, and my lips came alive.

Mouth kisses soon became neck kisses and collarbone kisses, and the kisses moved past the places I covered with my modest missionary clothing. In the dark of night, we would park just off an exit, lean back the car seats, and I would think of something my aunt said about the boyfriend who got her pregnant at the age of eighteen: *We wanted to be as close to each other as we possibly could.*

It's tragically ironic to me now, but the places we most often chose to be alone together were the places where we were supposed to be doing ministry: my apartment on the missionary compound and Dagi's office at the church. Once after service— after we had worshiped in the sanctuary, after we had prayed with the saints, after we had, perhaps, confessed, heads pressed to our knees in communion—Dagi and I found ourselves alone in his office, bound within each other's arms, lips against lips. Petrified of someone seeing us, I tried to listen for approaching footfall. Anyone—the pastor, a member of the youth group Dagi was mentoring, a fellow church member, one of my students—could have seen us pressed against a wall.

We were careful not to pass the boundary into sexual intercourse and kept some parts of our bodies off limits. Though the lines for appropriate touch can be gray, we knew without a doubt what we were doing was wrong. Fear warned first. I became afraid that my secret escapades would morph into missionary gossip, and my reputation would shatter. Looking back I'm astounded at our blindness. We parked in cars any compound missionary could identify, often off an exit just a few miles from where we lived. I'm sure colleagues drove past with their children, one of whom I signed up to mentor one year.

Bigger than the fear was the guilt. I would wake up after a night of intimate caressing and feel hungover with guilt. I would think of the high school students I taught, students I was supposed to be a model to. I was a missionary, charged with communicating the divine love and holiness of God through my mind, heart, words—and body. What would they say if they knew what I did after the sun slipped behind the mountains?

I would ask God for forgiveness again and again, but His grace became more and more cheap to me. I would entangle myself in Dagi's arms and kisses, knowing God would erase my guilt the moment I flicked a quick prayer heavenward. I began a habit of ignoring God, the tender nudgings of the Spirit.

Together we were building a habit of chasing our own desires for pleasure rather than sacrificing to meet the other's needs. We were hardening our hearts to compassion and gentleness. Though we knew we were creating sinful habits, we had no idea of their destructive, far-reaching effects.

Now years later, I wonder what ministry opportunities I lost through persistently choosing pleasure over purpose. But I was so addicted to the electricity of touch that I became willing to ruin my testimony, my platform for sharing the Gospel, the whole reason I'd left my parents' home in Indianapolis—for a few moments of physical thrills.

I wish I could say Dagi and I conquered this sin. I wish I could say we mustered up the strength to walk in sexual purity until our wedding day. But we didn't. And it almost cost us our relationship. After the incident with the police officer, I was deeply uncertain whether I should marry Dagi at all. My loving and godly mom, seeing our torment and wanting to protect us from further harm, encouraged us to call off the wedding. Other longtime family friends advised the same.

I can say God is merciful. Just a couple of days before the wedding, Dagi came into my bedroom, the one my mom had painted pink when I was a little girl. In the glow of the lamp that night, we sat on the bed and confessed our selfishness. He pressed me into his body in what was, perhaps for the first time, an embrace of true love. Held there, I whispered into his ear the words God was whispering into mine: "Behold I am making all things new." Dagi pointed to a book on my nightstand, Dallas Willard's *Renovation of the Heart*, and took it as a sign.

"It was God," my husband says. He is telling me what moved him to come into my room that night. Sitting together around a dish of warm butter cake, Dagi and I are celebrating our sixth anniversary.

"God is merciful," I say, at ease in the evening cool. We seek each other's hands.

Our marriage did not blossom into a fairy tale after the pastor pronounced us wed and Dagi kissed me in my frothy white gown. The selfish habits we had practiced for over a year of dating poisoned our first year of marriage. Looking back at the tortured months of consistent fighting, I see how feeble Dagi and I were to persevere together.

But God.

But God redeems.

But God redeemed our fragmented hearts and bodies.

Remembering our broken-and-redeemed love story overwhelms my heart with gratitude to God. Our story teaches me humility and grace, especially towards young people and missionaries struggling with temptation. It shows me how frail I am, how prone to wander, how profoundly in need of moment-by-moment grace like manna. It's also a story I've been able to share with other married friends, to remind them of the surpassing and infinite love of God. I know in the future, the God-Who-Redeems will continue to transform our story into bridges to reach those we seek to serve.

I cannot say I am courageous. I cannot say I found the strength in myself to overcome my broken ways. I cannot say Dagi and I saved our marriage through grit and determination. I can only say God is merciful. Without His grace, we would have walked away from the good gifts He had for us in our life together. The song I carry in my heart is that God is for us, He is for our marriage—and therein lies our hope.

—*Elise Tegegne*

Chapter 42

WHEN PAIN TURNS TO ANGER

It was autumn, but the heat of summer was nowhere near relenting. The pathetic ceiling fan in our tiny bedroom knocked about in circles, barely moving the air enough to evaporate the sweat from my back and neck while I sat on the floor repeating my new vocabulary words.

Perhaps my inferno of anger was the real source of heat. My language abilities were improving, and so was my comprehension of the violent realities being lived within the walls of my neighbors' homes and relationships. I could understand enough to learn that nearly all of the families I was interacting with had experienced extreme trauma and domestic violence. While some women's memories of life under the Taliban haunted them, others were still living a daily nightmare.

"Every man here hits his wife," one friend told me. "My father hit my mother, my husband hits me, and my sons will probably hit their wives too."

We're Going There

The heaviness of my friends' situations was bleeding into my own marriage too. I was stewing over an argument from the night before, mulling over what I *should have* said, the issues I needed him to understand, and the fact that nearly every aspect of the culture in which we lived was catered to the needs and desires of men. The men on my team, including my husband, seemed to be entirely oblivious to just how intensely the women all around them were suffering. But how could they know? Most of them had hardly spoken to an Afghan woman, let alone heard first-hand about the abuse one endured.

Afghan culture set strict boundaries on how men and women were permitted to interact. Women were simply not allowed to be seen or heard by men outside their immediate families. If this boundary was breached, the women would always be considered the guilty parties—and the price they paid was brutally high.

While the men on my team moved about without firsthand knowledge of the heavy burdens women were forced to carry, we ladies felt the ramifications of it daily as we tugged our burqas into place before stepping foot outside. Amidst the backdrop of a culture that allowed men to roam freely and kept women out of sight, my anger took aim at men.

As my frustration and loneliness intensified, I had a thought.

"Just have an affair with one of the neighbor women. They love you so much."

It was a thought unlike anything I had entertained before. It frightened me. I felt so confused by my own thoughts, wondering what was wrong with me that I would consider doing something so utterly destructive to my marriage, my neighbor, and myself. I had not felt sexual attraction to women before, but suddenly the thought of being passionately loved by someone who was not on the side of "Team Oppressor" felt appealing.

I never acted on that thought, but it easily could have been the start down a path of destruction. I'm grateful that Jesus spoke tenderly to me that day and in the days that followed.

"Come to me," He said. "You're weary from carrying these painful burdens."

The Lord showed me that my heart and mind needed tending. The anger and isolation I had been experiencing were more than just a few bad days. They were a serious reality within a culture of normalized abuse. My anger towards the men responsible for the abuse morphed into an anger towards all men in general. I was incensed with my friends' husbands, brothers, and fathers. I was resentful toward the incognizant men on my team, and I was angry that my husband was unable to fully understand what I felt. The evil one was exploiting raw wounds and pain with a plan to bring even more agony and destruction. I was aware enough of his schemes to recognize my thoughts for what they were: The voice of the deceiver offering destruction disguised as love.

Later that week, my husband and I had a serious talk about our need to be open with the difficulties each of us was facing in our separate spheres of ministry. I needed to start talking about the atrocities being recounted to me by Afghan women rather than trying to convince myself that this was just how life was in Afghanistan. The anger I felt towards men was compounded by anxiety that my sorrow was perceived as weakness. In my desire to appear resilient enough to handle the daily struggle that is life in Afghanistan, I believed that exposing my grief over the tragedies around me would be met with advice to "get used to it" or "toughen up." On some level, I was also trying to normalize abuse and violence in order to make myself resilient to the pain of it all. But painful things should hurt. Sin grieves the heart of the Father, and it should grieve mine as well. There is no weakness in feeling the pain of others.

Cole, my husband, needed to face the fact that he had been given way more responsibility than was reasonable. More than that, we needed to start noticing one another's needs. I desperately needed to know that Cole had affectionate thoughts and feelings for me. He needed to know that the difficulty of his daily responsibilities was seen, that his effort and personal struggles meant something. Slowly, we began making changes that would set us up to be more mindful of each others' needs, and we found unique ways to meet them in a place that was not exactly known for its romantic atmosphere. We decided, at the prompting of a seasoned worker, that we needed to actually have fun together. That meant more than just watching an episode of a sitcom while sitting next to each other, but actually doing something that allowed us to enjoy one another's company. Even though we were able to get our marriage on track, it would be another two years before I told Cole about my thoughts of becoming involved with a neighbor woman.

Why did it take so long for me to open up about something that was merely a thought? Why couldn't I tell someone immediately? The fact is, shame is a cruel and sadistic master. It convinces us that the secret is too ugly and destructive to let anyone know. Shame convinces us that it's better to just keep it quiet for the sake of protecting others—our family, our friends, our ministry. It keeps us covering, hiding, and fearful to the point of exhaustion. But Jesus is constantly breaking the shackles of shame and exchanging them for the exquisite garments of the royal family. This is who He is.

> *A slave is not a permanent member of the family, but a son is part of the family forever. So if the Son sets you free, you are truly free. (John 8:35-36, NLT)*

Another aspect of life that needed to change was how I was handling the burdens of my friends' painful stories. I had been going on visits to their homes alone or with my young daughter. Their difficulties and heartaches were more than I could bear alone. I began going on visits with teammates rather than by myself, which helped immensely with my ability to process the painful stories of Afghans.

We're Going There

The evil one wants to destroy us, to convince us that we are neither fit for the task nor worthy of the title of Daughter of the Most High King. The Father welcomes us with full knowledge of our past, our present tendencies, and our hidden secrets. His love covers all of it, and we don't need to tidy ourselves up in order for Him to call us worthy of participation in His Kingdom.

You, beloved daughter, are completely known and loved by the King. Your struggling, your hidden sin, and your dark nights do not disqualify you. Rather, it is in the acknowledgment of our weakness, shame, and helplessness where the perfect love of Jesus meets us in full. I would dare say that these are the moments we are most available to behold the miraculous. There is, perhaps, no better time or place for us to be used mightily by the King than when we come face to face with our frailty. It is in this sacred space where we see plainly that our skills, abilities, and expertise are actually worthless compared to the unrestrained love and power of Jesus.

—*Emmy Lopez*

Chapter 43

BE CAREFUL LITTLE FEET WHERE YOU GO

Elisabeth Elliot once described her husband Jim as she saw him in college: a serious-minded young man dressed neatly but simply, often carrying a stack of Greek flash cards to make use of spare moments in the cafeteria line. When I first read this description, I thought, "That's just like Joseph." Similar qualities attracted me to my husband in college: his brilliant mind cloaked in humility, his self-discipline, and his disregard for outward appearances in favor of pursuing study of God's Word. When we married three months after my graduation, we did so with dreams to follow God's call to the ends of the earth.

Six years later in the Middle East, we began full-time Arabic study—by any definition a beastly trial. And as if language school wasn't enough, I soon found myself embroiled in an unexpected, parallel struggle. Weekday mornings, as I climbed the stairs to my second-story classroom, my heartbeat felt light and butterflies danced in my stomach. While waiting for class to begin, I chatted with my fellow language learners while glancing toward the doorway, waiting until he walked in. But when I say he, I don't mean Joseph. I mean my Arabic teacher.

My crush on my language teacher was not just unexpected; it was downright embarrassing. I was married with a two-year-old, for cryin' out loud. I had dealt with brief attractions to male coworkers in the past, but with prayer and self-disciplined thoughts, I'd been able to quell emotions quickly. Now, two months into our first term as cross-cultural workers in the Middle East, I was blindsided by a powerful temptation that persisted day after day after day.

As I analyzed my infatuation with my teacher, an Arab Christian guy my age, I recognized what was happening. I needed to learn to communicate; he was teaching me how to say "hello," "how are you?" and everything after that. I needed someone to lead me through the culture around me; he was guiding me into the complexities of his world, answering my questions and helping me understand how our host country worked. And as an exhausted learner dealing with anxiety, I needed someone to fulfill the emotional needs that my equally exhausted husband wasn't meeting. My Arabic teacher was gentle, kind, and shepherding, consistently offering counsel and prayer for me and those in my class.

In short, I wasn't dealing with physical, sexual temptation in my attraction. I was lacking emotional and spiritual fulfillment, and to my weary heart—tired of constantly being on guard in the streets and shops, tired of lying in bed at night with Arabic grinding through my mind—dreamy thoughts about my teacher seemed an easy way to satisfy my needs and escape the often-boring reality of life.

Not that I wanted to surrender to these daydreams, no. I recognized that seeking to fulfill my desires for love and happiness in a man other than my husband amounted to emotional adultery. I was ashamed of my persistent attraction toward my teacher. I regularly came before God with my sin and even with my feelings that hadn't yet become sin but felt dangerously close. I wanted purity in my thoughts and an undivided heart for my husband.

Satan wasn't playing fair, and I hated it—hated that he and my flesh were ganging up to attack me at a vulnerable time.

After several weeks, when I saw that simple prayer and self-discipline were not winning the battle in my mind, I decided I had to confess. After our toddler was in bed, I sat with Joseph on the floor cushion in our family room and lay my struggle before him. My attraction felt silly, I told him, so teenage and trivial yet at the same time serious and overwhelming. With characteristic patience and love I can only describe as God-like, my husband listened and counseled and thanked me for not hiding from him. He told me I had broken the back of my sin by bringing it into the light.

Unfortunately, confession did not equal immediate resolution; weeks and months marched on, and I continued to fight for a pure heart. I ramped up my accountability by sharing my struggle with a woman in my class who'd become my prayer partner. When the semester ended and Joseph and I enrolled in a summer conversation course, I was relieved to be placed in the same classroom as him. At least he would be sitting beside me while our teacher stood before us, a present reminder of why I was fighting. In the summer I prayed fervently over our fall schedule, asking God to block me from being in this teacher's class again.

I emailed a group of women I was close with—friends who had interceded for me over difficult issues in the past—and requested their support in prayer. My mentor, who had served two decades in East Asia, recognized that although my problem sometimes seemed like a silly crush, it was nothing to giggle about and brush off. The enemy was attempting to undermine my marriage, and I needed to take that seriously.

As I reflect now, I see clearly that Satan assaults Christian marriages because the relationship between a believing husband and wife reflects the Gospel. Marriage is a living, breathing metaphor of the relationship between Christ and the Church. Satan wants to destroy this relationship—to introduce impurity, infidelity, or betrayal—in order to ruin this God-ordained magnifier of unfailing love.

Honestly, I easily forget this truth, and so I was grateful for my mentor's practical suggestions for guarding my marriage. She cautioned me to always consider where my feet would lead me, even to redirect myself from hallways or streets that would increase my chances of encountering my teacher outside of class time. She gave me the words of 2 Timothy 2:22: "So flee youthful passions and pursue righteousness, faith, love, and peace, along with those who call on the Lord from a pure heart" (ESV).

My mentor's admonishment went a long way, even stopping us from joining a Frisbee group so we would not run in the same circles as our teacher outside of class. Guarding the garden of our marriage—keeping the foxes out, as Song of Solomon puts it—required tremendous vigilance.

Often, as I waited for a class break to end, willing my feet from moving to where my teacher might be, I thought of the worship song "Christ is Risen" by Matt Maher. I took encouragement from the lyrics of the first verse, which reminds the sinner to fix her eyes on the cross.

Although I was "caught in sin" for a prolonged period, I felt Christ's great, great love for me and a new appreciation for the Gospel. I clung to Him who was tempted in every way, yet without sin. Often, when I sat still enough to listen, when I was able to quiet my mind that continually buzzed with verb conjugations, I could hear the Spirit whisper that I was fighting a good fight, that I was often tempted but not giving in to sin. He reminded me to give myself grace by carefully distinguishing between the temptation to sin and committing sin itself. Though weary and distracted, I pressed on in the Lord's strength.

How did it all end? After about a year, my feelings began to wane. My husband, son, and I had an unexpected detour in our missions journey, grounding us in the U.S. for more than a year, thus breaking all contact with our Arabic teacher. In a counseling session I shared my battle with our company's member care person, who asked good questions and provided practical suggestions for growth in our marriage. I had a dream of my teacher and my husband approaching me, and I joyfully chose Joseph and ran into his embrace. When we finally returned to the Middle East, I even attended my former teacher's wedding with great celebration and not a spark of jealousy in my heart. All glory to God.

How do we protect our marriage relationships while serving cross-culturally, especially in the early, draining days that utterly lack satisfying friendships and comforting routines? What can we do to prevent emotional and physical attraction to coworkers and nationals? I wish I had better answers to this conundrum. Joseph and I didn't fail entirely in this area, but neither did we completely succeed—the hurdles and hindrances to emotional intimacy were legion.

In our passport country, many advocate weekly date nights as the way to keep intimacy alive—or shared hobbies or holding hands in public or you-name-it. But what does one do when your idea of a shared hobby is reading (different) books in the same room and going out brings cultural stress and you can't hold hands in public anyway and babysitters are rarer than fresh milk and you already spend all your time together?

So much of what we hear about sustaining our marriages springs from secular cultural values and the entertainment industry. There's nothing wrong with a romantic date night, but do we require date nights to flourish as husband and wife? I think not. What we do require is consistent application of biblical principles in our marriages. We need to be tenderhearted toward each other, forgiving one another; we need to be thankful for one another; we need to believe the best about one another and serve and submit to one another out of love for Christ. Making the decision to love in these active ways will sustain our marriages cross-culturally because these choices are based on principles that transcend cultures.

Of course, we can and should establish routines that nourish our marriages. When we returned to the Middle East for our second term, Joseph and I established practices that worked for us in our specific context. We marked Tuesday nights as "Space for Us" nights, when instead of retreating to separate couches with books after putting our son to bed, we purposefully connected on a deeper level. We still have weekly comedy nights where we watch silly videos and stand-up on YouTube just to laugh. We pray together, which requires honesty and baring one's heart before God and one another. I've learned to see my husband's heart of love for me when he's washing the dishes or taking our son on errands, even if I wish he'd just sit to spend time with me instead. And we still go on dates, just not every week. We're doing well if we make it out once a month.

I wish one battle with temptation toward infidelity precluded further struggles, that all the safeguards we put up blocked future battles. But they didn't. I remember the very hour a second battle began: sitting on the floor cushions of a refugees' home, I watched one of my visiting partners tell a joke in Arabic and share the Gospel with a paralyzed elderly man. Something caught in my heart, and immediately I recognized—with a sinking feeling—what was happening and what might be ahead of me. Again, a cycle of confession, prayer, and accountability began as I committed my weekly interactions with this ministry partner to the Lord. Again, God proved faithful to guide me through an emotionally tumultuous season into wholeness and normalcy with this brother.

I'm so grateful that marriage is based on long-term commitment, not fleeting emotions. Unfortunately, our culture and the media we inadvertently absorb do not teach this. Commitment in marriage is underemphasized, but in my experience, seasons come when the best you can do is grit your teeth and flare your nostrils, as Joseph likes to say, and stick to your marriage vows. There are times when we must remember what we promised and cling to the covenant we made.

American singer-songwriter Andrew Peterson compares marriage to dancing in a minefield—one of the truest analogies about marriage I've ever heard. The bridge of his song contains a plea from one partner to another: a petition to seek him out when he's lost, to hold her close when she wanders. As cross-cultural workers, we will face marital challenges that require us to hold on to one another with determination. We will stand in the face of storms that force us to embrace our spouse (or be embraced by him) with all the unconditional, unfailing love of God for His wayward people. And although this is counter-cultural, perhaps these are the times when the Gospel shines most brightly in our marriages—not when we're smiling over a candle-lit table, but when one of us, a battered, hard-pressed sinner, is fiercely held and sheltered by the other, reflecting the perfect, pulsating love of the One who won't let go.

—*Esther Kline*

Chapter 44

GOD-GIVEN SEXUALITY

If only I had known. In one moment I saw the depths of my capacity for sexual sin, but it was years before I was able to see that my sexuality was a good gift that I could offer to God. Even now I am still learning to believe that I truly am fearfully and wonderfully made.

The summer after my sister and I graduated from university, she got married and I began my missionary training. She thought I would meet 'someone' very soon; I assumed I would be single for the rest of my life, and I was determined to treat it as a gift rather than a burden. After four months of training with no husband in sight, in January I flew to my host country.

I was pretty much halfway between the age of the parents and the children of the family who so warmly welcomed me. To me they were like an uncle, aunt and young cousins; the father called me 'little sister' and the girls saw me as a big sister! From their life and conversations I learned so much about missionary life and ministry, and even more about marriage and family. They courageously shared their own stories of brokenness and redemption and challenged me never to let myself think I was immune to sexual temptation. To this day they don't know what might have happened.

We had been living and working together for more than a year, and my 'uncle' and I had a business trip to make. As was his practice, he put shields in place: we did not travel alone together, and we stayed in the home of a family we both knew. But I had to walk past his bedroom to get to the bathroom, and as I did so I was almost drowned by a wave of longing to throw open the door and jump into his bed. Even while I was straining every muscle in my body just to walk past and not even look towards that door, I was filled with disgust at myself. How could I even contemplate such a thing? He was married, and I loved his wife and children dearly. I had never even found him physically attractive! It shook me deeply. The following morning I couldn't look anyone in the eye– which may well have passed unnoticed since there are strict cultural rules about such things–and to this day I put up an emotional wall every time I interact with him.

Although that situation never repeated itself, and in general I remained content with my single state, the bursts of longing for someone never fully went away. Periodically they would return in force, and to my shame I sought satisfaction in empty places, then wept as I pleaded with God to forgive me. Not once did I think to look for a pattern. If only I had known.

We're Going There

Five years later, my world was turned upside down by a wonderful young man who pursued me with the intent of marriage. Shortly before our engagement, my 'aunt and uncle' insisted on having the "birds and the bees" conversation with us. As they candidly shared about temptations and challenges, I shuddered to think how different things would have been between us all if I had allowed myself to be swept into that wave of longing. The disgust—and the guilt—had never left me. But suddenly the light burst in. As my beloved and I began to make practical preparations for our marriage, we discovered Natural Family Planning. This beautiful, earthy method revealed to me some of the mysteries of this female body God made for me, and it was during one of our discussions that that shady moment from my past was illuminated. We learned that the days around ovulation are marked by various physical signs, often including an increase in sexual desire. And as I looked back through my journals and thought back over those years, I saw that my pattern of temptation had indeed been closely connected to that other time of the month.

Believe me, my husband and I have used that discovery well! Under God's guiding hand, we carefully planned the timing of our first pregnancy. And, several years later, after almost three years without a period, weeks of asking God to give us a third child, and in the middle of the exhaustion of caring for two little ones, I recognized those all-but-forgotten signs of desire and made it clear to my husband that it was tonight or never! And by God's kindness we conceived our third child. I wanted to tell anyone who would listen–but my home and host countries agree on the taboo against talking about conception–so we keep the story between the two of us. In the quiet of our hearts and the exuberance of our celebrations of marital love, we marvel at God's incredible gift of sexuality and His beautiful redemption of the time of the month that had threatened to destroy everything.

A dear friend of mine, ministering in a very different context, is joyfully single but asked me to pray for her as she struggles with bursts of temptation. I cautiously shared my story and my discovery with her, and to her amazement she found the same pattern. As she testifies, the struggle continues, but it makes a huge difference to know that she is not alone – and to be reminded that God made her body and has given her the opportunity to offer it as a sacrifice of praise.

—Grace

Chapter 45

THE DAY I KEPT QUIET

We were all anxious for a bathroom break. The morning had been long, traveling on remote mountain roads, the kind with deep ruts and anything-but-smooth-sailing. Add to that the headache-inducing air freshener our driver had installed in his sturdy Toyota van, and every one of us was ready for a few moments outside the four tin walls with our feet on the actual ground, breathing actual fresh air. When our driver pulled over and motioned down the hill to the metal-roofed outhouse, everyone breathed a sigh of relief.

A teammate and I were joining a visiting short-term team as they traveled from village to village in our host culture. Earlier that morning, we had left one remote village where only one family of believers lived, and were now traveling to another one where we would help host an evening service for the small group of believers there.

But first, we needed a bathroom break.

I was one of the first down that hill, finding my way to the tin-roofed shack. From the outside, it looked like every other outhouse I'd seen in these remote stretches, but when I swung open that door, I was hit in the face with an image I couldn't un-see: the inside was covered from floor to ceiling with obscene, pornographic posters. It was shocking, so unexpected and overpowering in such a small space. I literally held my breath, averted my eyes, prayed for protection over my purity, and got out of that stinky outhouse as fast as I could.

And then I had a choice to make: do I tell the others? Do I warn them? Tell them to use the other one? Do I ask our driver to find another bathroom for us? My mind swam with options as I trudged back up that hill to the rest of the group. Should I just keep quiet about it, and let each person guard herself or himself on their own? How were they supposed to respond if I'd say something? Will I just make an awkward situation worse by talking?

I couldn't decide. The whole way up that hill thoughts banged around in my head. A determination that giving a warning was a way of honoring my brothers and sisters was immediately followed with the thought that I was making a big deal out of nothing and I should just keep mum.

So I stayed mum. I took the coward's way out and said nothing. *I acted as if nothing were wrong.* As if I had no responsibility whatsoever for the people entering that house of impurity after I did. A few minutes later, I looked down the hill to see a friend walking out of that bathroom. Something burned inside my belly—I knew what he had seen, and I had done nothing to help steer him away.

That incident happened more than a decade ago, and I still remember it clearly. And I deeply regret my silence. I remember it as the day when I did nothing to protect the sexual purity of my brothers and sisters. The day I allowed them to go into the lion's den, unprotected.

My host culture was many things. Welcoming, friendly, laid-back, beautiful. It brought me in like a welcome embrace and gave me a home. But it was also the keeper of dark secrets, a place of great idolatry, and deep brokenness. And it was highly sexually-charged. Pornographic images available all over town, solicitation on many street corners, sexual innuendo commonplace in everyday speech. A long-term worker once told me she feels there is a powerful sexual stronghold in that nation that I love so well, and I agree. It's everywhere, and free use of sexuality is celebrated. After a while, it became less glaringly offensive; my sensitivity to the sin began to wear down.

Living in a sexual war-zone takes resistance. First, it means surrendering to God's perfect plan for our sexuality and not bowing our knees to another definition. It takes holding firm to personal guidelines and a determination not to allow our standards of holiness to slip. This resistance must be built beyond just our own spiritual flexing. We need to band together to create a fellowship of resistance and help one another walk through in wholeness.

Paul spoke clearly and firmly to the church at Thessalonica about sexual purity. He calls for each one to stand firm in following God's guidelines for our sexuality, guarding our own hearts and avoiding exploitation of others. He wraps up this conversation by saying, "For God did not call us to be impure, but to live a holy life" (1 Thessalonians 4:7, NIV).

Throughout the whole of Scripture, community living is valued. Among many many other things, we are admonished to "bear one another's burdens" (Galatians 6:2), to "encourage one another" (Hebrews 3:13), and to "practice hospitality" (Romans 12:13). Walking with Jesus is not a solo gig; it's one meant to be lived together.

So then, is the fight for sexual wholeness. It's a fight we lend to our brothers and sisters. And I think we who live in foreign lands, especially those charged with sexual immorality at every turn, need to be especially aware of how we can fight for those in our families and on our teams.

Step one to solving a problem is identifying it. Let's identify it through conversation.

Conversation sets the stage for accountability. Maybe we're personally at a good place with this act of resistance, but someone across the table from us is not. Maybe he or she is slipping down the slide of immorality, one small action at a time. Conversation sets the boundary fence for all.

Conversation promotes vulnerability. The topic of sexuality needs to be handled with discretion and care, and this care can promote a spirit of vulnerability on our teams.

Don't follow my lead. Don't stay quiet. Don't do nothing.

Conversation promotes confession. While it's nearly a lost art in Christian circles today, public confession has long been a part of the church's history. Viewing it as public shaming is missing the point of what God created public confession to be: a moment of purification for an individual while inviting in the body of believers.

Let's silence the silence, and join the fight for the purity of those we rub shoulders with. Let's stop being quiet and avoiding the awkward conversations and engage in the battle for the sexual purity of those around us.

If I could go back to that sultry day in the Southeast Asian jungle, I'd do it differently. I'd take a stand for the resistance. Even a simple warning, a short "just so you know, you're entering a lion's den" would have communicated a sisterly love, care, and protection for those following me.

Engage, act, protect, defend.

We are called to holiness; let's help each other walk that path well.

—Maria Mullet

Chapter 46

SEXUAL STRUGGLES ON THE FIELD

Most of us avoid talking about our own sexuality. I do. It's hard to know what is normal or not when it comes to such a personal topic. I know I spent many years wondering and fearing that I wasn't normal. Though I have worked through so much, there is still a trepidation that creeps up even now as I put words to the page.

When I was deep in packing back in 2011, just a month prior to leaving for South Asia, I found myself suddenly experiencing an onslaught of perverted and blasphemous images coming to my mind every time I prayed and worshiped. It caused me to feel so ashamed and dirty. I had never been exposed to anything like these images I was seeing, and I knew these thoughts were from the evil one. However, they were so persistent and so vulgar that it was hard not to start believing that something was terribly wrong with me. They were interfering with the one place I felt safe: the Father's presence, and it felt like I couldn't even go to Him anymore without an epic fight. I talked and prayed it through with others and stood firm. Yet the thoughts were persistent. I left my home country wondering if I was worthy to be going, wondering if I had missed something huge in all my preparation. After my arrival, those thoughts, at least those particular kinds of thoughts slowed down and eventually stopped altogether.

Through that experience though, the Lord exposed some parts of my heart, parts I had not yet had the opportunity to see. I moved in with two other single women who were working in the area. I bonded with them quickly, finding them to be the kind of "kindred spirits" I had always hoped to meet. We all shared a love of history and eighteenth and nineteenth century literature, got a thrill out of learning languages, and were working in the same country with the same desire to reach and love the people around us. I could listen and talk with them for hours. Almost immediately, however, I found this odd fear creeping up into my mind. What if this is too close? What if the boundaries aren't clear? What if this turns into something impure? What if I can't be close to anyone because it will always become evil? What if there is something deep in me that is just evil and will soon be exposed?

The intensity of the thoughts was perhaps new, but the direction was not so unfamiliar. As much as I longed for and sought out deep friendship, there was always a fear in my heart—even in the most innocent of relationships—that somehow the relationship would not be safe, that somehow it could turn sexual.

Emotional intimacy felt dangerous. I talked to my mentors about this and prayed through all the issues as they came up. My childhood had not been easy, but there had never been even a hint of sexual abuse. Why was there this dark fear when that had not been my story? And yet, I realized it had been my parents' childhood stories. Close relatives. Trusted friends. Had they perhaps very unintentionally passed on some of their fears to me? Add to that some of the co-dependent relational patterns that had been part of my childhood experience, and I definitely had work to do in learning how to connect with others in healthy, life-giving ways.

The intensity of my new life gave a lot of context for learning to connect in a variety of relationships. One of the ladies in my house moved away, but the other stayed. I loved having a close friend, someone I connected with easily, and yet found myself terrified by it too at times. Whenever that old fear crept up, my instinct was to just run away. This must be bad. Run before it turns evil. Yet every time I talked to my counselors and mentors about it, the answer seemed to be, "Yes, be careful. Make Jesus your focus. But don't run away. How else will you learn to relate unless it's through relationships?" Close relationships exposed not only my fears about intimacy, but all my clingy tendencies, and my temptation to make others the center of my world.

As much as I enjoyed having close friendships, I still longed for a husband and children to fill my home. The Lord had not seen fit to give that to me, at least not yet. I wondered what relationships with others in a celibate life were supposed to look like. How close was too close? There was clear direction about the physical but what about the emotional and spiritual? There was such a deep need in my heart for intimacy. What was I supposed to do about that? And what was I to do with this longing for some kind of permanence? Usually the hardest part about being single was not the absence of physical intimacy, but rather the lack of having the right to make anyone stay in my life. With all the uncertainties of life overseas, it felt like my whole life and all my relationships could be ripped away at any time. Sometimes, I confess, that seemed unfair to me. Why did other women in my life get to take their families with them when they moved around the world, and I had no one to do that with?

I observed some other single women who seemed content with a somewhat distant attitude toward others. But, I was not wired that way. I needed people around whom I could be close with, like family. I knew Jesus was the ultimate answer to this deep loneliness, the only One who could truly satisfy my desire to be known and loved. But what did that really mean? And why had He created us with the need for relationships with others at all if it was so easy to make them idols? If He was really all we needed, why did we still need others at all? I wrestled with these questions again and again over the years.

And then, my life as I knew it was ripped from me. I lost my visa. I could not return to my home. I ended up in a remote location in another country where I had to start all over. While I had many lovely teammates whom I connected with in many ways, there was no one who "got" me, no one to share little inside jokes with, no one who sought me out just because they enjoyed my company.

That's when something biologically hit me hard and unexpectedly. Was it the fact that I was now thirty? Suddenly, it seemed like my sexuality had woken up in a new way and was demanding attention more loudly than ever before. The longing was so intense... and physical, and I did not know what I was supposed to do with it. My first reaction was shame, similar to how I had felt about the images sabotaging my mind. I felt so disgusted with myself for having these feelings I had no rightful way to fulfill. Yet somehow I knew that this time this was not just the evil one planting thoughts in my head. I couldn't fight this the same way I had fought sexual thoughts in the past. This was coming from a part of me that was real, something God had created. To just bash it would be killing something good, along with whatever was bad. No, I had to face this in a different way.

I nervously talked to a couple of friends and mentors about these thoughts and feelings and found them to be kind rather than judgmental. Sharing brought death to shame. One wise friend suggested I acknowledge the feelings, let myself feel them, and bring them to the Father rather than shamefully shushing them. Now I would lift my hands to the Lord, not hiding, not trying to defend myself, not even judging myself. I would just hold the thoughts up to Him and let Him do what He would, let Him change me.

We're Going There

My other friend talked about counting my current singleness and celibacy as part of the sufferings I was called to share in for Jesus. It was not that I had no legitimate needs. Rather, I was called to lay those down and suffer with Jesus. He would give me strength in that suffering. This helped me to understand why simply saying that "Jesus is all I need" had started to feel like more of a cliché than a reality. Indeed, I had been created with the need for close relationships and with the desire for sexual fulfillment. I was created with other needs as well—for food, water, and shelter. I would never deny that those needs were real. Now, I no longer had to pretend that the others were unreal either.

In Paul's well-known passage about contentment, he writes, "I know what it is to be in need, and I know what it is to have plenty. I have learned the secret of being content in any and every situation, whether well fed or hungry, whether living in plenty or in want. I can do all this through him who gives me strength" (Philippians 4:12-13, NIV).

What I realized as I studied this Scripture is that Paul is talking about a different kind of contentment than I had in mind. Being hungry and in want is not the same as being full. It is not putting on a brave front and saying, "I don't need anything." Paul's stomach still felt hunger when he didn't have food. He still had those needs, but regardless of whether they were filled or not, he had learned to draw on Christ's strength. I discovered I could live like that too—not denying the presence of needs but trusting Christ's strength even when those needs went unmet.

As I let go of my fears about intimacy and shame over my sexuality, I found there was a greater freedom to enjoy being who I was made to be. I did not have a husband or children, but this did not mean my womanhood was a waste. I could enjoy the rhythms of womanhood, the way my cycle works. There are times of fruitfulness and times of being dormant. There are other ways of relating and being creative and fruitful than only marriage. When desires that could not be fulfilled came up as they still would, I could keep offering them back to the Lord as a sacrifice, allowing Him to teach me how to rely on Him.

Quite unexpectedly, I had the opportunity to fall in love and get married. All the feelings that I thought were so intense at that time only intensified as I went through the process of a real romantic relationship! Looking back now though, I realize that the Lord had slowly been preparing me, helping me to deal with some of my hang-ups and fears. I still have loads to learn. But one of the biggest keys even now seems to be this dependency on Jesus. He won't make all my needs disappear, but He gives strength and His own fellowship in whichever situation He places me.

—RLS

Chapter 47

IRON SHARPENING IRON

One of the highlights for me of the 2020 Tokyo Olympics was the finals of the women's 400 meter hurdles. Being a University of Kentucky alum myself, I was keen to watch Sydney McLaughlin after her world record run of 51.90 seconds in the U.S. Olympic Trials. As the runners positioned themselves in their respective lanes, you could not only sense some anxiety, but also that this was going to be one for the record books.

The race started, and McLaughlin's teammate and former Olympic champion, Dalilah Muhammad, took the early lead. She would retain that narrow advantage until the very last hurdle. From there, it was a sprint to the finish. The two would remain neck-and-neck, but in the end, McLaughlin would edge out Muhammad shattering her own world record to win gold with a time of 51.46 seconds. Muhammad was awarded silver with a personal best of 51.58 seconds and Femke Bol of the Netherlands took the bronze medal.

In many of the post-race interviews after both the trials and the Olympic finals, McLaughlin quoted that familiar phrase from Proverbs 27:17 when referencing her camaraderie with Muhammad. "I just say iron sharpens iron. It's two people pushing each other to be their best," said McLaughlin. She goes on, "It's just two athletes wanting to be their best and knowing there is another great girl who is going to get you there."[12]

Well, I know a lot of great girls. Women who have trained and prepared and sacrificed just so that they could run this Christian race in their respective callings to this overseas life. Women whose faith is being tested on a trail marked with unfamiliarity, homesickness, and an unspoken loneliness that only those who know, know. Women whose hearts bear the burden of wondering if their children will grow up resenting God because goodbyes have become too common and deep connections too rare. Women whose lifework is to fill others with the restorative words of Christ but desperately need a refreshing themselves. Women who still smile a stoic brave on those days when the reflection in the mirror seems unrecognizable. Women who crave the intimacy once found in the community they've forsaken and who ache for another great girl who is going to get them there.

We all need someone to help us get there, don't we? Someone who has been there, done that. And even if they've not been there or done that, they are willing to go "there" with us. There in the scorn of our deepest hurts, in the chaos of our hardest days, and in the grit of our greatest triumphs. There to bring gut-honest truth to our ears, even when we don't want to hear it, and to offer love without condition. There to sit on the proverbial ash heap and cry with us and pray for us and just be. There to hold our arms when we tire, to cheer our minds when in despair, and to hold our lives accountable when we are waning. There to be as iron sharpening iron.

> As iron sharpens iron, so a man sharpens the countenance of his friend. (Proverbs 27:17, NKJV)

Let's take a moment to really ponder the imagery of the first part of this verse as penned by the wise man, Solomon. Then let's apply the imagery to the second part of the verse.

As iron sharpens iron...

For iron to effectively be sharpened with iron, a much harder piece must be doing the sharpening. The softer the iron being sharpened, the more time it demands. I can tell you, I must have been a *really* soft piece of iron for God to send me Kandi. And when I say send, I mean He physically uprooted her and her husband in their retirement and planted them in our country for a season of five years. They came with the intention of church planting. Instead, in her maturity and obedience, she spent most of her days grinding away in my areas of weakness and sharpening me with the Word of God.

She was wise, patient, and spoke the truth even if it made me uncomfortable. See, that's what happens when two individual, differently-composed pieces of iron come together—there must be friction. Friction in the form of my self-pity getting on her right-old nerves, and she'd let me know it. Friction when it was all I could do to keep from responding to her frequent reminder that the trial I was facing was "not about you."

Oh, the edging of those three words, they sharpened me, all right. She sharpened me, keeping me accountable to a calling that I honestly was not prepared to remain in. She taught me truths from the Word that made it make sense and gave me confidence to speak those truths over the anxiety, the fear, the guilt, and the doubt that had plagued me for years. She didn't mind showing tough love. Nor did she mind dropping everything to accompany me on shopping runs, calling them "divine appointments." We would talk over coffee, laugh over cheesecake, and cry over hands held. She was nearly thirty years my senior, and she was good at it. Somehow, the fire that had refined her in life brought out the best in me.

But she would tell you that I wasn't the only one who benefitted from our relationship. See, when iron is sharpened with iron, accountability to each other is reciprocated, and both pieces change. They become stronger, sharper, more nuanced tools ready to be used for their respective jobs in Kingdom work. In this instance, she as the mentor, me as the mentee.

We're Going There

So a man sharpens the countenance of his friend...

After the grinding and the sharpening are completed, the newly-sharpened piece of iron is often polished to enhance smoothness and to remove any minor mechanical deformities that may have occurred in the sharpening process. The polishing not only further readies the iron for use and makes it more aesthetically pleasing, but it also helps to reveal the metal's unique character.

Likewise, the sharpening that the Lord graciously used Kandi to do in me has strengthened and prepared me to be used by Him in this season, galvanizing my resolve to serve and improving my overall countenance. Had I gone at it alone, my demeanor would still be dull, depressed, and defeated. I needed the accountability. I needed the sharpening and the grinding and the polishing. I needed the wisdom, the admonition, the love of my experienced, more tempered friend to better me and bring me out of the pit of despair.

Just like David needed the reprimand of Nathan in 2 Samuel 12. Nathan begins the conversation with a parable that points directly to David's sinful act of adultery with Bathsheba and his subsequent murder of her husband, Uriah. Although the parable incited anger in David, he did not come under any conviction, nor did he repent of his own actions. Instead David pointed the finger to the man in the parable insisting he must make restitution. I'm pretty sure if emoticons were a thing in the Old Testament, Nathan would have inserted the "SMH," hand-over-the-face one *right here*.

Realizing David's hardness of heart, Nathan got straight to the point and strongly rebuked David with these four piercing words in verse 7, "You are the man!" (NKJV) He went on to chide him, "Why have you despised the word of the Lord by doing evil in His sight?" (MEV)

Iron sharpening iron.

David came under immediate conviction and repented. God forgave David's sin and allowed him to live, but his sin would come with the grave consequence of losing the son that he had conceived with Bathsheba. Despite this, Nathan's sharpening of the countenance of his friend would cause David to return to a place of worship, and the "man after God's own heart" would go on to pen the contrite prayer of pardon and accountability we so often pray ourselves from Psalm 51:

> Create in me a clean heart, O God, and renew a right
> and steadfast spirit within me.
> Do not cast me from Your presence and do not take Your
> Holy Spirit from me.
> Restore to me the joy of Your salvation and sustain me
> with a willing spirit.
> (verses 10-12, AMP)

David wasn't the only one who needed a Nathan in his life. Peter needed Paul to hold him to account for caving into social pressures and for his brief abandonment of doctrinal truths. Galatians 2:11-21 details Paul's public rebuke of Peter's legalistic display. Not only did Paul sharpen Peter's countenance as a key leader in the Church, but his words of reproach to Peter served to reinforce the free gift of salvation offered to everyone, Jew and Gentile, through the blood of Christ.

Sometimes, like Peter, we make rash decisions for fear of what others may think of us or because our current circumstances are not comfortable. It's in these times that we need a Paul to come alongside us and remind us that not only are we accountable to God *for* our decisions, but we are accountable for living out the truth of His Gospel *through* those decisions. And we will never be sharpened if we go at it alone.

That is why David needed Nathan.

That is why Peter needed Paul.

And that is why I needed Kandi.

We all need someone to help get us there. We will always need someone to help get us there. That is how God designed it. Ann Voskamp says, "We aren't here to one-up one another, but to help one another up".[13]

That's iron sharpening iron. And even if the Lord has yet to send you a Nathan or a Paul or a Kandi, there is a tribe of women who have served and struggled and succeeded in this overseas life that get you. Reach out to that community—a community such as this very one of Velvet Ashes. Or maybe your sending organization already has a community of mentors who have been there and done that and know the importance of accountability. Or maybe you're without a sending organization like me. Can I speak to your hearts specifically? Trust that God will provide someone who will be a safe space for you—a great girl who is going to get you there.

In the meantime, whether you are the iron that's being sharpened or the iron doing the sharpening, perhaps it would serve us all well to be reminded of a few Scriptures that give us a practical guideline for accountability as Kingdom workers. This is not an exhaustive list, nor is it in any order, but done daily, these measures will be sure to sharpen the countenance of any friend:

- Pray for one another (James 5:16)
- Confess our faults to one another (James 5:16)
- Love one another (1 John 4:7)
- Exhort one another (Hebrews 3:13)
- Encourage one another (1 Thessalonians 5:11)
- Forgive one another (Ephesians 4:32)
- Be kind to one another (Ephesians 4:32)
- Serve one another (1 Peter 4:9)
- Submit to one another (Ephesians 5:21)

Iron sharpening iron.

—Stephanie Prater-Clarke

Conclusion

I was sitting on a plane headed toward the States. Just two weeks earlier, this was not where I'd thought I'd be. I looked over at my daughter who was probably more scared than I was. What we thought was a parasite or stress from the civil war that edged it's way closer to us ended up being something more serious.

Yes, we knew she was losing weight. No, we didn't realize how serious it was until the hospital on the other end of the line said, "You have two weeks to be in the States. We will be expecting you."

Years earlier when we told our family and friends we were moving to South Sudan, many replied with, "I could never do that. You are so brave." I'm sure lots of you reading this have had similar things uttered to you as you live your life in various seasons of cross-cultural life.

To be honest I never felt brave. I didn't have fear of living in the bush in Africa five hours from the nearest reliable medical care (or seven, depending on rainy season). No, I didn't love the poisonous snakes that raised their heads to my back porch or curled themselves in sticky traps way too close for comfort, but I didn't feel super courageous for living in proximity to them.

But sitting here on this plane I was surrounded by the bravest people I knew.

Looking at her, I saw courage.

A seventeen-year old girl leaving a home she thought she had another year at and entering a hospital for three months after realizing she was anorexic and this was how to get well.

Looking over at him I saw courage.

My husband, team leader and overseer of lots of people and projects, leaving those he loved behind in the midst of a civil war that raged near our community.

Looking at my three younger kids, I saw so much trust and bravery.

They just packed up and didn't ask the questions they knew we didn't have the capacity to answer. They helped and smiled and hugged and snuggled. All the things we needed.

Thinking of them, I knew bravery.

Our teammates, who loved my daughter like she was part of their family, drove us to the airport and then turned back toward the work. Not knowing if we would ever be back, or if they were even safe, they stayed.

Our hope with this book is that through the real-life stories of other women serving cross-culturally, you will find courage for your story. Sometimes the courage you need is to stay and watch the Lord meet you where you are.

And sometimes the courage you need is for when you step foot on that plane to close a chapter that you hoped would last much longer.

Brave women are on both sides of this equation. And God is moving in all of them.

No matter where the new found courage from these stories takes you, we pray you will be able to say:

Whether I go or stay
Whether I see fruit or not
Whether I'm married or single
Have children or not,
Because He is good,
Because I know who has the victory
Because I know He is writing my story...

Yet I still hope.

—Denise Beck

Author Biographies

>)))/

Up the Mountain with Isaac

Abigail Rattin and her family have been striving to live with transparency, Biblical hospitality, and Christ-like love in Uganda since 2011. Abby and her husband have been entrusted with six precious and joyful children, including their oldest who has significant special needs. As a Gospel-centered medical doctor, she is especially passionate about ministry through the local church to families impacted by disabilities and epilepsy.

Anonymous: This summer marked 20 years for me of serving in Asia, first as a language student and then as an English teacher in a university. I love blue skies, mountains, photographing wildflowers, watching sports, eating noodles together with friends, studying the Word with my colleagues, and praying together with them to our faithful God of Peace and Hope!

Beth Barthelemy has called Southern Africa "home" for the last six years with her husband, Ben, and four daughters (though she's a Wisconsin girl at heart). Most of her time is spent writing, homeschooling, and sharing the goodness and grace of Jesus.

Carolyn Broughton and her husband have been living in a small village in Central Asia since 2005, where she homeschools their three children and enjoys drinking innumerable bowls of tea with local ladies. She thrills whenever someone is interested in hearing more about Jesus. Besides writing, Carolyn loves composing and recording music in her small home studio. Find out more on her website (CarolynBroughton.com), and look for her songs wherever you get your music.

Elisabeth (not her real name) and her husband have 3 children and currently live in a Scandinavian country. They have both worked with Youth with a Mission for several years in both Europe and the Middle East. Elisabeth loves discovering new countries and finding hidden treasures in cultures and languages. To relax she likes to drink tea, knit and crochet and read books set in the English countryside.

Esther Seifert: After unexpectedly and indefinitely having to leave their West Asian home of 10 years, Esther (not her real name) and her family have just completed their first year in a new West Asian country. Though her primary role is mothering their two daughters, Esther also enjoys consulting on literacy projects and leading prayer and worship at their small international fellowship. ame is also a pseudonym so she would like to add that to her bio. She has dedicated this piece to Rachel (not her real name), who has now gone to be with the Lord after a years-long battle with cancer.

Eva Burkholder's experience as a missionary kid, cross-cultural worker, and member care provider adds a global dimension to her study of scripture and storytelling. Through her blog, Pondered Treasures, and her book, Favored Blessed Pierced: A Fresh Look at Mary of Nazareth, Eva invites readers to pause, reflect, and apply God's Word. She and her husband live in Texas and enjoy spending time with their two sons and their wives.

Evangeline Chow is a Chinese American wife, mama, and teacher. She's been teaching in the Philippines at Faith Academy, an international school for TCKs, for the past decade. Her top 3 loves of the Philippines are: the people, the food, and the beaches! She is passionate about multicultural education and mental health.

Gwen Elm (not her real name) has made South Asia home with her husband for the last five years, and they recently welcomed a son. Gwen works alongside her husband to learn an remote, undocumented language, and they are moving towards literacy development for this language group. When not studying and concocting grammatical theories, Gwen can be found sewing, cooking, or trying out something new in their garden.

Jennifer Ball served with her husband and son in Botswana from 2013-2014 and 2019-2022. They lived in a village outside one of the game reserves. She enjoyed getting to see all the animals and the beautiful, open places. She has a passion for education and counseling. Currently her days mostly revolve around caring for her son which means staying very active.

Karen Lubbers-Odel, from Canada, and her Ugandan husband Moses serve together in Gulu, Uganda. Serving under MissionGo, Karen loves teaching, training, and discipleship. The Odels are passionate about music, adventure, trying new foods, and making friends. Karen enjoys knitting teddy bears, writing cards, telling stories, meeting with ladies for Bible study and sweet fellowship, and reading a good novel. Her life motto is "Riding in God's Palm"!

MaDonna Maurer is married to a German TCK and raising three TCKs in Asia, one which has special needs. Her passion is to help people navigate transitions in life whether that is moving, staying, or other life events that bring change. When not speaking or writing she can be found with an iced grapefruit green tea at the beach with her family.

Maggie V. has been a global worker on 3 continents serving in Senegal, Brazil and SE Asia. She is a widow and has 2 grown children. Maggie compares her experience to Psalm 66:12, having been through fire and flood, yet through it all, being ushered into a place of great abundance. Maggie's passion is making connections; the ultimate being connecting people to Jesus. Her global trek spans 35 years.

Michelle and her husband have been married for 11 years and served in Romania for 9 years. She is an introvert making a home in a communal culture, lover of cooking as long as she doesn't have to measure, and enjoys relaxing with watercolors and a good cup of coffee.

Nancy Haney is a wife and mother of three teenagers. After living in Southeast Asia for eight years, her family now resides in Tennessee. Nancy and her husband still travel back and forth to Asia, where they founded a school for Deaf children. As a songwriter, she loves to communicate everyday experiences of life and faith. You can find her music under Nancy Haney (Songs of Restoration) on most streaming platforms.

Ruth Potinu serves alongside her husband Simon and their three children in Papua New Guinea where they work among the vulnerable, especially widows and their children. She is the author of Permission to Mourn: Engaging with Culture, Story and Scripture in a Quest for Healing with Hope. Ruth enjoys a good cup of chai, stimulating conversations and writing whenever she can carve out the time.

Shirley Anne Jacobs lives in rural Paraguay where she works with low-language Deaf, using sign language as a means to build relationships and share who God is. She enjoys learning language and culture, drinking tereré (the local tea) with neighbors, reading, and spending time being active outdoors. Serving with SIM, she is passionate about helping the most vulnerable and forgotten learn of God's great love for them in Christ.

Collateral Damage

Abby Batson and her husband, Josh, live in Orlando, Florida. They recently relocated there for her husband's job. While moving to Florida was an adjustment, the hot, humid climate doesn't bother her because it reminds her of Thailand, where she served for 2 years. Abby is passionate about seeing women live out of their God-given identity. She loves connecting with people, Asian food of any kind, and hiking in the mountains.

Abuk (not her real name) and her husband and five children and have been serving with SIM in North and East Africa since 2012. They have lived both in the bush and in the city and enjoy board games, community, good food, hiking and laughter. Abuk enjoys reading, running, and mostly deep heart to heart conversations that give glimpses into others stories and how the gospel impacts faith, life and journeys. She loves serving in the realm of chaplaincy locally and globally and seeing how the good news of Jesus creates resilience in the unexpected.

Ashley Whittemore is a writer, poet, and recovering people pleaser. She, her husband, and their three children lived in the Amazon region of Brazil and Colombia for several years. While they no longer live there full-time, they continue to serve as part of the leadership of The Amazon Network, an organization they founded in 2013. In her free time, she can be found triaging the needs of her garden, houseplants, and chickens.

Autumn (not her real name) and her husband have three children and served in both Africa and Asia over a span of seventeen years. As a nurse and a mother, Autumn is passionate about women's health, healthcare equity, and mental health education–especially among marginalized communities. Her background includes community health education, women's health advocacy, and Scripture engagement training. Autumn currently resides in the US and works for a non-profit that focuses on mobility equity for people living with disabilities in under-resourced countries.

Caitlin Lieder has lived in Europe since 2006, most of her adult life. She and her husband have five kids and are currently church planting in northern Germany. While most of her energy goes into taking care of her family, she also loves filling in whatever gaps there are in church life, especially teaching the women and playing piano. When she has a free moment, Caitlin will be trying new recipes, running, or reading.

Emily Miller served in the Dominican Republic for 13 years with Kids Alive International. Along the way she met and married her husband and had two little boys. She moved back to the US in 2022 and continues to see God's provision in the re-entry journey. Emily loves the beach, the mountains, and good coffee, and she feels most at home with others who have lived and understand cross-cultural life.

Joy Smalley is a missionary kid from Outer Mongolia, a former missionary to Sumatra, Indonesia, current wife to Jonathan, and mother of four teenagers. Missions and ministry has been her life from the time she was five and she continues to grow in relationship with herself and with God as life throws challenges her way. She delights in books, in story, and the pursuit of healing, all while holding hope in a God that sees all, knows all and loves all.

Kara May (not her real name) spent five years delighting in iced coffee in Southeast Asia and sitting with neighbors to tell them about Jesus. While it has been challenging to leave that home to reside in her American home, she is grateful for the hard and beautiful lessons learned in that season. She is always on the hunt for a good book.

Karli VonHerbulis is a wife, mother, writer, and host of Third Culture Thriving Podcast. She and her family live in Kigali, Rwanda, where they homeschool, work with rural farmers, and run a popular ecotourism destination. You can catch Karli getting up before the sun, throwing themed parties, making lists, reading all the books, and pointing out cool birds.

Kathryn Hall: In the five years since she first moved overseas in 2017, Kathryn (not her real name) has come to love life in East

Asia's megacities, as well as all the particular joys and challenges that come with cross-cultural life and ministry. Currently based in Taipei, Taiwan, she particularly enjoys roaming Taipei's parks and trails, as well as train rides down the coast.

Laura Bowling spent ten years in cross-cultural ministry, serving in church planting and education in Portugal, South Africa, and Ireland. Between lesson planning and preparing crafts, she made lifelong friends and explored Europe. She now lives in Southern California with her husband, Chris, and works her new dream job as managing editor for an international ministry where her days now revolve around word choice, punctuation, grammar, and fact-checking.

Libby Wilkes and her husband have four amazing children. They have been serving with a local church in a big European city since 2018 and have grown to love the ever-changing sights, sounds, smells, and tastes that comes with living in a bustling, diverse, urban place. Libby loves spending time with local friends and neighbors, learning from them, listening to their stories, and sharing her own story of life with Jesus.

Linda K. Thomas authored *Please, God, Don't Make Me Go: A Foot-Dragger's Memoir* about her three years in South America, and *Grandma's Letters from Africa* about her first four years in Africa, both with Wycliffe Bible Translators. Her work has also appeared in newspapers, magazines, and anthologies. In addition to speaking, she teaches the craft of writing memoir to community and church groups and through her blog, Spiritual Memoirs 101.

Lynne Castelijn loves sharing about God's great faithfulness – and about 28 years of missionary adventures. (Her memoir series is enroute!) Lynne and her husband live with an indigenous group of the Philippines – church planting, Bible translating and doing community development. Having resettled four children into their homeland Australia, Lynne is looking for new adventures and lessons to be learned and shared. She can be found on the website under her name.

Nancy Rempel and her husband, Don, taught the Bible in the Urdu language for 28 years in Pakistan and India, where they raised their two sons. Currently, they are reaching out to Muslims in beautiful British Columbia. They love to hike, bike, and snowshoe. Nancy has begun writing stories from her life that communicate her passion for God's life-changing Word. To read more of Nancy's work, write to her at: ogogalnan@gmail.com.

Sarah Bliss: Currently living in Colorado, Sarah enjoys being a momma to her three-month old son, spending time in the mountains, and exploring countries she hasn't been to. She spent the last two years of university in Southeast Asia doing ministry while training with long-term missionaries, and Lord willing plans to return long term to the Muslim world, sometime in the future.

Stephanie Prater-Clarke is a pastor's wife and a thankful mom to two teenagers. She has lived and served alongside her husband in Barbados and the wider Caribbean region for more than 20 years. She has a passion to write with the hope of encouraging others and also loves her morning walks, capturing all things creation on camera, cheering on her children, family vacations, and a good cup of coffee.

Tricia Chen spent 15 years teaching English to University students in East Asia and now continues to invest in youth by working with InterVarsity Christian Fellowship in Canada. When not spending time with students, Tricia can usually be found reading a book, scoping out a new coffee shop with her husband, or playing at a park with her 3-year-old daughter.

We're Going There

Amber Taube enjoys ministry in Southeast Asia with her family of five. They live on the fifth floor of the camp and conference center they operate in a rural village just outside of the city, giving local believers a place to gather and worship in a safe and peaceful environment. She lives for good books and great conversation, both best served with a steaming cup of coffee or chai.

Christina M. Post is passionate about encouraging women around the world through intentional discipleship. As a missionary, writer, friend, and Bible study leader, Christina loves listening, encouraging, and praying for those God brings into her life. Christina and her husband James serve as missionaries supporting the work of Bible translation globally. She is a homeschooling mama of 6 children and enjoys reading, writing, hiking, and playing piano and guitar. Connect with Christina on her website www.christinamariepost.com, on Facebook, or on Instagram @christinamariepost09.

Dorette: After a decade overseas, Dorette ended up back in a small South African town. To her surprise, she loves her job as a kindergarten teacher while continuing to work as a part-time physical therapist, and raising two boys on her own. She hopes that her testimony can one day give others hope. Contact her on Instagram at @dorette_startover.

Elise Tegegne lives in Indianapolis, but considers Addis Ababa the other half of her home. A former missionary to Ethiopia, she writes on faith, culture, and the splendor of the everyday. She spends her days exploring the world with her toddler, dancing through life with her wonderful husband, eating squares of really dark chocolate, and seeking the breathtaking love of God pulsing in every nook and cranny of the universe. Connect with her at elisetegegne.com, on Facebook, or on Instagram.

Emmy Lopez and her husband have been living overseas since 2008 between Central Asia and the Middle East. She loves cooking spicy food, bird watching, and early morning runs. She spends part of her day chauffeuring her two children to school, but also can be found drinking an alarming amount of tea with Afghan and Pakistani women.

Maria Mullet finds herself at home in multiple places on the globe, both in Southeast Asia and her passport country, USA. These homes seem to have a common thread: a classroom. She loves her current job as a high school teacher in the USA but often longs for her far-away home and the invigorating world of cross-cultural life. Maria loves exploring new places, watching baseball, and defending the Oxford comma.

RLS has been working in South Asia for the past ten years. She married a guy from the local church at the beginning of 2021, and has now transitioned from being an English teacher to staying at home with their daughter. She loves drinking a good cup of coffee, shopping at the second hand bazaar, and cooking or baking up delicious food.

Stephanie Prater-Clarke (bio listed on previous page)

Endnotes

1. Douglas McKelvey, Every Moment Holy, Volume 2, (Nashville, TN: Rabbit Room Press, 2021). P. 303-304

2. Ibid

3. Ibid

4. Ibid

5. Ibid

6. J. Calvin and W. Pringle, Commentary on a Harmony of the Evangelists Matthew, Mark, and Luke Vol. 1 (Bellingham, WA: Logos Bible Software), 77.

7. Bob Sorge, Dealing with the Rejection and Praise of Man (Kansas City, MO: Oasis House, 2009), 10-11.

8. Why Does a God of Love Allow Suffering - Dr Helen Roseveare 2/4 [Video] Retrieved July 6, 2022 from https://www.youtube.com/watch?v=G9bTBimRvjw

9. Ibid

10. Richard Plass and James Cofield, The Relational Soul (Downer's Grove, IL: InterVarsity Press, 2014).

11. Ruth A. Tucker. Guardians of the Great Commission: The Story of Women in Modern Missions (1988), 17.

12. Amy Tennery, "Athletics-'Iron sharpens iron': McLaughlin, Muhammad hurdle to new heights," Reuters, August 4, 2021, https://www.reuters.com/lifestyle/sports/athletics-iron-sharpens-iron-mclaughlin-muhammad-hurdle-new-heights-2021-08-04/.

13. Ann Voskamp, The Broken Way (Grand Rapids, MI: Zondervan), 91.

Acknowledgements

This book was a team effort and we are so thankful for each person that gave time and expertise along the way!

When we started to dream about what this project could be, Joy, Karen, Elizabeth, Maria, Kelsey and Jill sat with us on Zoom calls and shared from their heart about what they wanted to see in this book. Their ideas and encouragement helped shape the structure of this book from the beginning.

We are grateful to Laura for her expert eye in copy editing. Thank you, Laura, for pouring over the words in this book and adding all your thoughts in the editing phase!

Abby, thank you for creating the beautiful cover that captures the heart of this community. We love it!

Jenny put up with all our questions about publishing options and content, so graciously chatting with us multiple times throughout this process. We are especially grateful for her help in formatting and getting the book ready to be in your hands!

The Velvet Ashes Board of Directors asks the tough questions only because they want the absolute best for this community. Kim, Laura, Jenny, Bayta, Carol and D'Arcy give their time, expertise and support in so many different ways and we are grateful for their undergirding in this project.

And to the women in the Velvet Ashes community, those who shared their stories in the pages of the book and who share their lives with us and each other, thank you. You inspire courage in us as we see you walking in obedience and loving Jesus right where you are.

May you continue to say, "Yet we still hope."

VELVET ASHES IS A COMMUNITY OF WOMEN SERVING CROSS-CULTURALLY, DOING LIFE TOGETHER ALL YEAR ROUND.

There are several ways you can join in! From online retreats and connection groups to monthly resources and quarterly webinars, we work to create space for women serving all over the world to find community, spiritual renewal, and resources for their journey right where they are.

Follow us on Facebook and Instagram
or join us in our membership site to be part of this sweet community of women.

HEAD TO VELVETASHES.COM
TODAY TO LEARN MORE.